Praise for *The Biggest Year in American Birding*

What an interesting quest to establish a benchmark record by adding current U.S. territories in the Caribbean and Pacific [to the USA]. This is a fun read reliving iconic birding sites and opening our eyes to novel birding locales in our territories.

—Peter Alden (Author, National Audubon Society regional field guides)

Do you want to break a Big Year birding record? Nick Komar shows you how. Start by ignoring any handicaps—for him, it was Parkinson's disease. With fine wit, he introduces you to birds, birding hotspots and birders across the USA, including the territories from Puerto Rico to Guam. Birding is addictive, and after you read this book, you'll want to do your own Big Year!

—Oliver Komar (Author, Peterson Field Guide, Birds of Northern Central America)

Nick redefined the geographic limits of the *Big Year*. His journey took him to spots I had to Google. Yes, he set a precedent, but it's more than numbers. It's a well-written story of challenges and experiences all birders will love!

—Laura Keene (Big Year birder and Photographer)

Every bird has a story to tell,
and it's our duty to listen and learn.

ROGER TORY PETERSON
1908–1996

NICHOLAS KOMAR

THE BIGGEST YEAR IN AMERICAN BIRDING

A QUEST TO FIND 900 BIRDS
IN THE USA AND ITS TERRITORIES

BOHANNON HALL PRESS

Illustrations © by Sarah Robin Coleman
Cover Photo © by Nicholas Alexander Komar
Most Interior Photos © Nicholas Komar
Other photos with permission: see Photo References
Cover Design by Bohannon Hall Press
Edited by Richard Wilks Taylor

Library of Congress Control Number: 2025919253

Publisher's Cataloging-in-Publication Data

Komar, Nicholas, 1965-
    The Biggest Year in American Birding: A Quest to Find 900 Birds in the USA and
    Its Territories / by Nicholas Komar ; illustrated by Sarah Robin Coleman.
    Niceville, FL: Bohannon Hall Press, 2025.
    314 p.: illustrated- ; 23 cm.
    First edition.

1. Birds—Counting. 2. Bird Watching—Anecdotes 3. Birds Watchers—United States--
Anecdotes. I. Title. II. Illustrator-Sarah Robin Coleman, 1977- III. Editor-Richard Wilks
Taylor, 1953-
QL682.K66 2025   2025919253

ISBN 978-1-962995-12-2 (softcover)

Published by Bohannon Hall Press

*I dedicate this book to my family and friends who
put up with my birding obsession for many years,
supported me during my Big Year competition in 2023,
and helped me confront my issues with Parkinson's.*

I love you all.

TABLE OF CONTENTS

[1] Contributed by Nicholas Alexander Komar
[2] Contributed by Oliver Komar
[3] Contributed by Oliver Komar
[4] Contributed by Nicholas Alexander Komar

PROLOGUE
Setting the Stage

On the day I turned 57, I awoke from an anxiety dream in which I was giving a presentation for the Fort Collins chapter of the Audubon Society. My wife Maribel was shaking me.

"You were having a nightmare. Your flailing arms almost hit me. What was it about? Do you know anyone who calls you Captain?" she queried.

Parkinson's disease is known to cause vivid dreams. Patients like me often act out the movements they are dreaming about because they are reacting to stimuli that seem real. Normally I cannot remember my dreams. This one was different. The details were fresh. I reviewed them over and over again to burn them into my memory bank.

In my dream, I was nervously presenting slides on gull identification through a remote computer video connection. I looked down and noticed I was naked from the waist down. I thought I could get away with this as long as I didn't stand up. The audience was remotely linked. Suddenly, technical difficulties interrupted the presentation. The chapter president asked me to drive over to the local senior center to finish delivering the talk in person.

In my haste I forgot to get dressed appropriately and was standing behind the podium at the senior center still half naked.

Then suddenly I was on a pelagic boat trip. I was the leader pointing out seabirds to a dozen other birders on the small fishing vessel off the Pacific coast. I was still half naked, so I grabbed a blanket to cover up. Then a large wave washed over the boat, and I lost my balance trying to hold the blanket in place rather than holding onto a rail. The boat pitched and I toppled over the side rail into the stormy sea.

I struggled for a while underwater but couldn't seem to figure out which way was up. After about 20 seconds the air supply in my lungs was depleted. I gave up struggling and felt myself sinking deeper underwater, the life draining out of me.

1

I felt a pair of arms grab me. It was a beautiful mermaid, with long flowing auburn hair. She hugged me to her humanoid chest and pressed her lips against mine. I had never been hugged so tightly. She breathed air into my lungs. Her whole body was intertwined with mine. I could feel her life force surging through my body. I never felt more alive or safer than at that moment with this mermaid stranger. Together we moved in unison toward the surface. As she gave me one last deep breath, our bodies writhed together.

I emerged from the deep feeling stronger than ever. Somebody threw a ring buoy and I was hauled onto the boat by other birders. Now I had clothing on. I looked back to wave goodbye to the mermaid. "Good luck, captain" she mouthed to me, and then she morphed into a dolphin and swam around the boat a couple of times. I felt lucky to be alive. At that moment I felt inspired to do just about anything. Even something as intense, daring and foolhardy as a *Big Year*.

In the USA birding world, a Big Year is an annual competition to see the most species of birds in a particular geographic region. Traditionally that region is the American Birding Association's *ABA Area,* a combination of the Lower 48 states plus Alaska and Canada. In 2016, ABA expanded the definition of the area to include the State of Hawaii. Other popular birding *Big Years* are state and county level, in which birders compete for the largest annual list of species observed within those areas. I wanted to take the ABA Area Big Year competition to the next level and create the *Biggest Year in American Birding.*

So, what is a *Biggest Year*? First, a little history to set the stage. The American Birding Association was founded in 1969. The first Big Year attempt of the modern era was orchestrated by Ted Parker at the age of 18. In 1971, he reported 636 species. In 1973, Kenn Kaufman and Floyd Murdoch challenged Parker's record, observing 666 and 669 species respectively. Kaufman wrote about his low budget quest in his novel *Kingbird Highway* in which he hitched rides to his next birding destination, survived on cat food and slept under bridges. Benton Basham was the first to break the 700 species barrier in 1983 (710). In 1987, Steve Perry reported 711 species but was topped by Sandy Komito with 722. In 1998, Komito broke his own record with 748 species. He had competition from two other birders, Greg Miller

(715 species) and Al Levantin (711 species). The three-way competition was popularized in a 2004 book by Mark Obmascik, which became a 2011 movie by the same name, *The Big Year*.

In 2016, with the addition of Hawaii to the ABA Area, 800 species in a year became achievable in the USA. John Weigel reported 836 species in 2016. Laura Keene reported 815 species and set the unprecedented standard of physically documenting 802 of them. She took identifiable photos of 790 species! In 2017, Georgia birder Yve Morrell tried to break Weigel's record, but fell short with 816, the best for that year. Similarly, Nicole Koeltzow posted the 2018 top list with 830. Today dozens of competitive birders each year attempt to break Big Year birding records. As of 2022, the record holders for the ABA Area (Continental) and Lower-48 Big Years were John Weigel and the Stoll brothers (Ruben and Victor) with 784 and 751 species, respectively (source: Wikipedia: *Big Year*). Including Hawaii, the ABA Area record was 840 species set by John Weigel in 2019.

To my knowledge, no one has attempted to see 900 species in a calendar year in the United States and the USA territories (American Samoa, the Commonwealth of the Northern Mariana Islands, Guam, Puerto Rico and the US Virgin Islands). This expanded geographical region, *USA and Territories*, hosts approximately 100 additional species available for observation, thereby earning such a Big Year attempt the unofficial title of the *Biggest Year in American Birding*. Starting on January 1, 2023, I initiated a year-long attempt to accomplish this feat for the first time.

You might be wondering, who is Nicholas Komar? And why did I think I could be the first to observe 900 species in the USA and Territories? I became a birder more than 50 years ago, when I was seven. Birders who start young often become ornithologists, and that is what I did. My path to becoming an ornithologist was indirect. Before graduating from high school, I applied for admission to Cornell University where many aspiring ornithologists study. However, my B-level performance in high school did not impress Cornell nor three other Ivy League schools I had applied to. Instead, I attended the University of Massachusetts at Amherst where I graduated with an honors degree in Biochemistry. My honors research project was development of a subunit vaccine for Japanese encephalitis (a brain infection caused by a mosquito-borne virus).

In 1991, I was accepted to the doctoral program at the Harvard School of Public Health. I earned my Doctor of Science degree in Tropical Public Health with concentrations in Infectious Disease and Epidemiology in 1997. My project studied the ecology of another mosquito-borne virus called eastern equine encephalitis (EEE). This deadly virus lurked in the freshwater swamps of the eastern and southeastern seaboard of the USA. I operated field sites in Southeastern Massachusetts at Hockomock Swamp where the virus's natural vertebrate hosts were birds. My project was to determine which birds were responsible for amplifying the virus to epidemic levels. I studied under the late Andy Spielman who was a medical entomologist. Andy's roots were in ornithology. He studied the Cliff Swallow at Colorado College before becoming an expert on *Culex* mosquitoes at Harvard. My doctoral dissertation was titled *Reservoir Capacity of Communally Roosting Passerine Birds for Eastern Equine Encephalitis (EEE) Virus.* The work at Harvard led to a 25-year research career in Fort Collins, Colorado, where I worked for the Centers for Disease Control and Prevention. I studied the interactions between birds and mosquito-borne viruses, such as EEE, St. Louis encephalitis, West Nile and others.

In 2004, at age 38, I was diagnosed with early-onset Parkinson's disease, a progressive neurological disorder that affects movement and cognitive abilities due to insufficient dopamine production in the brain's substantia nigra. This led to my early retirement at the end of 2022, at the age of 57. All along this journey I nurtured my passion for birding. My two kids, Angela and Nick, left the nest and have careers of their own. My wife Maribel and I were expecting to become grandparents sooner rather than later. I figured 2023 would be the one year I could seriously attempt a birding Big Year. In competing for the *Biggest Year in American Birding*, I intended to make my mark on USA birding with "a bang, not a whimper."

The story you are about to read is true. The people, places and birds named are all real.

CHAPTER 1
Birding with Parkinson's Disease

*P*arkinson's disease (PD) is not a death sentence. Many people with this disease lead productive lives. In writing this book, I hoped to show that PD can be overcome. I decided early on, following my diagnosis in 2004, I would not let my illness interfere with my plans and dreams. My approach was to ignore it. I avoided talking about PD or discussing it. I controlled the symptoms of stiffness and movement dyskinesias such as tremors by taking synthetic dopamine, the neurotransmitter required for muscular innervation and hence, movement. My motto became *work hard, play hard*. Between 2004 and my retirement from my federal biologist position, I published over 90 scientific articles and was considered an expert in my field during my career at CDC. I also started a side business (Quetzal Tours) running birdwatching tours throughout the Americas.

I stayed physically active playing softball and baseball throughout the year. And I birdwatched daily, contributing my checklists to eBird.org. I photographed unusual birds to document their occurrence and also audio-recorded bird sounds. I became active in birding organizations in my home state of Colorado, ultimately becoming the president of the Colorado Field Ornithologists from 2019–2023. Eventually PD would slow me down, but still my approach was to ignore it.

Some aspects I could not ignore. My hands and arms trembled, making binocular use very difficult. I got around this hindrance by using battery-powered image-stabilized binoculars. I used a Canon model but half-way through 2023, I switched to Opticron 14×30 binoculars, which were considerably lighter.

Other physical issues I dealt with included balance disorder, slowness and weak vocal cords. This meant that when I hiked, I needed a walking stick or hiking poles, especially at night. I would fall more than most people. My balance on boats was atrocious. I needed to always hang on to something or someone. To communicate with others, I needed to conscientiously enunciate my words and belt them out if I wanted people to understand what I was saying. My slowness affected me most when getting in and out of vehicles. Also, on hiking trails, I tended to move quite slowly. Moving slowly through the landscape was a way of seeing more birds. Or rather, detecting more birds, not necessarily seeing them. My eye movements and connecting my eyes to my binoculars or telescope were also slower. This made it difficult for me to spot birds moving through vegetation. Fortunately, my hearing was still sharp. During my 2023 Biggest Year, I relied heavily on my ears to hear and to track the movements of birds.

You may be thinking that symptoms I described are common among the elderly. Indeed, loss of dopamine is a natural part of aging. Just as we all age in unique ways, all PD patients suffer in unique ways. What worked for me might not work for other patients. It is a progressive disease and different patients progress at different rates. Fortunately for me, progression was slow.

I ran into some other issues during my Biggest Year effort in 2023. Most notably, I found that my muscle tone for controlling my plumbing had decreased. Thus, when I felt the need to relieve myself, finding a nearby bathroom took on a new urgency. Sometimes, mother nature provided the only available toilet.

One thing I found interesting was that my body had difficulty coping with stress. I felt my stress levels would rise much more readily with my advanced stage of PD. Situations I handled stress-free 20 years ago now caused me great anxiety. For example, eating and swallowing food, interacting and conversing with people, typing a message on my telephone or personal computer and public speaking were all high stress activities for me now. Early in my career, I often gave public lectures and felt little stress about it. However, throughout my life I never panicked, even in situations where many healthy people would.

I would have to face my stress and physical obstacles and move forward in my mission despite them. I felt up to the task. When January 1, 2023, loomed large, I thought to myself, *Bring it on.* I was ready.

CHAPTER 2
Strategic Planning

A successful birding Big Year could not happen without a plan. I began
scheming up a strategic plan for my *Biggest Year in American Birding*
around my 57th birthday, in August, 2022. I was driving home from a day of
birding with David Wade in Jackson County, home of Colorado's North
Park. Dave was a birding buddy from Fort Collins. Our styles of birding
were similar so we often birded together. We were about the same age too.
Crossing Cameron Pass at 11,000 feet into Larimer County, David asked me
about my retirement plans. Truthfully, I had not yet given the matter any
serious thought. I didn't even have a retirement date yet, although my
supervisor told me to plan on December 31.

Pondering David's question, I looked around at the spectacular scenery
and felt inspired to think big. I remembered my anxiety dream. I blurted out
"I've always wanted to do a Big Year." As we snaked downhill following the
curves of the Cache La Poudre River for roughly 50 miles, I brainstormed
my plan, bouncing ideas back and forth with Dave. Over the next several
months, I honed the plan during discussions with other lifelong birders, such
as Rob Raker, E. J. Raynor, Alfred Wilson and John Vanderpoel.

Skill, time and financial resources (and perhaps a little luck) were the
main ingredients for a successful Big Year. I possessed skills in bird finding
and bird identification. These are skills I honed during 50 years of avid
birding. A great way to learn bird identification is to teach it, and I had been
teaching others through leading bird walks for local bird clubs since I was 12
years old (Brookline Bird Club, Needham Bird Club, Fort Collins Audubon
Society, Colorado Field Ornithologists [CFO], Western Field Ornithologists).
More recently I taught bird identification workshops for CFO, Denver Field
Ornithologists and Denver Audubon Society.

I would also need skill in logistics and planning. I developed these skills
through my side business (Quetzal Tours) operating birding tours since 2010.

Retiring from my full-time job as a biologist, I would have the time needed to dedicate a full year to birding. Parental duties were minimal now that my two kids were in their late twenties/early thirties and live on their own. Spousal duties were, well, negotiable. Fortunately, my wife Maribel agreed to support me, at least for now.

Financial resources would be a limiting factor as federal agency biologists don't have large salaries. My small retirement nest egg needed to last for several decades. So, I would need to protect it. These factors led me to develop a plan. I would subsidize the cost of my travel to multiple birding destinations by offering simultaneous tours to locations I needed to visit. This would slow me down somewhat, but having multiple sets of eyes searching for target species should offset the hindrance of necessary bathroom and meal stops required to appease tour customers. The tours would be designed to see most of the resident species of the USA and its territories. Destinations for small group tours would include California, Texas, Arizona, Florida, Minnesota, Puerto Rico, Maine and Alaska.

I would need to hire drivers for each of the tours. My Parkinsonian tremors and dyskinesias eroded customer confidence in my ability to drive safely.

An ongoing debate among Big Year birders is whether to prioritize travel for resident species or for vagrant species. One school of thought prioritized resident species, ticking off any vagrants that are convenient to chase along the way. The alternative prioritized chasing vagrants and picking up resident species along the way. The American Birding Association provides a code for every species on the official *ABA Checklist* (1,124 species in 2023). Codes 1 and 2 were reserved for the resident breeders that were easiest (Code 1) or more difficult (Code 2) to find. Codes 3–5 were vagrants (unexpected visitors or wanderers) that occur with diminishing frequency. Code 6 birds are extinct. Many Hawaiian species were Code 6.

John Vanderpoel did his own Big Year in 2011. He found 44 Code 3+ species, when he achieved second place all-time in the ABA Area (Continental) with 744 species observed in the USA and Canada (excluding Hawaii). John Weigel, the current record-holder for the ABA Area (840 species) recorded about 100 ABA Code 3+ species. Because my approach involved the Territories, the ABA Area codes were not as meaningful. For example, a Bananaquit in the ABA Area is a Code 4 species. However, in Puerto Rico, Bananaquit is abundant. I decided to set a goal of 40 ABA Code 3+ species within the ABA Area. Since chances of winning the competition increased with a higher number of vagrant species detected, I would design tours prioritizing the more difficult resident species (ABA Code 2) with some flexibility for deviating from the itinerary for chasing vagrants should they be reported nearby. One way to maintain flexibility was to avoid reserving hotels in advance.

Because my goal was to establish a new world record, I wanted to document my observations with photographs and audio files, at least once for each species, and to record my observations using eBird.org. This would permit me to keep a careful record of all observations, back up all my observations and documentation and allow others to follow my progress.

eBird was created in 2004 to convert recreational observations of birds by birders and birdwatchers into scientific data of use to scientists, conservationists and land managers. I began using eBird around 2010 and it has transformed my birding listing activities from a selfish hobby into what I hope is socially responsible community-based *citizen science*. Several years ago, I pledged to submit at least one checklist to eBird every day as a way of making eBird use a chosen lifestyle. I kept up this commitment for more than six years until I began writing this book. For me writing requires a huge mental focus, even more now that my Parkinson's disease is advanced. Recently, I gave up creating daily checklists in order to reduce distractions and finish this book.

I had hoped the eBird team at Cornell Lab of Ornithology would embrace my project and create a listing category for *USA and Territories* so that my followers could track my progress through time during 2023. I spoke with Marshall Iliff, the director of eBird operations. He agreed to create the category but would not commit to a time frame. Hopefully soon, so that my world record was established and visible and other competitive bird observers could attempt improving on my record. I look forward to my record being broken. I support competition in birding, as long as the competition is healthy (i.e., constructive rather than destructive) and is generating data or funding that is useful for bird conservation.

Almost 20 years after its release, eBird has grown exponentially and is now used by over a million observers worldwide. The data are expected to be analyzed by scientists and conservationists. However, the creators intended for birders to also use the data for their birding goals as well. Thus, the eBird software also tracks list totals of users, and serves as a planning tool for birders seeking target species or organizing birding trips. Contributors to the database must establish a free account at www.eBird.org. A free mobile app can be downloaded onto a smart phone of any type for easy use in the field. To submit a checklist to eBird in the field, an observer first establishes the location by comparing GPS coordinates to established eBird *hotspots* and existing *personal* locations. Clicking the start button initiates a timer that measures the duration of the observation. GPS technology in the smart phone maps your track which helps scientists determine how to analyze the checklist data. These can be entered via a variety of data entry protocols, such as *Stationary* or *Traveling*. If observations are incomplete, users must check the appropriate box. Incomplete data may also be submitted using *Incidental* or *Historical* protocols. Once the checklist is finalized, comments may be added for the list in general, or for specific species entries. Photographic and audio files may be attached as well. Species flagged as unusual are vetted by local volunteer reviewers before being accepted into the scientific database.

Many competitive birders submit all their checklist data to eBird.org so that eBird totals reflect their true list totals. This practice makes species totals publicly accessible through the eBird website. For those interested in using eBird for the first time or need a refresher course on how to use eBird, check out the help section of the website.

I planned also to use eBird to develop trip itineraries in real time and to maximize the probability of finding target species. eBird location-based *needs alerts* and *rare bird alerts* would help me learn about real-time potential new targets being seen in a region where I may be located. Third party apps that use eBird data would also serve me well, particularly the BirdsEye app which mines eBird reports for location-specific rare bird alerts and generation of personalized needs lists.

I was off and running. I published my schedule of tours on my Quetzal Tours Facebook page on December 22, 2022. My first tour was scheduled to begin January 7, to Southern California. This was just a couple weeks for advance notice. On New Year's Eve, I did not yet have any customers. I crossed my fingers that customers would sign up and went to bed. The next day (January 1, 2023) would be a big day for me, the first day of my Biggest Year.

Great Horned Owl
1 Jan 2023, Larimer County, Colorado

CHAPTER 3
The Christmas Bird Count

*I*n 1900, Frank Chapman initiated the tradition of counting birds during the Christmas season. This was an act of conservation value, as it intentionally challenged the practice of the Christmas Hunt, a popular competition to kill the most birds using shotguns on Christmas Day. Today, Christmas Bird Counts (CBC) are held on a specific day during a three-week period between December 14 and January 5. Each circle has a 15-mile diameter and is divided up among teams of observers who record every individual bird seen and heard. The data are used to monitor population trends of winter resident birds. This CBC for 2023 was the 123rd annual event sponsored by the National Audubon Society. The number of count circles across the nation has increased over time.

Though I have been participating in these counts for the past 45 years or so, I started participating in the Loveland, Colorado count with Tony Leukering in 1999. In recent years we made it a tradition to hold the count on New Year's Day. The CBC account for a significant portion of December and January birding, which is generally depressed in the cold gray winter months of the Northern Hemisphere. While most birds tallied during these counts may seem mundane, on occasion rarities appear and are subsequently sought by birders and by Big Year competitors. During this Christmas season, I participated in four counts, all located in Colorado within an hour's drive from my home. These included Fort Collins on December 18, 2022, Rawhide Energy Plant on December 31, 2022, Loveland on January 1, 2023, and Rocky Mountain National Park on January 4, 2023.

I began the Loveland CBC counting owls in the Masonville area. I was joined by Loveland birder Irene Fortune before sunrise. Irene was active in the birding community. In addition to serving as treasurer for the Colorado Field Ornithologists, she was also the president of the Foothills Audubon Club.

In the frigid pre-dawn darkness, Great Horned Owl and Eastern Screech-Owl launched my USA and Territories Biggest Year list. Then, as the sky lightened, we visited Carter Lake to pick out gull species roosting communally on the reservoir before they flew out to remote feeding locations for the day. I added Ring-billed, California, Herring, Lesser Black-backed and Iceland Gulls. The latter two species were flagged as rare in eBird and thus required a comment on the checklist, or photo documentation, to be vetted by a volunteer eBird reviewer before being entered into the scientific record for use by scientists.

Many birders are intimidated by eBird's rarity flag because they feel like they could be opening themselves up to judgement, doubt, ridicule and/or public humiliation by others, such as an eBird reviewer or the birding public. I didn't worry about such insignificances. On the contrary, I enjoyed reporting eBird rarities. I felt like when an observation was flagged, it was a way of saying that the record was important for science. If the record merited scrutiny, I felt like I had made an important discovery and I enjoyed providing the requested documentation.

Gulls are notorious among birders for being difficult to identify. This is partly because there are numerous species with cryptic plumages. For example, adult California, Ring-billed and Herring Gulls all look similar to each other, at least superficially. Yes, they all have white underparts with gray upperparts, white heads with brown streaking in winter, white tails and black wingtips. But there are subtle differences in body size and shape, coloration of bare parts such as legs, feet, eye, *orbital* (eye ring), bill shape and color and gape color, as well as shades of mantle plumage and wingtip pattern. Immature plumages are even more cryptic. All of this presents great challenges for birders. Personally, I liked the challenge.

I am what you call a *larophile*. Don't worry, it is not illegal or immoral. It just means I love gulls. I joined Irene at Carter Lake because I was a larophile and I was looking for love before dawn the morning of January 1.

I found it in the form of Lesser Black-backed Gull and Iceland Gull. Irene is not a larophile, so she asked me to assist with the gull identification. She will tell you she is not a gull lover, but I think secretly she has some larophilic tendencies. She has asked me on more than one occasion to review gull identifications with her and to look for gulls with her at Lake Loveland and Horseshoe Lake. I've even run into her at the Larimer County Landfill watching gulls. She could become a larophile if she was not careful. I once was with her when she spotted a rare Laughing Gull flying overhead near Bogotá, Colombia. All gulls are rare in the high Andes. She looked at it, recognized it as a gull and called it out to me and others in our group. Like I said, larophilic tendencies. Many birders hate gulls and would not have paid it any attention, once they realized it was a gull.

There is a long-entangled history between gulls and the Loveland CBC. Tony Leukering wanted to capture data on wintering gulls in Northern Colorado and was aware of the diversity of gulls appearing at the Larimer County Landfill, which is located about a mile outside of the Fort Collins CBC circle. So, he resurrected a defunct Loveland CBC that had been active in the 1940s. He shifted the center of the circle to ensure the CBC area encompassed the landfill location as well as foothills and prairie habitats. A new Loveland CBC was born in 1999. A handful of observers participated that first year. Tony did not live close so he asked me to become the compiler in 2000, the first official year of the current Loveland CBC. I organized the event up until 2019 when I turned over the reins to Loveland birder Denise Bretting. I still function as co-compiler most years if I am not traveling. Participation has grown over the years. We now have typically 60 to 70 participants counting more than 100 species each New Year's Day. Up to ten percent of the species are gulls some years.

Some of the rarer gull species that have turned up on Loveland CBCs during the last 25 years include Short-billed, Glaucous, Iceland (both Thayer's and Kumlien's subspecies), Glaucous-winged, Great Black-backed, Lesser Black-backed, Bonaparte's and Franklin's Gulls. Slaty-backed, Kelp, Sabine's, Laughing and Little Gulls have occurred in Loveland but not yet on the CBC. One overdue species that has not yet been sighted in Loveland, or anywhere in the State of Colorado, is the Black-tailed Gull, a vagrant from Japan. I hoped to find one someday, perhaps during my Biggest Year attempt in 2023!

Fast forward to 2023. I left Irene at Carter Lake where she would meet the remainder of her Loveland CBC team. Carter Lake is a massive deep-water irrigation reservoir that seldom freezes. Aside from the gulls that roost communally—sometimes more than 1,000 overnight in the center of the lake—many fish-eating waterfowl are also attracted to this inland sea. It has a surface area about 12 square miles and is nestled in the foothills between two ridges. A count of the birds utilizing the surface of Carter Lake was likely to find ten or more eBird rarities! Typically, half those rarities are in the gull family, so I make an effort to situate myself there at dawn and dusk to help identify any vagrant gulls that join or leave the communal roost.

Once the gulls departed Carter Lake, I detoured to the foothills west of the city of Loveland, where I located Pinyon Jay, a nomadic species I might have trouble finding again for my Biggest Year. I then met up with Texan Stephan Lorenz at 8 AM. Stephan is an expert birder who guides professionally in Alaska and several international destinations. He was in the area visiting family for the holidays. I invited him to join me for the bird count. We were assigned the Larimer County Landfill area by compiler Denise Bretting.

Stephan and I tallied over 2,200 individual birds in our assigned area, including Snow, Canada and Cackling Geese, Sharp-shinned Hawk, three species of falcons (American Kestrel, Merlin, Prairie Falcon), Black-billed Magpie, Horned Lark, Bushtit, Townsend's Solitaire, Lapland Longspur and American Tree Sparrow. We picked up some additional species outside our assigned area including Northern Shrike, Evening Grosbeak and Bohemian Waxwing.

The following day, January 2, I tried to see species that were reported by others during the Loveland CBC that I had missed in my assigned count area. E. J. Raynor and I visited Cattail Pond where we relocated Redhead and Ring-necked Duck. Later in the day, Greg Osland and I tried to find a roosting Long-eared Owl but turned up a Northern Harrier instead. Greg and E. J. are expert birders who live near me in Fort Collins and often accompany me on short outings.

On January 3, during a return visit to Carter Lake, I spotted Bufflehead, Eared Grebe and Common Loon, three species of waterfowl that are flagged rare in eBird.

On January 4, I joined Loveland newlyweds Joshua and Katie Smith and Estes Park birder, Marc Hemmes. We were assigned to tally the birds around Lake Estes for the Rocky Mountain National Park CBC by compiler Scott Rashid. We tallied 28 species that day, including several new for my year list: Lesser Scaup, Hooded Merganser, Bald Eagle, Pygmy Nuthatch and American Dipper. On the way back home to Fort Collins I added a Long-tailed Duck (rare) at Carter Lake.

I was glad to have spent that morning with Marc Hemmes. Marc was new to birding but was quite skilled. He had made a name for himself finding rarities at Lake Estes over the past couple of years. I had heard a rumor he had been diagnosed with cancer. He quit at lunchtime because he was feeling too weak to continue. A few weeks later, at just 48 years of age, he died from colorectal cancer, which I learned had been diagnosed three years earlier. While new to birding, he took great care to document any unusual sighting with photos and audio recordings, which he dutifully submitted to eBird.org. Perusing his eBird profile, I noticed that he had submitted more photos than checklists! What dedication. His final eBird checklist was this morning counting birds with Joshua, Katie and me. The birding community will miss Marc.

Over the next couple of days, I continued to chase birds reported during the various local CBCs. In Fort Collins, I recorded Cooper's Hawk, Trumpeter Swan and Greater White-fronted Goose at Warren Lake. Then I recorded Lesser Goldfinch and a vagrant Northern Cardinal at Red Fox Meadows Natural Area (less than a mile from my house). In Loveland, I added Virginia Rail, Wilson's Snipe and a vagrant Eastern Phoebe.

During the two January counts, I personally tallied about 60 species, roughly half those encountered by all participants. During my free time that week, I chased down another 20. Most of these were common species that I would eventually see many times during my Biggest Year competition. Several were considered rare in winter, representing unusual species for

January in Northern Colorado. These important CBC counts might play a crucial role in my Biggest Year attempt again at the end of the year as scores of participant eyes are able to detect rare vagrants I might have missed.

Pygmy Nuthatch
4 Jan 2023, Estes Park, Colorado

CHAPTER 4
Southern California
The Adventure Begins

I chose Southern California as my first tour destination because I knew that during the winter months San Diego County traditionally hosts over 250 species which represented twice the number recorded during January where I lived in Larimer County, Colorado. Furthermore, the Salton Sea in Imperial County usually harbored a rarity or two during winter. Indeed, local birders had recently reported Yellow-footed Gull and Rufous-backed Robin, two Mexican vagrants I might not find elsewhere during the year.

Rarities reported to eBird.org during the first week of January 2023 in San Diego County included a bunch of pelagic species blown on-shore during strong winds on January 1 (Buller's and Short-tailed Shearwaters, Northern Fulmar, Red Phalarope, Nazca Booby, Leach's Storm-Petrel) at the Point La Jolla sea-watch hotspot. Also reported were Eurasian Wigeon, Yellow-billed Loon, Little Stint, Greater Pewee and Tropical Kingbird—an impressive list.

Several resident species in Southern California were not easily seen elsewhere, so they too were on my target list: Ridgway's Rail, Sagebrush and Bell's Sparrows, Tricolored Blackbird, California Gnatcatcher, LeConte's Thrasher, as well as some exotic species that were established in Southern California like Lilac-crowned Parrot and Scaly-breasted Munia.

On January 7, four of us (Charles Wood of Oregon, Pamela St. Clair, driver Scott Rashid and me, all of Colorado) started the six-day tour at 11 AM. A visit to a private residence near the San Diego Airport produced good views of Allen's and Anna's Hummingbirds. At Mission Bay, just north of downtown San Diego, we missed the staked-out Yellow-billed Loon. But we did find Brant, Heermann's Gull, Brandt's Cormorant, Brown Pelican, Black Skimmer and Pacific Loon. At Famosa Slough in Point Loma, we missed the staked-out Swamp Sparrow and Tropical Kingbird but picked up Marsh Wren and Common Yellowthroat. A few minutes away, at the San Diego

River mouth, we added Greater Scaup, Red-breasted Merganser, Long-billed Curlew, Little Blue Heron and Reddish Egret. At 4 PM, we cut short this productive visit in order to reach the parrot roost at the El Cajon courthouse before dark. The roost did not disappoint, and close views of Lilac-crowned and Red-crowned Parrots dazzled us.

On January 8, we started at 7 AM at Point La Jolla. Aside from spectacular close-up views of roosting Brandt's Cormorant, Brown Pelican, Black Turnstone, Black Oystercatcher, Western and Heermann's Gulls, we also found large numbers of Black-vented Shearwater and Bonaparte's Gull beyond the surf. I also added Cassin's Auklet and Scripp's Murrelet.

A late-morning visit to Terra Nova Park in Chula Vista produced several California endemics such as California Scrub-Jay, California Thrasher and California Towhee. A gnatcatcher in the shrubs on a hillside turned out to be a Blue-gray Gnatcatcher rather than our target California Gnatcatcher. Other year-birds here were Nuttall's Woodpecker, Cassin's Kingbird, Wrentit and Bewick's Wren.

We spent the afternoon south of San Diego. At the visitor center of Tijuana Estuary National Wildlife Refuge (NWR), we were treated to spectacular views of Ridgway's Rail and Yellow-crowned Night Heron. A visit to the nearby San Diego Bay NWR added Long-billed Dowitcher and Black-necked Stilt to the list but did not turn up the recently reported Little Stint, a vagrant from Eurasia that preferred San Diego for its winter territory for the last six years rather than hang out with its conspecifics in Vietnam. Instead, a small flock of exotic Burrowing Parakeet, an introduced transplant from Southern Argentina, entertained our group. At dusk, a visit to the Tijuana River Valley Bird and Butterfly Garden failed to reveal the resident flock of Black-throated Magpie-Jay, an introduced transplant from Jalisco in West Mexico, but we found our first of three rare White-tailed Kite.

January 9 began at Harry Griffen Regional Park in El Cajon. This was a birdy spot, but we could not find Scaly-breasted Munia or Lawrence's Goldfinch, both targets recently reported at the park. We did find Red-shouldered Hawk and Cedar Waxwing. Next stop was 20 minutes away, an eBird hotspot called Rangeland Road. Several eBird rarities were easily found here, including Greater White-fronted Goose, Snow Goose and Zone-tailed Hawk. We also added Tricolored Blackbird and Ferruginous Hawk to the list.

We arrived at our next destination after lunch—Lake Hemet, nestled at 6,000 feet in the San Jacinto Mountains of Riverside County. Here we had our second encounter with the rare White-tailed Kite and were surprised by a vagrant Yellow-bellied Sapsucker. We were also greeted by several California specialty species including Oak Titmouse, Wrentit and Nuttall's Woodpecker. As night fell, we bunked down in a rustic cabin by the lake.

January 10 started off with steady rainfall. Lake Hemet was besieged by a low rain cloud. The conditions prevented us from finding additional montane targets White-headed Woodpecker, Red-breasted Sapsucker and Mountain Quail. An enormous flock of 200 Tricolored Blackbird, an endangered species, was a welcome sight in the campground village. To escape the rain, we headed east out of the San Jacinto Mountains. As we descended via a slow winding road, the vegetation became more and more arid. The road dumped us into the Anza-Borrego Desert and guided us toward the Salton Sea.

The Salton Sea is one of my favorite birding locations in the USA. This enormous lake in a vast desert valley was formed in 1905 by a freshwater flood event. Salts from the soil seeped into the lake creating a brackish water habitat similar to an estuary. The lake and surrounding plains, now irrigated for agriculture, feed thousands of wintering ducks, grebes, pelicans, waders, cormorants, shorebirds and gulls. The lake has receded in recent years and smelly algal blooms can keep recreational tourists away.

After lunch, a visit to the southern shoreline of Salton Sea at Lack Road was inadequate for detecting vagrant Yellow-footed Gull. The Sonny Bono Salton Sea National Wildlife Refuge headquarters building was birdy, with several new species for the trip including Ross's Goose among a flock of several thousand Snow Goose. Here we also found Gambel's Quail, Verdin, Black-tailed Gnatcatcher, Abert's Towhee and our third encounter with a rare White-tailed Kite. We left around 5:00 PM and retreated, driving a couple hours west to the charming town of Julian in the San Diego hill and wine country for our final two nights of the tour. We stayed at the Apple Tree Inn, a quaint motel in a quiet rural getaway for West Coast city folk.

After an unsuccessful attempt to find Spotted Owl and Western Screech-Owl before sunrise on January 11, we drove northeast for another visit to the Anza-Borrego Desert. Recent rains had turned the desert green, and we encountered a flock containing dozens of birds including American Robin, Say's Phoebe, Costa's Hummingbird, Cactus Wren and Black-throated Sparrow, as well as eBird rarities Mountain Bluebird, Sage Thrasher, Bell's and Sagebrush Sparrows. In the town of Borrego Springs, we added Greater Roadrunner. We spent our final afternoon racing back to Lake Hemet in the San Jacinto highlands. We arrived in time to see a Golden Eagle and hear a Purple Finch but alas, our Lake Hemet targets (Mountain Quail, Red-breasted Sapsucker, White-headed Woodpecker) were still missing in action.

We began the final morning of the tour at another regional suburban park, Lake Murray, on the outskirts of San Diego. Three hours here produced about 50 species of birds of which several were new, including Least Bittern, Lawrence's Goldfinch (I missed this one) and Scaly-breasted Munia. Then, en route to the airport for a 2 PM drop-off, we returned to the San Diego River mouth. This second visit was more leisurely. We added a few new shorebird species: Whimbrel, Dunlin and Snowy Plover. A complete accounting of the 177 species observed during the tour is available as an eBird trip report on-line at: https://eBird.org/tripreport/100217.

After dropping off the tour participants for flights to Colorado and Oregon, I returned to San Diego Bay to search (unsuccessfully) for Red Knot and Little Stint. After sunset, I drove two and a half hours north to Lytle Creek, a small community nestled in the San Bernardino National Forest, where I visited with my friend Joe Burns. During this drive on multilane expressways, I found myself struggling to keep the car from straying across lanes, a reminder of my Parkinson's disease and that I needed to hire drivers when possible.

Joe Burns and I worked together on the West Nile virus field investigations in New York City from 1999 until 2001. Joe studied Spotted Owls earlier in his wildlife career and thought he knew a nearby spot where

I might find an owl. I had arranged an 8:30 AM appointment the following morning at a private residence three hours farther north to view a staked-out Streak-backed Oriole that had strayed north from Mexico.

Streak-backed Oriole
13 Jan 2023, Lone Pine, California

After a late dinner and short night, we departed Lytle Creek at 3:30 AM, arriving at a trailhead at 4 AM. We hiked for an hour through ideal habitat in a moonlit canyon, but alas, no Spotted Owl. A makeshift walking stick prevented me from tumbling downhill a couple of times in the darkness.

Joe drove for me on the wild oriole chase. The homeowner in Lone Pine, California, a biologist named Russell Kokx, welcomed us to his yard, replete with bird feeders of various types, as well as suet and orange halves. Birds were everywhere. Large flocks of Brewer's Blackbird and House Sparrow joined small flocks of Eurasian Collared-Dove, Pine Siskin and Lesser Goldfinch. It was a chilly morning. The surrounding hills of the Eastern Sierra were shrouded with recent snowfall. On a clear day, the town of Lone Pine lay in the shadow of Mount Whitney, the tallest peak in the contiguous United States. However, it was a wintry morning. Birds were everywhere around the feeding stations. Russell pointed at the orange half and said, "There she is."

The female Streak-backed Oriole (ABA Code 4) had shown up right on cue. This was an important species for my Biggest Year, as I would not see another in the USA and its territories this year. This pale orange bird with a black chin, gray wings with thin white wing-bars and thin dark streaks on its dull gray back is a vagrant from tropical thorn forest habitat in Northwest Mexico. Also seeming out of place on such a cold morning was a hummingbird visiting a nectar feeder, a beautiful adult male Costa's Hummingbird with bright purple feathers decorating its beard and crown as if it wore a helmet of shining armor.

Joe and I retraced our steps back to Lytle Creek, stopping briefly in a sea of desert creosote to photograph and audio-record a singing LeConte's Thrasher. Then in Lytle Creek, Joe pointed out flocks of Band-tailed Pigeon. I walked through the town but, unfortunately, I could not find any other year-birds, even though White-headed Woodpecker and Lawrence's Goldfinch were supposed to be common there. I dropped off the rental vehicle at 6 PM in San Diego after another harrowing solo drive and flew home to Colorado.

It was only January 13. With 211 bird species now on my list for 2023, I was among the top 30 eBirders in the USA (Lower 48 states) for the year. I felt like the species seen during this first of many Biggest Year tours provided a good start for my year-long effort.

Back home in Colorado, I kept a close eye on the local text chatter for rare bird species I could add to my year list. On January 14, a report of Bohemian Waxwings caught my attention not because I needed it for a year-bird (I saw them January 1 during the Loveland Christmas Bird Count) but because it is one of my favorite birds. In the same Fort Collins neighborhood as the waxwings, I discovered a rare Winter Wren skulking along Spring Creek.

Later the same day, I was joined by local Colorado birders David Wade, Kyle Carlsen and Lori Pivonka for an owling field trip in the foothills and high, snowy mountains west of Fort Collins. Playing recordings, we heard calls of a responding Boreal Owl along State Highway 14 in Jackson County and a couple hours later, a singing Northern Saw-whet Owl along the Rist Canyon Road just west of Fort Collins.

The next day, E. J. Raynor joined me at Hamilton Reservoir north of Fort Collins. Here the water is heated by the Rawhide Energy Plant so the lake never freezes. I added Horned Grebe and Tundra Swan. Over the next few days, I successfully chased a couple of rare sparrows reported by others at Red Fox Meadows Natural Area in Fort Collins, Harris's Sparrow and Swamp Sparrow. On January 16, a visit to the Larimer County Landfill to look for rare gulls paid off. A Franklin's Gull was either a straggling fall migrant or an early spring migrant. This species nests in Canada and winters in South America normally. On January 19, I flew to South Texas.

Costa's Hummingbird
13 Jan 2023, Lone Pine, California

CHAPTER 5
Touring South Texas

*T*he Rio Grande Valley of Texas is one of the most exciting birding destinations in the USA and a mecca for USA birders (and especially Big Year birders). Why? Because of its proximity to the subtropics of Mexico, the prospect of finding a Mexican vagrant is tangible (only a few hours are required to drive to the cloud forests of the Sierra Madre Oriental in Tamaulipas, Mexico). In recent years such strays have included Social Flycatcher, Bat Falcon, Stygian Owl, White-throated Thrush, Bare-throated Tiger-Heron, Black-headed Nightingale-Thrush, Black-vented Oriole and Amazon Kingfisher.

Some tropical species are becoming regular visitors to "the Valley" as it is known locally. For example, Mexican Violetear, Tamaulipas Crow, Brown Jay, Blue Bunting, Crimson-collared Grosbeak, Roadside Hawk, Rose-throated Becard, Tropical Parula and Golden-crowned Warbler have each occurred multiple times in recent decades. Certain tropical species have actually adapted their populations to breed and prosper in South Texas. These include Hook-billed Kite, Green Parakeet, Great Kiskadee, Tropical Kingbird, Audubon's Oriole, Altamira Oriole, Morelet's Seedeater, Red-crowned Parrot, Clay-colored Thrush and Ferruginous Pygmy-Owl.

An entire economy based on visiting birders has developed in South Texas, complete with a network of bird sanctuaries called World Birding Centers, each charging a small entrance fee. Winter is the popular season for birding in the Valley, in part due to the mild weather. Many northern birders come to the Valley for the winter, like migratory birds. These fair-weather birders are known as *snowbirds* in the Valley. During the summer, the heat can be unbearable. I visited the Valley several years ago in July and found the heat tolerable, and the birding was just as fabulous. I appreciated having the trails to myself without the throngs of visiting birders. However, for this visit, I would appreciate large groups as the extra eyes could help track down species needed for my Biggest Year.

I had scheduled a tour from January 19 to 26, 2023, and would be accompanied by John Vanderpoel, a seasoned Big Year veteran from Niwot, Colorado. Also joining me were my son Nick (living in Austin, Texas) and Irene Fortune of Loveland, Colorado. Irene and I served together on the Board of Directors of the Colorado Field Ornithologists. We would rely on John for guidance with the itinerary and many other pearls of wisdom related to his successful Big Year in 2011, when he observed 744 species in the ABA Area (Continental), which excludes Hawaii. In 2011, he finished the year in first place, and second place all-time, just four species behind Sandy Komito's record 748 species.

Audubon's Oriole
21 Jan 2023, Hidalgo, Texas

We began the tour at the McAllen airport on January 19 with 219 species on my Biggest Year list. John and I arrived in the morning with a few hours to kill until Irene would arrive. Having driven down from Austin, Nick picked us up in his Subaru Forester mini-SUV and whisked us off to the nearest World Birding Center which was Quinta Mazatlán in McAllen. At the parking lot, John spotted the first cool bird of the trip: Yellow-throated Warbler.

Walking the trails, we encountered many of the common South Texas target species such as Plain Chachalaca, Inca Dove, Buff-bellied Hummingbird, Gray Hawk, Golden-fronted and Ladder-backed Woodpeckers, Great Kiskadee, Tropical Kingbird, Green Jay, Black-crested Titmouse, Long-billed Thrasher and Clay-colored Thrush. Nick spotted a Black-headed Grosbeak, a local rarity. I spotted another rarity, Winter Wren! Yellow-bellied Sapsucker, Blue-headed Vireo, Carolina Wren, Curve-billed Thrasher, Summer Tanager and Nashville Warbler were also noteworthy during our three-hour stay.

After collecting Irene at the airport, we drove an hour east to Brownsville and stationed ourselves at Oliveira Park waiting for the arrival of roosting parrots. We expected to see hundreds of resident Red-crowned Parrot with some exotic species mixed in, but the parrots never showed up, leaving us (and about 20 other birders) disappointed. My year-birds at the park included Black-bellied Whistling-Duck, Anhinga, Roseate Spoonbill and Vermilion Flycatcher. We settled in for the night at our roost site in Harlingen.

On January 20, we returned to Brownsville, arriving at the local University of Texas campus hoping to find the resident Social Flycatcher, a Mexican vagrant, which had been missing since January 7. It remained missing but we did get killer views of several dozen raucous Red-crowned Parrot. The campus was birdy. We assembled a list of 42 species for eBird, including three year-birds, but nothing unusual.

We spent the rest of the morning exploring some under-birded hotspots along the Rio Grande River east of Brownsville at Sabal Palm Sanctuary and Southmost Nature Preserve. Year-birds included Olive Sparrow, Chihuahuan Raven and Hooded Oriole. We grabbed a quick lunch from a Hispanic market in Brownsville. I bought a chicken breast and wing. John had a turkey leg. Nick and Irene passed, worried about maintaining their wiry figures perhaps. After taking one bite of my chicken, I thought better of it and donated the rest to the scavengers at the Brownsville Dump.

We headed to the Laguna Vista Nature Trail on South Padre Island, on the shores of the Gulf of Mexico, in an unsuccessful attempt to find a staked-out

Tropical Parula. However, we added White-tailed Hawk, Ringed Kingfisher, Harris's Hawk, Altamira Oriole and American Oystercatcher.

After transferring to the Alamo Inn (a fabulous lodge run by birder Keith Hackland specifically for birders), we were better situated to search for our most wanted bird targets: Hook-billed Kite and Rose-throated Becard at Bentsen Rio Grande Valley State Park and Morelet's Seedeater and Groove-billed Ani at Salineño Wildlife Preserve.

On January 21, we drove 30 minutes west to Bentsen where we met Mark and Joanie Hubinger, local *snowbirds* hailing from Michigan. They lived minutes from the park and knew the daily habits of both target species there. First, we would station ourselves at the Familia Nature Center waiting for a brief appearance by an immature male Rose-throated Becard. After about 45 minutes, I spotted the becard (ABA Code 3) and about 20 assembled birders let out a collective sigh of relief. We then hopped on the tram that would take us about a mile to the vicinity of the hawk watch platform where seven Hook-billed Kites had taken up residence to reduce the copious tree-snail population in that part of the park. Here we met several more groups of birders all seeking the same thing. David Koehler of Idaho showed us a photo he took of a flyby kite earlier that morning. We also met David and Tammy McQuade of Florida, prominent Big Year birders who managed to find over 700 species in the ABA area annually. They also encountered flyby kites. We were not so lucky. After a couple of hours of searching, we gave up and got lunch. We did however add another rare Winter Wren and a Swamp Sparrow to the trip list, as well as important South Texas targets Least Grebe and Green Kingfisher. Nick re-found the becard and I was able to obtain a photo which I uploaded to the eBird checklist.

After lunch, Nick began his five-hour drive home to Austin. I was sorry he couldn't remain with us on the trip. However, he and I would have the pleasure of birding together for a week at the peak of spring migration on the Upper Texas Coast at the end of April. Think *spring migration fallout*! Because Nick had provided transportation thus far, our gracious host Mark dropped us at the airport where we rented a new vehicle. Mark then guided us to another target species, a beautiful Audubon's Oriole at the National

Butterfly Center. With just a couple hours of daylight left, we decided to return for another attempt to find elusive snail-hungry kites. Irene and I speed-walked two miles from the parking area at Bentsen and were rewarded with a couple of flyby Hook-billed Kite (ABA Code 3) but unfortunately no photos. John had stayed back at the headquarters/visitor center building because he was feeling under the weather, and didn't think his bum knee would tolerate the hike.

John, Irene and I departed the Alamo Inn early on January 22 for the 90-minute drive upriver to the typical border hamlet of Salineño. Here we met the McQuades again who got our hopes up when they told us they had already found our target species, the seedeater and the ani, just ahead in the trail. However, after two hours of searching, we only added one species, Couch's Kingbird. We headed west to Falcon Reservoir State Park where we found Northern Bobwhite visiting the park's bird-feeding station.

Acting on a tip from a birder we met earlier, we checked near the boat ramp for Sprague's Pipit. To find a pipit, we gathered a group of birders including David Koehler and JoJo and Steve Audet, a couple from Maine. Creating a line of walkers spaced 25 feet apart, almost immediately a candidate was spooked from the short grass. It flew only a short distance, characteristically undulating as it flew, and showing off white outer tail feathers. Its visibly thin bill ruled out similar Vesper Sparrow, and a second bird flew overhead vocalizing. Photos and audio file were added to the eBird checklist. Adding this Sprague's Pipit to my Biggest Year list took a group effort. It was a *lifer* (a life bird) for David, JoJo and Steve, making it even more satisfying.

We headed west to the small lakeside city of Zapata where we had a picnic lunch at Bravo Park. I should say that Irene and I ate while John spent most of the time in the latrine, wishing he had not eaten that turkey leg on our first day in Brownsville. He was apparently suffering from *Santa Anna's Revenge*. While we picnicked, we added Wood Duck and Eastern Bluebird to the trip list and to my year list. Exploring the park after lunch, I found one of our most challenging targets—a drab female Morelet's Seedeater (ABA Code 3) which popped up in front of me as I tried to photograph a Blue-headed Vireo in a thick tangle of shrubby vegetation. With this feather in our

29

caps, we altered our plan to visit Laredo farther west upriver, and instead began the three-hour drive east across the arid uplands of South Texas to the bustling port city of Corpus Christi. We made several pit stops along the way for John's sake.

We spent the next two nights in a no-frills motel on Mustang Island, about a half hour south of Port Aransas, along the coast of the Gulf of Mexico. On January 23, after finding the pair of Aplomado Falcon perched on their hacking platform just north of our hotel, we visited the Leonabelle Turnbull Birding Center in Port Aransas. There we added the endangered Whooping Crane. After a celebratory sit-down lunch, we got lucky chasing a previously reported Groove-billed Ani at Oso Wetlands Preserve and Learning Center near Corpus Christi. The ani, a migratory species in the northern extreme of its range, was rarely found in Texas outside of summer. They usually retreat to Mexico in winter. I went to sleep quite satisfied with the day's achievements.

January 24, our final morning in the Corpus Christi area, was rainy but productive. I added several species including Piping Plover and Gull-billed Tern but missed an overwintering vagrant Bar-tailed Godwit near the Texas A&M Corpus Christi Campus. We then headed south to drier climes at Laguna Atascosa National Wildlife Refuge, where we successfully scored two important South Texas targets, Northern Beardless-Tyrannulet and Tropical Parula (ABA Code 3). I also found a third Winter Wren for the trip! We returned to the Alamo Inn for our final two nights in South Texas.

January 25 was enormously successful. We joined several dozen birders scouring the trails at nearby Estero Llano Grande State Park. Here we tallied 70 species including Fulvous Whistling-Duck, Common Pauraque, Ruby-throated Hummingbird, Stilt Sandpiper and a staked-out Dickcissel (rare in winter) coming to a feeding station at the park headquarters. I helped identify an immature female Broad-tailed Hummingbird (arguably the rarest find of the trip so far). After a sit-down lunch at John's favorite local barbecue just up the road from the park, Irene and I dropped John off at a health clinic in Weslaco to get him checked out.

Frontera Audubon Sanctuary was right around the corner from the clinic. Irene and I headed there. This small thicket surrounded by neighborhoods was infamous for harboring vagrants although nothing unusual had been reported there lately. We added Green Heron. Here I spotted another candidate for the rarest bird of the trip, Bay-breasted Warbler, which should be wintering in South America. This unseasonal warbler was potentially even rarer than the vagrant Broad-tailed Hummingbird, seen earlier, which normally winters in Mexico.

John had passed the test at the clinic. At dusk, he took us to the H-E-B supermarket in McAllen. What were we shopping for? You guessed it! Year-birds. We found two, Green Parakeet and Bronzed Cowbird, among the thousands of communally roosting Great-tailed Grackle that draped telephone wires and decorated car rooftops throughout the parking lot.

January 26 was our final morning. We had until 2:30 PM to return our rental vehicle. We added Yellow-headed Blackbird at the Progreso Granary in Mission and Monk Parakeet in Hidalgo (where a flock of six Long-billed Curlew landing on a residential street was an interesting spectacle). At Anzalduas Park along the Rio Grande River, we added an adult male Northern Parula. At mid-day we met up with Mark and Joanie Hubinger again at the National Butterfly Center where Mark showed us a roosting Eastern Screech-Owl. The last bird of the day ironically was a beautiful Yellow-throated Warbler at Roselawn Cemetery. Irene spotted it. She had not yet joined the trip when John spotted the first one at Quinta Mazatlán World Birding Center a week earlier. I had hoped to reach 200 species for the trip but was content with 195.

I returned home to Fort Collins with 306 USA year-birds, which put me on the leaderboard (in third place for ABA Area behind David and Tammy McQuade). During this trip to Texas, I added 87 species to my Biggest Year list. The hordes of species observed during this pilgrimage to the mecca that is South Texas launched John and Irene into the *Top 100* of eBird users for the ABA Area for 2023, as well. Site-specific checklists with photos and audio files attached can be reviewed at https://ebird.org/tripreport/102615.

CHAPTER 6
Pajareando in Puerto Rico

*T*he Commonwealth of Puerto Rico has been a territory of the USA since the Spanish-American War resulted in its independence from Spain in 1898. Its residents are US citizens but those who live on the island for more than six months of the year are ineligible to vote for president. Its location 1,000 miles southeast of Miami at the eastern end of the Greater Antilles made it a valuable source of species for my Biggest Year. The eBird app lists 324 species for Puerto Rico. Many of these are Neotropical migrants that pass through Puerto Rico or that winter on this Caribbean island. There are roughly 50 species occurring in Puerto Rico but not in the ABA Area. This includes 19 island endemics, about a dozen additional Caribbean regional endemic species and numerous naturalized exotic species. Three smaller islands are included in the Commonwealth—Vieques, Culebra and Mona.

My Biggest Year tour to Puerto Rico got off to a rocky start. Frontier Airlines canceled my flight connection from Orlando to San Juan, the capital of Puerto Rico. I was traveling with Cliff Hendrick from Fort Collins. We found a later flight, but we missed the first afternoon of the tour. Any instability caused by the delay was easily handled by the experienced guiding skills of Julio Salgado, one of the premier birding talents in Puerto Rico and owner of the local business called Puerto Rico Birding Trips. I had set up a five-day tour designed to find all 19 island endemic bird species as well as about a dozen Caribbean endemics. In addition to Cliff Hendrick, Dana Hiatt of Colorado, James Nealon of New Hampshire and Howard Youth of Washington DC joined me on the tour. While all four had return flights scheduled for five days later, I would stay on the island an extra week in order to celebrate my 32nd wedding anniversary (Maribel would arrive February 1 at the end of the birding tour) and to play in a baseball tournament (Men's Adult Baseball League 45+ division February 2–5). Birding and baseball have always been my two biggest hobbies. Birding keeps my brain sharp while baseball keeps me physically fit.

Because of the mechanical issue on our Frontier Airlines flight from Orlando, Cliff and I missed the pickup at the airport at 1 PM on January 28. We joined the group by nightfall at the Manatí Hyatt Place Hotel by spending about $600 on new flights and a costly hour-long Uber ride from the airport in San Juan to Manatí. Upon our arrival, Julio delivered some great news. None of the species seen that afternoon, including eight endemics, would be difficult to re-find along the route.

White-winged Tern
30 Jan 2023, Punta Boca Morena, Puerto Rico

Furthermore, he received news that a pair of vagrant White-winged Tern were discovered close to our route and stuck around throughout the day. We hoped to find them in Mayagüez at the west end of the island in two days' time. This tern is classified as ABA Code 4, although Puerto Rico is not in the ABA Area. However, it is probably as rare in Puerto Rico as in the ABA Area so it would be important for me to chase these birds. I landed in Puerto Rico with 309 Biggest Year-birds, having added Wood Stork, Fish Crow and Boat-tailed Grackle at the Orlando International Airport while waiting for my flight to San Juan.

On Sunday, January 29, stepping out the hotel door, we added two endemics, Puerto Rican Mango and Puerto Rican Spindalis, as well as Zenaida Dove, Scaly-naped and White-crowned Pigeons, Gray Kingbird, Red-legged Thrush, Greater Antillean Grackle and Bananaquit, several of which are Caribbean endemics. Our first destination was Cambalache State Forest along the north coast of the island. The dense tropical forest was teaming with bird life. Here we added ten more island endemics: Green Mango, Puerto Rican Lizard-Cuckoo, Puerto Rican Owl, Puerto Rican Tody, Puerto Rican Woodpecker, Puerto Rican Flycatcher, Puerto Rican Vireo, Puerto Rican Oriole, Adelaide's Warbler and Puerto Rican Bullfinch. Key West Quail-Dove (heard only) was a Caribbean endemic. Smooth-billed Ani, Mangrove Cuckoo, Black-whiskered Vireo, Cape May and Magnolia Warblers, and Chestnut-sided Warbler (local rarity according to eBird) were also new for my Biggest Year list.

Before breaking for lunch, we toured some farm ponds at nearby Sabana Hoyos and added West Indian Whistling-Duck, White-cheeked Pintail, Loggerhead Kingbird, Shiny Cowbird and two species of Grassquits, Yellow-faced and Black-faced. After lunch and a brief siesta, we picked up Sandwich Tern and Magnificent Frigatebird at the Port of Arecibo. A late afternoon visit to Rio Abajo State Forest scored two important endemics, Puerto Rican Emerald and the critically endangered Puerto Rican Parrot.

On Monday, January 30, we returned to Cambalache State Forest for a second unsuccessful attempt to see Key West Quail-Dove. However, we added White-winged Parakeet (a naturalized exotic). En route to the west end of the island, we observed displaying White-tailed Tropicbird at a coastal nesting site, Los Merenderos de Guajataca. This was one of the tour highlights.

While lunching on empanadas along the island's west coast at Añasco, we added Cave Swallow, Pearly-eyed Thrasher (a Caribbean endemic) and Venezuelan Troupial (a naturalized exotic). A quick stop near the city of Mayagüez was sufficient to tick the Palearctic vagrant White-winged Tern at Punta Boca Morena. We found endangered endemic Yellow-shouldered Blackbird at the Cabo Rojo National Wildlife Refuge salt flats where Semipalmated Sandpiper was also new. A visit to Rice Tech (grassland habitat) produced Northern Red Bishop, Scaly-breasted Munia and Orange-cheeked Waxbill, three naturalized exotic species. We ended the day with Caribbean Elaenia, Puerto Rican Nightjar (a Puerto Rican endemic) and the Puerto Rican subspecies of Clapper Rail at Parguera, where we would stay for the last two nights of the tour.

On Tuesday, January 31, we visited the hills of Southwestern Puerto Rico at the Maricao State Forest where we added our final three endemic species, Puerto Rican Tanager, Elfin-woods Warbler and Puerto Rican Euphonia. While watching the beautiful euphonia, a colorful small finch, a car sped past us. I heard my name and then the passing car screeched to a halt. A young man jumped out from the back seat and walked toward me. Did I know him?

"Hi Nick, I thought I might run into you. How is your Big Year going?"

It was Skyler Bol, a 20-something biologist from Fort Collins. I knew him from his high school days when he participated in the Fort Collins Christmas Bird Count with his parents who are well-known wildlife photographers. What a small world! He explained that he was part of a team monitoring the nests of Sharp-shinned Hawk, a threatened endemic subspecies on Puerto Rico. We agreed to get together for birding after my tour finished.

Back in the coastal lowlands, we visited Boquerón National Wildlife Refuge, adding Least Grebe, Sora, Limpkin, Osprey, Lesser Antillean Pewee (a Caribbean endemic), Northern Waterthrush and Black-and-white Warbler. We spotted a Brown Booby at our lunch spot, Annie's Place Restaurant in Cabo Rojo. After a siesta, a visit to Laguna Cartagena NWR turned up tons of birds, including several Least Grebe and Least Bittern, but only Purple Gallinule was new for the Biggest Year list. Here we missed Masked Duck and Yellow-breasted Crake. A Prairie Warbler in the mangroves at Parguera was new.

On Wednesday, February 1, we added Antillean Crested Hummingbird at Salinas on the island's south shore, Plain Pigeon flying high over Caguas in the island's interior, and Green-throated Carib feeding at ornamental flowers near Viejo San Juan before ending the tour at the airport at 11 AM. These three species are Caribbean endemics. In all, the tour participants observed 120 species of birds, including 19 Puerto Rican endemics, 13 Caribbean endemics and one Palearctic vagrant species that would be unique for my USA and Territories Biggest Year list.

Over the next week, birding was secondary to baseball and anniversary activities, but I would manage to add several species to my Biggest Year list including Solitary Sandpiper (with Skyler Bol at Arecibo), Blue-and-yellow Macaw (a naturalized exotic at Guaynabo), Ruff (an eBird rarity from Europe, staked-out on Vieques Island; considered an ABA Code 3 in the ABA area), Wilson's Plover (on Vieques Island), Bridled Quail-Dove (on Vieques Island, a Caribbean endemic) and Bronze Mannikin (a naturalized exotic). We were not able to find Scarlet Ibis or American Flamingo. A possible Cory's Shearwater flyby was left unidentified.

I ended the visit to Puerto Rico on February 8, 2023, with 379 species on my Biggest Year list. Because there were several species I missed during this trip to Puerto Rico, I planned to come back. A couple of species are only in Puerto Rico during the summer breeding season, such as Caribbean Martin (a Caribbean endemic), Roseate Tern and Antillean Nighthawk. There was still a long list of exotic species that could aid me in my goal of reaching 900 species, including Orange-fronted Parakeet, Orange-winged Parrot, Yellow-collared Bishop, Pin-tailed Wydah and Indian Silverbill. There were some migratory species that I might have good luck finding in Puerto Rico such as Connecticut Warbler, Fork-tailed Flycatcher and Vervain Hummingbird, as well as some low-density residents that I missed during this initial visit (Masked Duck, Yellow-breasted Crake, Scarlet Ibis, American Flamingo, Ruddy Quail-Dove). Julio believed that the Ruddy Quail-Dove was extirpated from the island after Hurricane Maria caused massive destruction of the forest habitat in Puerto Rico in 2017, but there have been some undocumented reports scattered over time and space that provide hope for a comeback.

More details about the birds seen in Puerto Rico, including photos and audio files, may be found at https://eBird.org/tripreport/108325. Many thanks to Julio Salgado for leading a fabulous tour; to the tour patrons Jim, Howard, Cliff and Dana for supporting (and subsidizing) my Biggest Year; to Manuel and Mabel Amador for hosting Maribel and me for several days in Guaynabo and for showing us around Vieques; to Nancy Rios for hosting us and showing us around Viejo San Juan; to Freddy Martinez for allowing me to fill a spot on the Team Colorado roster; and to Maribel for being my biggest fan and coming to all my games.

30 Jan 2023, Group Photo Overlooking Cabo Rojo, Puerto Rico.
From Left: Howard Youth, Dana Hiatt, Cliff Hendrick,
Julio Salgado, James Nealon, Nick Komar

CHAPTER 7
Sax-Zim Bog
A Winter Wonderland

*T*he next big adventure of my Biggest Year would take me to Northern Minnesota, home to the famous Sax-Zim Bog, a managed black spruce–tamarack birch wilderness where Great Gray Owl can be reliably found throughout the year. In winter, these majestic owls are joined by Northern Hawk Owl, Boreal Owl, and several other northern species like Pine Grosbeak, Common Redpoll and Boreal Chickadee.

I was joined by Joe Kipper and Kathy Kay on a week-long road trip to see these species and others. I had invited Joe to be the local guide and driver for this tour as he had birded the bog the previous year. Joe is a young (20 years old) talented birder from Fort Collins who had impressed me with his birding skills and independence and who I was mentoring to become a tour leader and guide for Quetzal Tours. Kathy is a soft-spoken homemaker from Denver. I met her about a year earlier while chasing a Eurasian Wigeon in Boulder County. She is an active member of the Colorado Field Ornithologists (CFO) and I ran into her at various CFO events during the prior year. She had been a client on my Quetzal Tours trip to Oaxaca just a few months earlier in November 2022. I was happy to have her as a returning customer.

I had advertised this trip on Facebook and was disappointed that others had not signed up. This meant that I would take a financial loss on this trip. Kathy kindly offered her car for the long drive and paid for her lodging in addition to the tour fee (which was supposed to include lodging and transportation). I wondered why she was willing to join the trip given the added expenses. She revealed that she too was on a Big Year mission in 2023. She had set herself a goal to photograph all 19 species of resident owls in North America. This trip was necessary for her to photograph the Great Gray Owl and the Northern Hawk Owl.

A couple of Kathy's birding buddies (Adrian Lakin and Valentina Roumi) were also planning to be there but would fly from Denver to Minneapolis and rent a car for the final two hours of driving to Duluth. Kathy planned to share sightings with Adrian and Valentina, which would increase our chances of finding all our target species.

I started the trip with 380 Biggest Year-birds after adding a Northern Goshawk with Greg Osland in Fort Collins on February 17. Kathy picked up Joe and me at 4 AM on Saturday, February 18, driving her Mazda CX-9 SUV. We headed east on Colorado Highway 14 through the Pawnee Grasslands before the sun appeared on the horizon. Our first destination was the sandhills of Logan County in Northeast Colorado where Joe had seen several Short-eared Owl in January. We arrived before dawn at a wetland area north of Highway 138 but the *shorties* failed to appear. Instead, we found plenty of Ring-necked Pheasant and Rough-legged Hawk. I led the group to a mature shelter belt along a county road where I had seen a roosting Barn Owl several years earlier hoping for a similar experience. As we rolled slowly along the mile-long juniper and Russian olive shelter, Joe spotted an owl at eye-level. Using the vehicle as a blind, we got excellent photos of Long-eared Owl.

Back on the road, we sailed eastward across Nebraska on Interstate 80, and then turned north on Interstate 35 at Des Moines, Iowa. We made a birding stop from 4 to 6 PM at the Ada Hayden Heritage Park in Story, Iowa. We hoped to find a resident pair of Eurasian Tree Sparrow, an exotic species originally introduced to St. Louis, Missouri. We could not find this target but we did add Red-bellied Woodpecker in a section of deciduous forest.

Continuing north after dark, we drove for hours. We arrived at our destination—the Quality Inn in Virginia, Minnesota—after midnight. About 50 miles from the Canadian border, we were in the Northwoods of Minnesota above Duluth and Lake Superior. About a foot of snow blanketed the ground. The air was frigid.

On Sunday morning, February 19, we arrived at the Sax-Zim Bog area by 7 AM. The bog was situated in a square of managed lands about 15 miles on each side and is serviced by the Friends of Sax-Zim Bog for the enjoyment of birders. Numerous seed and suet feeders are situated throughout the eastern half of the bog to facilitate good views of the resident birds for birders and photographers. A welcome center at the south end provided shelter, bathrooms and free coffee, tea and hot chocolate. Staff members keep tabs on recent sightings of rarities, especially the two stars of the show: the Great Gray Owl and, when present, the Northern Hawk Owl. Chatter on a local text chain informed us that both stars were present this winter, but the hawk owl had been unreported for several days. We traversed the bog by driving the few maintained roads on the way to the welcome center, stopping along the way at several feeding stations for birds. Year-birds picked up along the route included White-winged Crossbill, Canada Jay, Ruffed Grouse, Pine Grosbeak, Pileated Woodpecker and Boreal Chickadee.

Ruffed Grouse
21 Feb 2023, Lake County, Minnesota

At the welcome center, we interrogated the clerk for any information we could get to track down the two targeted owl species. Frank Nicoletti, a well-known birding guide that we met there, suspected that the one wintering hawk owl had probably been killed by a goshawk. Searching along the network of roads that crisscrossed the bog region turned up nothing new during the afternoon.

On Monday morning February 20, we waited for a Great Gray Owl to appear at the east edge of the bog, but it never did. A lone Common Redpoll was new. Since the owls were unlikely to be found in the middle of the day, we headed to the Duluth area where we successfully chased a pair of Eurasian Tree Sparrow at Superior, Wisconsin, and a photogenic Snowy Owl at the Duluth Airport. We returned to the bog at dusk but still no Great Gray Owl.

Tuesday morning February 21, we decided to look for another target, the Spruce Grouse. Looking on eBird.org, there were recent sightings about a half hour north of the little town of Virginia near Cook. If we did not find it there, we might have better luck an hour farther east along Route 2 in the Superior National Forest, in Lake County. Near Cook we found more Boreal Chickadee and had great views of a very cooperative Ruffed Grouse, but no Spruce Grouse.

We headed east to Route 2. At a burn scar from a past forest fire, we encountered another target species, the Black-backed Woodpecker. At 2 PM, we received some welcome news on the local text chain. A Northern Hawk Owl had been sighted back at the bog, about 90 minutes away. We charged off, hoping the report was legitimate. We also checked in with Adrian and Valentina, who had just landed in Minneapolis. They were thrilled with the news and were speeding north on Interstate 35. Fortunately, the sighting was legit. The hawk owl was still alive after all, or this was a newly discovered bird. We joined about a dozen other birders lined up in four or five vehicles, happily clicking our cameras as the owl perched atop a pine tree watching for prey in the gloom of the late afternoon.

Adrian and Valentina arrived a few minutes after we did. A storm was brewing. Low clouds were moving in. The owl might have sensed the onset of stormy weather and had begun hunting earlier in the day than usual. This Northern Hawk Owl was a life-bird for most of the observers that day. I had seen two others in my lifetime.

Northern Hawk Owl
21 Feb 2023, Sax-Zim Bog, Minnesota

After an hour or so, more good news came through the text line. A Great Gray Owl had been seen 30 minutes away at the opposite end of the bog area. Off we went. It flew before we arrived, but we persisted. Our patience paid off. The massive Great Gray Owl reappeared just before dark. I had seen just four others in my lifetime.

Wednesday morning, we checked out of the hotel at 5 AM and returned to Lake County before dawn. Playing a Barred Owl recording was uneventful, so we began driving Route 2 headed north slowly, intently watching for grouse along the road. Bingo! At 6:45 AM, a small dark grouse perched at the roadside. By 7 AM the dim morning light was sufficient to recognize the beautiful polka-dotted plumage of a male Spruce Grouse. We watched it fly into the lower boughs of a spruce and begin to feed on the nascent buds.

We also added another woodpecker species, the American Three-toed Woodpecker, based on its unique drumming which starts slow but ends fast. We only heard this species. But fortunately, I would see it in April in Colorado and again in August.

After the morning in the Superior National Forest, we headed to Duluth hoping to find some new trip species along the north shore of Lake Superior. Glaucous Gull at the Superior Landfill, on the Wisconsin side of the lake, was new for the list. The threatened snowstorm began in earnest around 4 PM so we delayed our departure back toward Colorado by 24 hours.

Thursday was a snow-day. We searched for birds around Duluth but found nothing new for my Biggest Year effort. When the storm subsided, we headed toward Fargo, North Dakota, a five-hour drive.

Friday morning, we successfully chased a recent report of Gray Partridge, an introduced species, just north of Fargo. Then just south of Fargo, after hiking through Gooseberry Mound Park on the Minnesota side of the Red River, Kathy spotted a perched Barred Owl from the back seat of the Mazda as Joe was driving away from the park. Snow Bunting made a good showing in farmland near Strasbourg, North Dakota. We pulled into North Platte, Nebraska, about 2 AM for our last night of this trip.

We started the final day of the tour on Saturday, February 25, around North Platte. Here we found a flock of 120 overwintering Sandhill Crane. In the same wheat field, we spied a half dozen Greater Prairie-Chicken. After a few more stops en route to the Front Range of Colorado, we saw an eBird report of Short-eared Owl at Lower Latham Reservoir from earlier in the day. Arriving at dusk, we found two Short-eared Owl hunting the marshes and meadows of Beebe Draw near the south shore of the reservoir. Thanks to Chris Wood, one of the founders of eBird, for reporting his sighting in a timely fashion!

Special thanks to Joe and Kathy for their partnership in my Biggest Year endeavor and their good company and long hours of birding during this eight-day road trip to Sax-Zim Bog. I was happy for Kathy who got excellent photos of five owl species. More photos of birds from this trip can be viewed in the eBird trip report online at https://eBird.org/tripreport/108290.

With just three days at home before my next trip, I was sure to keep my commitment of eBirding daily. On February 26, I checked on an over-wintering Rock Wren in Bellvue, Colorado, I had discovered during the Fort Collins Christmas Bird Count. Sure enough, it was still there more than two months later. On February 27, I checked on an Eastern Screech-Owl along the Poudre River at Lee Martinez Park in Fort Collins. On February 28, I accompanied my birding buddy David Wade and my wife Maribel on a hike up the Young Gulch Trail in the Cache La Poudre Canyon to look for a territorial Northern Pygmy-Owl. Maribel loves owls. The Northern Pygmy-Owl cooperated for us and was USA and Territories Biggest Year-bird 405. The next morning, Maribel and I flew to Boston.

Eastern Screech-Owl
27 Feb 2023, Fort Collins, Colorado

45

CHAPTER 8
Massachusetts
Return to My Roots

My mother Karen introduced me to birdwatching before I can even remember. I was an infant in the suburbs of Philadelphia in Southeastern Pennsylvania. I would not consciously appreciate birds until I was older. When I was three the family packed up our Volkswagen bus and drove north to Eastern Massachusetts where my parents had bought a small house in Newton (a suburb of Boston). At age seven, I consciously became a birder, having been influenced by a pair of *spark birds* perched together during spring migration. These two beauties were the Baltimore Oriole and the Rose-breasted Grosbeak, both males in their stunningly beautiful breeding plumage. I was able to appreciate their beauty while peering through binoculars at the canopy of a tall tree along the Charles River, where my father had taken us three children on a bird walk. My twin brother Oliver was equally affected by this experience, whereas my older brother Ned, already a young teenager, was oblivious to the joy that birding could inspire.

During the next ten years, Oliver and I became expert birders. We attended weekend field trips with the Brookline Bird Club, visiting well-known birding destinations such as Plum Island (Parker NWR), Great Meadows NWR and Cape Cod. Longer outings included the Berkshire Mountains of Western Massachusetts, the islands of Nantucket and Martha's Vineyard. Our birding hobby became too much for our parents to handle on their own, so we developed many adult mentors in the birding world. Our relationship with these mentors was mutually advantageous. They provided knowledge, experience and, most important, transportation. We provided sharp eyes and ears. By age 12, we were leading field trips for the Brookline Bird Club. During our teenage years we began birding during the week as well, visiting the numerous parks and gardens around Newton. We found that the birds frequenting our local birding patches were just as exciting as those at the better-known hotspots. Some of the unexpected species we found in the neighborhoods of Newton included Tundra Swan, Least Bittern, Ruffed Grouse, Northern Goshawk, Buff-breasted and Baird's Sandpipers, Pileated and Red-headed Woodpeckers, Yellow-breasted Chat, Connecticut Warbler, Lark Sparrow and Dickcissel.

After graduating from Newton South High School in 1983, I left Newton to pursue higher education elsewhere in Massachusetts, and then a career in Colorado. My mother still lives there in the same house where I grew up. Early in 2023, I decided that my family needed a trip to Massachusetts to celebrate her 87th birthday. We planned to fly into Logan International Airport in Boston on March 1, 2023, and celebrate her birthday the following night. We would stay through March 6, so I began scheming ways to add new species for my Biggest Year. Several people had reached out to me (or perhaps I reached out to them) and had offered to help me get around the area looking for rarities, including Jim Nealon of New Hampshire, Mike Greenwald in Western Massachusetts, and Alf Wilson in Marblehead on Metropolitan Boston's North Shore. One recent rarity I had hoped would stick around was a Steller's Sea-Eagle, last reported in Georgetown, Maine, on February 14. But alas, it hadn't been seen since that day. Fortunately, there were plenty of other rarities being seen that would keep me occupied during the days, while I kept busy with family obligations in the evenings.

I made a list of the highest priority species being reported within a couple hours of Boston. These included Barnacle Goose in Woburn, Black-headed Gull on Cape Cod, Common Gull in Northwest Connecticut, Tufted Duck near the Rhode Island border and Razorbill at Cape Ann. I would aim to pick up several other lower priority species as well, such as American Woodcock, Northern Gannet, Purple Sandpiper and American Black Duck. I had also hoped for Smith's Longspur, Pink-footed Goose and Northern Lapwing but these three vagrants had all moved out of their Massachusetts winter stakeouts. All these species would be difficult to find in other locations and seasons, except for Northern Gannet and Razorbill, which I expected to see during a planned trip to Maine led by Eric Hynes, June 25–30. Well, that was my plan anyway. But you know how plans fare. I like to say, *the best-laid plans of mice and men oft go awry*. Wow that is catchy. Maybe I will write a book about my Biggest Year experiences and lead off with this sentence. I could title the book *Of Mice and Men*. Of course, I will check first to make sure that title hasn't already been used.

I started my trip to Massachusetts with 405 species on my USA and Territories Biggest Year list. Arriving in Boston with my daughter Angela and wife Maribel, we were picked up on Wednesday, March 1, by my son Nick and his girlfriend Heide. They had arrived from Austin about an hour earlier. We stopped for lunch at a restaurant overlooking Boston Harbor, where I spied a few American Black Duck. After a quick meal, we headed west about 30 minutes and checked in to our small two-story rental (an Airbnb) in Waltham, overlooking a lagoon off the Charles River. Here there was a nesting pair of Mute Swan. Nick offered to drive me to Horn Pond in Woburn first thing the following morning to look for the Barnacle Goose which had been roosting there, although there were no confirmed sightings there since February 20. I ticked White-throated Sparrow there first thing on Thursday, March 2, in pouring rain, but we found no sign of Barnacle Goose.

We had offered to pick up my niece Yvonne (Oliver's daughter) at Endicott College in Beverly at 3 PM but everyone had work obligations that morning, so I got dropped off in Cape Ann with Alf Wilson at 10:30 AM to go birding while others set up workstations in a Rockport coffee shop.

The rain subsided and birding Cape Ann was productive. At Fisherman's Monument in Gloucester, Alf and I saw plenty of Common Eider, black and white diving ducks of seacoasts with a green patch on the nape and greenish bills. We also had Surf and White-winged Scoters, Great Black-backed Gull and a recent spring arrival, the Common Grackle. We scoured Gloucester Harbor for Razorbill and glimpsed a candidate as it dove near the Jodrey State Fish Pier, but then subsequently disappeared before we could assign an identity to it. We could not come up with a sure Razorbill, despite many recent reports. At the Eastern Point Jetty, we got close-up views, photos and audio of a flock of Purple Sandpiper. At Bass Rocks in Gloucester, a lone Red-necked Grebe disappeared before I could photograph it. We finished up our outing at Granite Pier in Rockport where we observed an adult "Kumlien's" Iceland Gull, numerous Harlequin Duck and a pair of Great Cormorant.

That day with Alf reminded me of my early days birding in the 1980s when I was a student. Alf had been one of my teachers at Meadowbrook Junior High School, and later at Newton South High School, where he taught social studies and coached the varsity soccer team. He was British so knew *football* well. He had also dabbled in *twitching* as birding is called in England, where it had become quite popular (and competitive), much more so than in the USA. In 1982, Alf and I were assigned to a small territory in Newton and Brookline for the Greater Boston Christmas Bird Count. On that day in December, at the Brookline Recycling Center, he found a small sparrow that he didn't recognize. I identified it as Henslow's Sparrow, and it soon became the first documented winter record for the species in the State of Massachusetts. News spread quickly of our discovery and over the next month, the rare sparrow was observed by hundreds of local birders.

After graduating high school, my brother Oliver became business partners with Alf and created the *Gone Birding VCR Game*. In 1989 their company, Rupicola Productions, Inc., hired me as Sales Director, a position that I held for about a year. Fast forward to 2023, Alf still spoke with a heavy English accent and was in great shape, despite his 75 years. He even played soccer most Sundays with opponents half his age. Alf was excited to help me during my Biggest Year effort in 2023. I would meet up with Alf again three more times in Massachusetts (in July, September and December), and also during August in Arizona and in December in Puerto Rico.

The next day, Friday, March 3, I set up the family at a daytime work-station at a coffee shop in Salem and then headed out on my own to explore the coves of Salem and Marblehead for a couple of hours. I hoped to find Razorbill, a penguin-like seabird found only in the North Atlantic Ocean. It winters in ocean waters off New England, and summers on coastal cliffs and islands mainly in Canada. Remaining unsuccessful in my search for a Razorbill, I made one more birding stop after ferrying family members to various places. I visited Cold Spring Park in Newton where a woodcock was heard calling several days earlier. The American Woodcock is a forest sandpiper that returns north from the Southeastern USA in late winter to breed. I hoped that the individual reported here was not a migrant but rather had returned to its breeding territory and would vocalize and conduct its aerial display flights at dusk. It was getting dark when I arrived at the park. Any resident woodcock might have a couple more display flights planned for the evening.

"I will be back in ten minutes," I announced to Maribel and Angela who were my passengers, as I parked at a back entrance to the park. I hurried down a dim trail to a swampy area. The evening was dark and dreary with low cloud cover and no moonlight. Twenty minutes later it was pitch dark and all I could hear was silence over the suburban traffic noise in the distance. I didn't have a flashlight, but I was able to rely on my memory of the trail system from 40 years ago to guide me through the woods and back to the parked car, where Angela and Maribel were impatiently waiting for me.

"I hope you saw your bird," my wife said with a sarcastic tone which she uses when my passion for birds seems obviously selfish. "Nope, not yet," I muttered as I guided the car toward our evening destination at my mom's house a mile away. Angela, sensing an awkward moment between her parents, broke the tension by asking me questions about woodcocks.

On Saturday, March 4, Massachusetts was under a winter storm watch, and I awoke to rain, sleet and snow falling throughout the state. The wind was forecast to reach 40 MPH out of the northeast by 1 PM. I could not be happier. The strong easterly winds should be a gold mine for ocean birds blown to the coast including Razorbill and rarer seabirds such as Dovekie and Atlantic Puffin. I reached out to several contacts who might want to accompany me for a stormy sea watch. Peter Crosson of Barnstable had the same idea and invited me to join him at Sandy Neck Beach on Cape Cod at 1 PM.

I left Newton at 9 AM, and stopped at Lake Pearl in Wrentham, near the border with Rhode Island. Here, through falling snow, I observed year-birds Tufted Titmouse, a common songbird of the Eastern USA forests, and a staked-out overwintering female Tufted Duck (ABA Code 3), a European vagrant!

As I continued driving south and east toward Cape Cod, the snow turned to rain and the wind picked up strength. Peter called me from Sandy Neck and reported that the winds were not as effective as he had anticipated so he redirected me farther east to Corporation Beach in Dennis. I arrived at 1:15 PM and immediately noticed three Black-legged Kittiwake resting on the beach. This species normally winters at sea. Despite being the world's most abundant gull, it is rarely seen on land away from its massive breeding colonies on remote coastal cliffs. However, other oceanic birds were absent except for a lone Northern Gannet that made a pass unusually close to shore, struggling in the wind.

I decided to check out the south side of Cape Cod and headed to Craigville Beach, where a veteran Massachusetts birder, Chris Floyd, had reported a Black-headed Gull the previous day among a flock of roosting Ring-billed Gull. The smaller Black-headed Gull is a common Eurasian species, but only a handful stray to the Northeastern USA each winter. These birds may actually come from a small breeding population in the Canadian Maritime Provinces, which is why the ABA classifies it as Code 2, and not Code 3+. Despite the offshore wind, or maybe because of it, Buzzards Bay appeared quiet. I noticed a Red-throated Loon swimming parallel to the beach in the calm bay waters. As the sun sank in the western sky, it eventually fell below the storm clouds, which cheered up the gloomy afternoon, and gave a false impression that the storm was over.

One very pale gull on the beach looked like an adult Glaucous Gull with snow white wingtips, but its tiny bill and large dark eyes led me to a different conclusion: a *nominate* Iceland Gull, subspecies *glaucoides*, presumably from Iceland itself. These palest of the Iceland Gulls normally winter in Europe, whereas the Canadian breeding *Kumlien's* Iceland Gull winters in coastal Northeastern USA and carries darker gray pigment in its wingtips. Farther west, *Thayer's* Iceland Gull has even darker wingtips, which appear black when at rest, causing it to be confused with Herring Gull. Ironically, this European vagrant would not count for my list as it is a subspecies of Iceland Gull. I had already recorded Iceland Gull on my Biggest Year list, having seen the *Thayer's* Iceland Gull in Colorado in January, and the *Kumlien's* Iceland Gull in Massachusetts earlier in the week.

After the *nominate* Iceland Gull flew east disappearing down the beach, I refocused on the growing number of Ring-billed Gull arriving to roost for the night. The flock of 50 eventually grew to 500 as the sun fell below the horizon and then I found it. A smaller gull with a thin bill and a black ear spot—the Black-headed Gull had returned to roost. Unable to get a documentary photograph in the fading daylight, I retreated to my vehicle and drove two hours back to Newton through more wind, rain and snow.

On Sunday, March 5, the weather was much improved. I started birding early at Crystal Lake in Newton, where my brother Oliver found the Barnacle Goose in December. It wasn't there today. I then picked up my mom in Newton Highlands and we returned to Cold Spring Park hoping to run into that American Woodcock, which didn't happen. Dropping off Mom, I returned to my Airbnb via Newton Cemetery. This was another hangout for the overwintering Barnacle Goose, but not this day.

Thick-billed Murre
5 Mar 2023, Boston, Massachusetts

We checked out from the Airbnb by 10 AM. I dropped off the family at the Freedom Trail in downtown Boston and headed to Draw Seven State Park, a tiny urban park along the Mystic River in Somerville. I arrived around noon, and quickly spotted the big attraction, a staked-out Thick-billed Murre, as well as an overwintering Eastern Towhee. Other rarities here included a small flock of Red Crossbill and an early migrant Osprey. It is unusual to find any rare bird species, but here I found four in one small park—a lucky day! As luck would have it, I ran into another birder at this park. It turned out to be an old friend/mentor from my early birding days in Massachusetts—Bob Stymeist. We spent a while reminiscing about the good old days, including the day Alf Wilson and I reported the Henslow's Sparrow. Bob was the compiler of the Greater Boston Christmas Bird Count, so he remembered it well.

While I was chatting with Bob, I noticed a report on the *Rare Bird Alert* in my BirdsEye App. More luck! The Barnacle Goose, another stray from Iceland, had been re-found 30 minutes away, in Concord! Bob encouraged me to go for it. An hour later, I spotted the diminutive Barnacle Goose (ABA Code 4) among a group of 150 Canada Goose feeding in a fallow farm field along the Concord River. I didn't have much time and rushed back to the Bunker Hill Monument in Boston to pick up my family at the end of the Freedom Trail.

I needed to return my niece to Endicott College in Beverly, which gave me another chance for Razorbill. Checking BirdsEye, I found an eBird report of Razorbill from earlier in the day at Halibut Point State Park, Rockport, a 30-minute drive from Endicott College. After parking, I began the long walk to the shore. I had forgotten that I would need to hike a half mile to the coast. It had been a long day. My tired legs felt stiff and my feet were dragging. I reflected on my luck and wondered if the Razorbill would finally cooperate for me now. Would the Razorbill become a nemesis bird for me? I hoped not. The sun was almost setting by the time I arrived at the rocky shoreline of Halibut Point. Here I encountered dozens of Harlequin Duck, dozens of Long-tailed Duck and about a hundred Black Scoter, but alas, no Razorbill. I settled for the stunning scenery as consolation. Returning to Newton for our last night in Massachusetts, I devised an itinerary for my final day of this trip to New England.

5 Mar 2023, Halibut Point, Rockport, Massachusetts

On Monday, March 6, I left Newton at 5 AM with my mom, driving west on the turnpike (Interstate 90). We turned south at Sturbridge, on Interstate 84, toward Hartford, Connecticut. Daylight was encroaching so I took the first exit onto US20 and then Route 49 and followed signs into Wells State Park. I was looking for woodcock habitat. When the road crossed a low wet spot in the forest I pulled over. The dawn chorus was exuberant. My Merlin app alerted on about a dozen species of birds, including Pileated Woodpecker and Golden-crowned Kinglet but woodcock would elude me again. After enjoying the menagerie of bird calls and songs for about 20 minutes, we forged farther south, arriving in Connecticut and finally stopping at a shopping center in Mansfield.

We were searching for a staked-out rarity—another European gull species called Common Gull. Perhaps common in Europe, this species (recently split off from its Western North America counterpart, Short-billed Gull, by the North American Classification Committee of the American Ornithological Society) is exceedingly rare in the New World. Several Ring-billed Gull were around, so I began offering breadcrumbs to the flock.

Within a few minutes about a hundred *ringers* were at our feet. Sure enough, one of them was different—a tad smaller, with a slightly darker shade of gray on its upperparts. Instead of a yellow iris, the eye color was entirely dark, and the eye appeared larger than the beady eyes of the Ring-billed Gull. The bill was thinner and lacked the obvious black ring. This was the Common Gull (ABA Code 3).

I returned to Colorado by nightfall having added 23 species to my Biggest Year list, including three ABA Code 3+ rarities, all while juggling family responsibilities. More photos and audio files from species observed during the trip can be found on my Massachusetts trip report, available online at https://eBird.org/tripreport/112270. I observed 77 species of birds. The trip helped me in my quest for 900 species in the USA and its territories in 2023 and helped me stay competitive in the regular Big Year categories of ABA Area and Lower 48. In eBird's *Top 100,* I was ranked fifth in each of those categories.

Common Gull
6 Mar 2023, Mansfield, Connecticut

CHAPTER 9
Central California

I wrote earlier that Christmas Bird Counts would play a big role in my Biggest Year effort. In Central California, several rarities had been discovered during the CBC period including Rock Sandpiper, Ruff, Curlew Sandpiper, Little Stint, Wood Sandpiper and Red-flanked Bluetail. All of these were on winter territories. I wanted to visit the region before they left to breed in Alaska or Siberia. Three paying customers from Colorado (Patricia Cullen, Dana Hiatt and Greg Osland) and a local guide from San Francisco (Logan Kahle) joined me for a week of birding from Sacramento to Los Angeles March 8–16.

We arrived around noon at Sacramento and reviewed our itinerary with Logan over lunch. A major Pacific Ocean rainstorm was forecast to reach San Francisco within 24 hours so we scratched plans to bird in Marin and Sonoma counties and cancelled a scheduled whale watch out of Monterey Bay. During the calm before the storm, I picked up Red-breasted Sapsucker and Yellow-billed Magpie (a California endemic) in Sacramento. Then at San Francisco Bay, we added Fox Sparrow, Golden-crowned Sparrow, Clark's Grebe, Glaucous-winged Gull and Short-billed Gull as the sun set. Dana and Pat had never birded the west coast, so they were enjoying many new species for their life lists. I enjoyed helping them interpret their new discoveries.

We began March 9 at dawn in calm weather at Lighthouse Field State Beach in Santa Cruz. We were the only birders on site to find the overwintering Asian mega-rarity Red-flanked Bluetail. An Old World chat-flycatcher from China or thereabouts, this species had only occurred in the continental USA a handful of times. Logan pointed out the thicket where it usually appeared around 9:30 AM each morning. The hunt was on. While searching, I added two year-birds, Brown Creeper and Chestnut-backed Chickadee. The Red-flanked Bluetail (ABA Code 5) appeared right on cue around 10 AM making us all very happy. This was a rare lifer for Greg, who is a well-traveled and seasoned birder.

And then the rain started. We decided to try a sea watch from Point Pinos at Monterey Bay before the storm became too severe. This was a good move, although we got soaked in the rain. I added numerous year-birds including Common Murre, Rhinoceros Auklet, Pigeon Guillemot and Pelagic Cormorant as they flew low over the Pacific past the point. Several Surfbird foraged and rested on the rocks as well. These rotund sandpipers were in their dull gray winter plumage. By mid-afternoon, we headed inland to California's Central Valley hoping to escape the torrential rain, gale force winds and flooding expected near the coast.

Arriving at Merced National Wildlife Refuge near dusk, we drove the auto route in light rain and enjoyed a great diversity of waterfowl and shorebird species (including a rare Ruff, ABA Code 3, found by Logan's sharp eyes) despite the thick cloud cover and gloomy aura of the storm. There were two year-birds here: Cliff Swallow, an early spring migrant and Swainson's Hawk, an overwintering bird. While most of the population of this grassland-associated hawk winters in the Argentine pampas of South America's southern cone, a small percentage avoid the long voyage, taking advantage of the mild California climate for their winter home.

On March 10, we began the day in the desert near Bakersfield in Kern County, hoping for respite from the rain. Here we were rewarded with numerous singing Bell's Sparrow and one LeConte's Thrasher. A male Lawrence's Goldfinch gave some of us brief but excellent views when it perched on the seed stalk of a desert plant. Later, we made a pass through the grassy hilltops of Bitter Creek National Wildlife Refuge hoping to find the endangered California Condor on the wing, but these magnificent aerialists seemed to be grounded by the stormy weather conditions. Next stop was a search for exotic species in the city of Bakersfield where we added some rain-soaked Rose-ringed Parakeet. We then headed a couple hours south to Los Angeles County to a stake-out for a vagrant Tundra Bean-Goose at the Lancaster Water Reclamation Plant. But the goose, a stray from Eurasia, did not cooperate. We ended the birding day at nearby Apollo Community Regional Park, home to many lost geese. No bean-goose here, but we did find a locally rare Neotropic Cormorant!

We started March 11 at a dairy pond in San Bernardino County, 10 minutes from our motel. The pond hosted a rare Eurasian Wigeon as well as a staked-out Ruff (ABA Code 3). Being close to Los Angeles, we decided to dedicate the rest of the day to finding exotic species that are considered countable by the American Birding Association because they have reached the status of *established populations*. Without much trouble we added Yellow-chevroned Parakeet, Egyptian Goose, Red-whiskered Bulbul, Indian Peafowl and Red-masked Parakeet. We found two of these species at the Los Angeles County Arboretum and Botanical Gardens, where we spent an hour. Unfortunately, I spent most of the hour on a Zoom call with the Colorado Field Ornithologists Board of Directors organizing the upcoming annual convention scheduled for July.

Red-flanked Bluetail
9 Mar 2023, Santa Cruz, California

On March 12, we began the day with a longish (about an hour) drive from our hotel in Chino to the San Jacinto Wildlife Area in Riverside County. A normally closed section would be open today to accommodate birders interested in viewing two Asian shorebirds that had overwintered, Little Stint and Wood Sandpiper. The stint evaded us, hiding among thousands of like-plumaged Western Sandpiper. We managed great views of the Wood Sandpiper (ABA Code 3). Other year-birds included Canyon Wren, Rufous-crowned Sparrow and White-throated Swift. After receiving a *rare bird alert* that the Tundra Bean-Goose had returned to the Lancaster Water Reclamation Plant, we headed that way for a literal *wild goose chase*. This time was a success! By mid-afternoon, we found the rare goose (ABA Code 3) foraging with a small group of Canada Goose. We ended the day after sunset in Thousand Oaks, Ventura County. A visit to a county park gave us several nocturnal species, including Common Poorwill, Western Screech-Owl and Barn Owl.

On Sunday, March 13, we had reserved passage on the Channel Islands Ferry from Ventura Harbor to Scorpion Anchorage on Santa Cruz Island. With an hour to kill before boarding the ferry, we visited Mission Oaks Park where we found Lawrence's Goldfinch, Scaly-breasted Munia (an exotic), Western Tanager, Bullock's, Orchard and Hooded Orioles and Hermit Warbler. At Ventura Harbor we added Wandering Tattler. We departed the harbor at 9:30 AM and landed at Santa Cruz about 75 minutes later. A brief visit to this unique island was adequate to add the endemic Island Scrub-Jay. From the return ferry I got lucky when a northbound Ancient Murrelet crossed the bow. Later in the afternoon, back on the mainland, we added Lewis's Woodpecker and Greater Roadrunner to the trip list.

We dedicated March 14 to target birding in Orange County where we visited San Joaquin Marsh & Wildlife Sanctuary, Upper Newport Bay Nature Preserve, Santa Ana River mouth and Bolsa Chica Ecological Reserve. Highlights included California Gnatcatcher, Swinhoe's White-eye (another exotic), Hutton's Vireo, Elegant Tern, Black Scoter, Ridgway's Rail, Snowy Plover and Reddish Egret. All were additions to the trip list.

On the morning of March 15, we headed into the foothills of the San Gabriel Mountains and the Angeles National Forest. Here we found California Thrasher in the shrubby understory of the live oak scrub forest. Mountain Quail calls echoed from various canyons in these foothills.

When we entered a pine forest, we were thrilled to spot a White-headed Woodpecker flying in front of our minivan. Logan slammed on the brakes in time for all of us to get stunning looks and even photos of this target species which I had missed farther south in January. We returned to Bitter Creek National Wildlife Refuge again hoping to find the condors but found thick fog instead. A backup choice was Lake Piru. There, finally, we found 11 majestic California Condor soaring high overhead.

On the final morning of the tour, we were treated to a staked-out Burrowing Owl at Ontario Airport just before dropping off our three customers for their return flight to Colorado. They seemed satisfied by the productive trip. We had tallied 237 species for the eBird trip report which can be viewed on-line here: https://eBird.org/tripreport/112559.

My California trip, however, was not yet finished. I still needed to return our rented minivan to the airport in Sacramento and our guide to San Francisco! This gave me an opportunity for more birding. Over the next 36 hours I would add ten more species to the trip list total, all found north of San Francisco in Marin and Sonoma counties: Northern Saw-whet Owl, Varied Thrush, Pileated Woodpecker, Sooty Grouse, Pacific Wren, Cackling Goose (*Aleutian* subspecies), Tufted Duck (a staked-out Asian stray at the Petaluma River, ABA Code 3), Iceland Gull (pointed out to me by my friend Noah Arthur) and Black Rail (at Petaluma Marsh).

Coming to Central California in late winter/early spring paid off in terms of the number of species found here. I added 61 species for my USA and Territories Biggest Year, including three new ABA Code 3+ species. These additions placed me firmly among the top five in the eBird leaderboard for the ABA Area. For a few days during this tour, I reached the top position. Many thanks are due to my three customers, Pat, Dana and Greg, for their excellent companionship and to our able birding guide and driver, Logan. I considered all of them my friends.

CHAPTER 10
Rare Birds Are Common!

O n my recent Biggest Year trip to New England, the rarest bird was a Common Gull (*Larus canus*), a diminutive white-headed larid from Europe that was staked out with a group of our familiar Ring-billed Gull (*L. delawarensis*) in a Connecticut shopping center. Encountering gulls in a paved parking lot away from the seacoast is mundane, i.e., it happens all the time. Both Ring-billed Gull and Common Gull are well adapted to habitats dominated by humans (such as big box strip malls and restaurant parking lots). These birds were not picky eaters. They eat human garbage (such as leftover food from household meals and restaurant kitchens) as well as fish and crustaceans found in ponds, lakes, bays and oceans. These gulls were also happy to accept food donations and would gladly devour any morsel of food offered by humans who passed nearby to their hangouts. In certain places, gulls had become quite confiding and would attempt to steal food from picnic baskets or even from your hands if you were not paying attention. French fries seemed to be highly valued by Ring-billed Gull. For this reason, *ringers* (as they are commonly called) often hung out near fast food venues.

I suspected this to be true for gulls not only in North America but also on other continents. In the case of Common Gull, I found them abundant in city parks in Iceland, England and Germany during past visits to those European countries. Outside cities, the Common Gull was numerous in agricultural settings where flocks with hundreds of birds foraged in recently tilled fields, hoping to find crop residue from recent harvesting operations or worms and grubs exposed by tractors turning the soil. The same was true for Ring-billed Gull in the farm belts of the USA.

As human populations grew, the numbers of human-adapted gull species also grew. A small portion of these explored new migration routes or accidentally crossed the oceans during storms. Some were assisted by ships.

The odds of finding one outside its normal range is purely a question of mathematical probability, a numbers game. Because the number of observers has increased, previously rare sightings of misplaced species in new locations are now commonplace. Considering that there are many abundant species eligible to become vagrants to the USA and the increasing number of skilled birders watching for these misfits, the probability that any one birder may see these oddities has increased. My trip to New England seemed to confirm this assessment. In just under a week, I saw Barnacle Goose, Black-headed Gull, Common Gull and Tufted Duck, all vagrants from Northwestern Europe. Not to mention the nominate subspecies of Iceland Gull, a vagrant from Iceland.

It was ironic that the common name for *Larus canus* is *Common Gull* given its rarity in the USA, where it is decidedly not common. Of course, this is due to a confusing aspect of the English language. There are at least three different meanings of the word *common*:

1. Abundant; occurs at high frequency or present in high density

2. Widespread

3. Mundane; vernacular

The Common Gull was so named not because of its abundance but rather because it was widespread. It bred and wintered across the Old World from the Atlantic coast to the Pacific coast. In the New World, however, it is fair to say, "Common Gulls are rare." I should point out the Short-billed Gull (*L. brachyrhynchos*), a common species of gull that breeds in the northwest of the North American continent, was long considered to be a subspecies of Common Gull, until 2021. The North American Classification Committee of the American Ornithological Society upgraded its taxonomical status to full species level. In the field, they are almost inseparable. Morphologically, they are practically identical.

Another species that is rare in North America is the Common Crane (*Grus grus*) which also is found across the Eurasian continent. For several decades, one or two individuals of this iconic Old World crane species have been appearing annually in the USA during winter, hanging out with and migrating with flocks of Sandhill Crane (*G. canadensis*). Some Sandhills migrate northwest across the Bering Strait to breed in Eastern Siberia. There, the ranges of these two crane species overlap. Apparently, a few Common Cranes of Eastern Siberia migrate southeast with Sandhills rather than southwest with their own kind. The phenomenon has continued for years.

On Thursday, March 16, 2023, a report surfaced of a Common Crane among tens of thousands of northbound Sandhill Cranes that had settled to roost along the North Platte River near the village of Lewellen in Garden County, Nebraska. I received this news from my friend David Wade about noon on March 18. Lewellen is just over three hours if driving the speed limit from my home in Fort Collins. I immediately texted friends who might want to go on a wild crane chase. One responded favorably, and by 3 PM, Cole Wild and I were racing (at the speed limit, of course) across the eastern plains of Colorado hoping to reach Lewellen before sunset. We hoped the roosting cranes would be within view of a public road. We could not count on local intelligence from birders because this part of Western Nebraska is largely unpopulated. This under-birded part of Nebraska is located about 20 miles north of the northeast corner of Colorado.

We arrived about an hour before dark and quickly found a large flock of foraging cranes in wheat stubble near the river. We carefully studied each bird, searching for the black neck unique to the Common Crane. Not having any luck, we arrived at the highway bridge over the river and watched as dozens of crane flocks, each with hundreds of birds, passed high overhead from all directions settling in to roost for the night in the shallow river. Finding this vagrant Common Crane was going to be more difficult than we realized. We pondered our strategy as we drove to the nearest motel 30 miles away.

The following morning (Sunday, March 19, 2023), we began our search at sunrise from the bridge. There were about a thousand cranes still in the river, but too distant to study. We began driving country roads looking for foraging flocks. Several hours passed and we had observed several thousand birds with no luck. Then at 10:30 AM, we noticed an exodus of cranes from the corn and wheat fields, returning toward the river. We followed them and found a massive flock of about 10,000 cranes packed together in a grassy field adjacent to the river. We had about an hour until we had to return to our families in Colorado. We searched and searched and searched, assessing every individual crane, using spotting scopes. At 11:40 AM, Cole calmly announced "Got it!" Sure enough, he had spotted the needle in the haystack. And just in time for us to meet our family obligations. To see photos of the Common Crane (USA and Territories Biggest Year-bird 489, ABA Code 4), check out my eBird checklist on-line: https://eBird.org/checklist/S131299323.

Common Crane in Flock of Sandhill Cranes
19 Mar 2023, Lewellen, Nebraska
Photo by Cole Wild

The Common Crane and the Common Gull are two examples of *common* birds that are rare in the USA. But one concept that my Big Year experience has reconfirmed for me is that the opposite is equally true: Rare birds are common. Everywhere I have traveled for my Big Year, I have encountered species classified as rare in eBird. Many of my checklists include a rare species or two. Sometimes even more. My friend John Vanderpoel observed about 40 vagrants during his successful Big Year effort in 2011. These were mega-rarities, birds classified by the American Birding Association (ABA) as Codes 3, 4 and 5. During the first quarter of 2023, I had seen more than a dozen, putting me on track for well over 40.

Of course, not all birds flagged in eBird as *rare* are ABA mega-rarities. eBird considers seasonality and geography such that a species may be considered rare one week and common the next week, or rare in one county and common in the next. Oddly, I've noticed that a relatively small percentage of birders ever report rarities. I believe this is because the concept of rarity implies that a species does not belong and therefore encountering one does not compute in the brains of many birders. To find a rarity one must keep an open mind to the possibility of its occurrence. It's actually just a numbers game. I think of it this way. A frequency of one per 1,000 or lower is what I would consider rare. So, in a flock of 1,000 geese, I expect to find one rare goose. A mudflat crawling with a thousand shorebirds may host a rare one among them. In my home county of Larimer in Northern Colorado, we regularly expect to find about 300 species each year. That leaves over 600 species from the *ABA Checklist* for the USA to occur as a rarity. So, while it would be unexpected to observe any one of these, I would expect to find some of these each year just because of the number of birds that pass through annually.

I typically report an eBird-flagged rarity about once per five or ten checklists. I suspect many timid birders are hesitant to claim a rarity observation because of the interpretation of eBird's requirement for comments as questioning their integrity or their birding skills. But my message to all birders is this: Expect to find rare birds as rare birds are actually relatively common. And if all birders reported the rarities they observe, we would find that they are even more common than we thought.

CHAPTER 11
Southeastern Arizona

*A*t 2:45 AM on March 21, 2023, Joe Kipper picked up my friend Scott Rashid and me in his vintage Jeep Cherokee. Joe's license plates read **G Y R F L C N**, a reference to the Gyrfalcon, North America's largest falcon and one that I longed to find in 2023. He dropped us off at the Denver International Airport at 4:30 AM for our 6:30 AM Southwest Airlines flight to Phoenix Sky Harbor International Airport. By 9 AM Scott and I were rolling in our rented Nissan Rogue mini-SUV. I had asked Scott to drive for this tour because I knew he loved hummingbirds and owls. Southeastern Arizona is known for both. Several Mexican species occur only as far north as the *sky islands* (sky islands refer to cool, wet, isolated mountain ranges that rise out of the sea of hot, dry desert). Scott is a self-taught ornithologist who studies hummingbirds and owls in Rocky Mountain National Park. He has published several books on the owls of Colorado. When no one else registered for this tour, we decided to go anyway, splitting the costs evenly.

Our first stop was Veterans Oasis Park in Chandler, a Phoenix suburb. What a great park, with managed desert habitat and a series of lakes. A Rufous-backed Robin, a stray from Mexico, had been spotted here about ten days earlier and reported to eBird. No luck finding that bird, but we did spot 49 other species here in two and a half hours. This was a good start to our week-long trip through Southeast Arizona. USA and Territories Biggest Year-birds were Gila Woodpecker, Dusky Flycatcher and Lucy's Warbler. I then guided us to my favorite location for Bendire's Thrasher at Red Mountain Park in Mesa, Arizona near the eastern edge of the Phoenix metropolis. The thrasher cooperated for us and Gilded Flicker was new also. A quick stop at Arizona State University Research Park in Tempe netted us another target, Rosy-faced Lovebird, an established exotic originally from Africa. Having nailed my two Phoenix area targets (the thrasher and the lovebird), we jumped on Interstate 10 and headed south toward Tucson and the famous sky islands. We arrived at dusk and spent our first evening in an overpriced motel in Green Valley south of Tucson.

On March 22, we started early in Madera Canyon in the Santa Rita Mountains, the most accessible of the sky islands. These high-altitude extensions of the Sierra Madre Occidental serve as a natural corridor for species that have their core populations in West Mexico. Either we arrived too late in the morning to hear nocturnal owls and nightjars or these birds had not yet returned to their breeding sites in the canyon. The dawn chorus was quiet too, giving us the impression that it was still winter in the canyon. Several year-round resident bird species were present, including Mexican Jay, Bridled Titmouse and Painted Redstart. At the Santa Rita Lodge bird feeders, we added Rivoli's Hummingbird, Arizona Woodpecker and Hepatic Tanager. These were all great birds we expected to find easily in the sky island ecosystems, which combined desert grassland with arid scrub/thorn forest, pinyon juniper forest and pine-oak forest at higher elevations. The riparian creeks hosted massive, white-barked sycamore trees whose leaves were weeks away from emerging.

Montosa Canyon, a couple drainages to the southwest, had recent reports of Black-capped Gnatcatcher, so we went there next. The gnatcatcher remained elusive, but we added Crissal Thrasher, Red-naped Sapsucker, Canyon and Green-tailed Towhees. Farther south along the Santa Cruz River, we targeted a recently staked out Thick-billed Kingbird at Roger Morriss Park but, unfortunately, without success. There we found Zone-tailed and Common Black Hawks, Broad-billed Hummingbird and a migrant Western Kingbird among the resident Cassin's Kingbird.

Continuing south to Nogales on the Mexico border, and then east skirting around the Santa Rita Mountains, we found ourselves at the Patagonia rest area where we made a quick stop to pay homage to this iconic birding location made famous by Kenn Kaufman in his book *Kingbird Highway*. Our destination however was the Paton Center for Hummingbirds a short distance up the road in Patagonia, Arizona. A Violet-crowned Hummingbird was wintering there, and it made a brief appearance for us shortly after our arrival. We also added Lazuli Bunting. Birds were seemingly everywhere as the sun disappeared, so we made plans to come back first thing in the morning.

On the morning of March 23, birds and birders abounded. We met Louie Dombrowski, the manager of the Center, who pointed out a White-throated Sparrow (rare) in a brush pile and informed us about a pair of rare Sabine's Gull he had found the previous evening down the road at Patagonia Lake. We also met Richard Fray, a local birding guide from Rio Rico, who gave us status updates on most of our target species.

Sabine's Gull
23 Mar 2023, Patagonia Lake State Park, Arizona

We checked out of our hotel in downtown Patagonia where I was surprised to hear and see Northern Beardless-Tyrannulet, a bird I had already encountered in January in Texas. At Lake Patagonia State Park, we found more birders, many of whom had come specifically to chase the Sabine's Gull. The gulls cooperated for great views. One of them was in full alternate (breeding) plumage. We were able to obtain excellent photos at close range.

A singing western Bell's Vireo was also new. I ran into Texas snowbirds Mark and Joanie Hubinger here. They hosted me during my trip to the Rio Grande Valley the previous month. What a small world!

The next birding stop was the San Rafael Grasslands east of the Santa Rita Mountains. We hoped to find wintering Baird's Sparrow and longspurs but settled for Savannah Sparrow and Chihuahuan Meadowlark. From there we headed north to Graham National Forest near Safford, Arizona. We had received a tip about a Spotted Owl located near a campground, but we found nothing upon our arrival at dusk. After dark, we eventually spied a large owl perched atop an oak tree along the road.

"Stop the car!" I shouted. "We just passed an owl on the left." Scott obliged, and whirled around in his seat as he brought his binoculars to his eyes. "Holy f—g s—t, that's a fricking Spotted Owl!" Scott often cusses when he gets excited. The magnificent owl flew off before we could get photos.

On March 24, we returned to the Mount Graham National Forest campground hoping for a daylight view of Spotted Owl but again we came up empty. We did find an unexpectedly large flock of 18 Yellow-eyed Junco. We then headed southeast to Portal and checked in at the Portal Peak Lodge at the eastern foot of the Chiricahua Mountains. By late afternoon we had tracked down Mexican Chickadee and Olive Warbler. Owling in the evening yielded Northern Saw-whet Owl (rare), Whiskered Screech-Owl and Great Horned Owl.

Spending the next day, March 25, around Portal was productive as we were able to find Hammond's Flycatcher, Gray Catbird (rare), Pyrrhuloxia, Rufous-winged and Black-chinned Sparrows, Scott's Oriole, Juniper Titmouse, Rivoli's Hummingbird and Blue-throated Mountain-gem. We left the area somewhat frustrated that we could not turn up Montezuma Quail. Apparently, several years of drought had suppressed the population considerably.

Our target for March 26 was Rufous-capped Warbler, another Mexican species like Five-striped Sparrow and Black-capped Gnatcatcher that barely extends its population into the USA among the canyons of the sky islands. The species had not been reported recently in eBird. Then on March 23, a pair was discovered singing in an under-birded area called Ramanote Canyon west of Rio Rico (and west of the Santa Rita Mountains). They were relocated in the same area by two independent birders on March 25. This was music to my ears as I figured there was a good chance that they were establishing a breeding territory, and they would be advertising their position through song. We drove 90 minutes to the parking area and hiked 30 minutes to reach the canyon. Along the way we added two new trip species, a locally rare Harris's Hawk and Phainopepla.

Once at the canyon, we found running water and lots of birds. We hiked about a mile upstream and another mile downstream, spending about five hours searching for Rufous-capped Warbler, but to no avail. Year-birds were Ash-throated Flycatcher and Cassin's Vireo. We retreated from Ramanote Canyon, frustrated but satisfied that we had searched the area adequately and headed back to Madera Canyon in the heart of the Santa Rita Mountains.

We checked into the Madera Kubo Cabins for our final two nights of the trip. The sun was setting so the time was right to try nocturnal birding again. We started at the bottom of the canyon at Proctor Road overlooking the grasslands north of the canyon entrance. We could see the distant lights of Tucson across the desert, in front of a large shadow that was Mount Lemon. A distant Montezuma Quail sang once, to our delight! An invisible Barn Owl flew over the grassland, screeching once every few seconds, presumably advertising for a mate. We played recordings of Mexican Whip-poor-will and Buff-collared Nightjar but received no response. Moving uphill we played a recording of several small owls and nightjars at Whitehouse Picnic Area, and one Western Screech-Owl obliged us by calling back. We followed its soft voice to an oak tree across the main canyon road until it was right above us. Shining our flashlight into the branches we watched it as it hooted at us, as if to say, "OK you got my attention, now what is it that you want?"

Farther up the canyon at the Santa Rita Lodge, we listened intently for owls. Small owls are known to sing frequently here and we didn't feel that playing a recording was necessary or appropriate. In fact, we did hear a distant morse code tooting of a Whiskered Screech-Owl and a brief series of high-pitched shrieks from the miniscule Elf Owl.

On March 27, we started our birding day at dawn at our cabin, hoping to hear the barking of an early migrant or wintering Elegant Trogon. No barking. Then we returned to Proctor Road and listened intently for more song bursts from Montezuma Quail—none. We kept driving downhill into Florida Wash and turned onto Box Canyon Road, heading east. After five miles, we parked at the steep ravine known as Box Canyon and searched a short stretch of the curvy dirt road and the adjacent hillside for Five-striped Sparrow. A small group had been discovered here earlier in the winter and were being reported by birders almost daily. Several other birders arrived to join the search. Unfortunately, we came up empty after patiently searching for several hours.

Next, we returned to Roger Morriss Park along the De Anza Trail in Tubac, Arizona. One of the birders we met told us that a pair of Short-tailed Hawk had been hanging around the park. We found a Zone-tailed Hawk and several Gray Hawk but had no luck with the rare Short-tailed Hawk. A drake Mexican Duck in the Santa Cruz River was new for my year list in eBird. We returned to our cabin with plenty of time to prepare for the evening owl show. Unfortunately, there was no further sign of any Elf Owl activity, and a couple of Whiskered Screech-Owl tooted only briefly but remained distant.

March 28 was our final morning of birding before flying home from Phoenix. We started before sunrise at Box Canyon hoping the Five-striped Sparrow would be singing. Not so. We then drove an hour northeast toward Paige Creek near Benson. We were following an eBird *Rare Bird Alert* for Nutting's Flycatcher, another Mexican vagrant. As we neared the national forest where the flycatcher had been seen, we came to a creek crossing that seemed too deep for our vehicle. We didn't want to risk getting stuck on our last day. Instead, we diverted to Benson to look for Scaled Quail. We found Gambel's Quail and many other birds around the cemetery there.

Our final birding stop was in Tucson's Reid Park, where we hoped to track down some lingering winter residents, including Wood Duck, Lewis's Woodpecker, Greater Pewee, Plumbeous Vireo and Red Crossbill. We meandered through the park and eventually found two drake Wood Duck, a singing Plumbeous Vireo and nine Red Crossbill.

We ended the trip with 179 species. More details including photos and audio are available from our Arizona trip report, which can be found online at https://eBird.org/tripreport/115162. I was satisfied with 43 year-birds, bringing my Biggest Year total to 532. At least 25 of these were species that I was unlikely to find anywhere outside Arizona. We missed many of the rarer species that we chased, including Rufous-backed Robin, Black-capped Gnatcatcher, Five-striped Sparrow, Rufous-capped Warbler, Short-tailed Hawk and Nutting's Flycatcher. In fact, this trip produced no ABA Code 3+ species. Fortunately, I would have more opportunities to add most of these species to my Biggest Year list when I returned to Arizona in August and October. Special thanks to Scott Rashid for his companionship and assistance.

Yellow-eyed Junco
24 Mar 2023, Graham County, Arizona

CHAPTER 12
Colorado Grouse

*T*he grouse are among the most difficult orders of birds to see in North America. They are large birds but because of their status as upland game birds, they have learned to avoid humans and have adopted stealthy behaviors to avoid detection. Furthermore, their camouflage plumage—an adaptation evolved to avoid predation—allows them to blend into their surroundings perfectly. To see all 27 ABA Area species in the order Galliformes, which includes typical grouse, pheasants and quail, I needed to visit Alaska, Arizona, California, Hawaii, Minnesota and Nevada. However, the largest number of these species were found in my home state of Colorado because of its centralized position on the North American continent. In fact, Colorado in April has become a popular destination among birders keen on adding many of the Galliformes—up to 13 species—to their life list in a single trip.

During the spring mating season, many of the grouse species form social *leks* where males dance and strut and generally show off for females which gather to select a suitable mate to fertilize their eggs. Most of the major birding tour companies offer a Colorado Grouse tour (also known as a *chicken run*). My first professional gig as a birding tour guide was leading one of these 2,000-mile, seven-night van tours in 2004. Bob Odear, the founder of the *North American Rare Bird Alert,* had two tours scheduled back-to-back for his target birding company OBServTours, and had become ill with flu-like symptoms after the first trip. He called the American Birding Association headquarters for help. Chuck Bell, ABA's travel director, suggested me as a replacement guide. I led five of these tours over the next three years before starting my own company, Quetzal Tours.

Fast forward to April 2023. I had two grouse tours scheduled, both of which were rescheduled events that had been postponed since 2020 when the COVID-19 pandemic caused Colorado tourism to be put on hold. The first tour was for a photographer from Thailand. We spent six days together

April 5–10. Then I guided a Partnership in International Birding group of six birding clients mostly from Great Britain, April 12–20. During these two gigs, I added several species to my USA and Territories Biggest Year list, including: Clark's Nutcracker and Brown-capped Rosy-Finch at Scott Rashid's feeder in Estes Park on April 5; Mountain Plover and Thick-billed Longspur at the Pawnee National Grassland on April 6; Greater Sage-Grouse at North Park, April 9; and Chestnut-collared Longspur from the Pawnee National Grassland on April 12.

The next day, April 13, my group visited the Nature Conservancy's Smoky Valley Ranch in Western Kansas where local guide Jim Millensifer showed us a lek site on the prairie with a dozen dancing, stamping, jumping and dueling Lesser Prairie-Chicken all trying to impress a female or two that were hidden nearby in tall grass. There was a single intruder Greater Prairie-Chicken as well that tried to steal the show. The ranch is located in a small region of range overlap between these two similar species. Nearby in Oakley, Kansas, I added Baird's Sandpiper, a northbound migrant.

Greater Prairie-Chicken
13 Apr 2023, near Oakley, Kansas

The following morning, April 14, I added White-tailed Ptarmigan, a grouse species found above the tree line, at Loveland Pass, west of Denver. Unlike the other grouse species, the ptarmigan were in snow-white winter plumage to blend in with their snowy surroundings.

Following the successful encounter with ptarmigan, I took the group to the residential neighborhood of Wildernest on a mountainside overlooking the town of Silverthorne. Several houses there attracted birds to feeding stations. This was a good location to find a variety of winter finches such as crossbills and grosbeaks. A noisy flock of crossbills flew overhead. I recorded their vocalizations using my cell phone. The sonogram of their flight calls confirmed the presence of both Red and Cassia Crossbills.

The next day, en route to Craig in Northwest Colorado, I would pick up Barrow's Goldeneye at Windy Gap Reservoir, a migrating Gray Flycatcher in Steamboat Springs, and Sharp-tailed Grouse at an evening lek site in a hayfield north of Milner. On April 17, I added Chukar, an introduced species originally from North Africa, and a migrating Virginia's Warbler in an arid wash at Coal Canyon in Cameo, Mesa County (Western Colorado). The same day we found Gray Vireo singing on territory in junipers at Colorado National Monument near Grand Junction.

At dusk, we visited Black Canyon of the Gunnison National Park but could not find Dusky Grouse at their usual booming grounds among the Gambel oak shrub-forest along the south rim of the spectacular canyon. As a consolation, however, we were serenaded by the eerie hooting of a Long-eared Owl after sunset. The next morning, we returned to the beautiful canyon for a second attempt to find the Dusky Grouse. The scurrying Mountain Cottontail got us excited on several occasions. But alas, no grouse!

April 19 was our day to use the Waunita Hot Springs blind (the Brits in our group called it a *hide*) to observe a lek for the threatened Gunnison Sage-Grouse. It was a relatively warm morning 30 miles east of Gunnison, with no wind and some clouds but no precipitation. The grouse put on a great show for us with 38 males dancing for 9 females. I had never seen so many birds at this lek. The total population of this species reached a low of only 2,000 birds remaining in 2022.

The Sisk-a-dee organization volunteer (Kaitlin Harvey, a grad student in ecology at Western Colorado University) told us the population in 2023 appeared to have doubled.

After the successful lek visit, we headed north from Gunnison to look for rosy-finches at feeders around the Crested Butte ski resort. By spring, these montane finches retreated into the high alpine forests, but storms could bring them back to backyard feeding stations in mountain towns all over Western Colorado. Snowflakes were falling so we hoped for a large flock that might contain small numbers of wintering Gray-crowned and Black Rosy-Finches. However, only four Brown-capped Rosy-Finch showed up.

A few hours later we encountered a stronger snow squall at Sally Waterhouse's feeder in Nathrop. Right on cue, a swirling flock of rosy-finches arrived to refuel, with about a hundred Brown-capped but again no Gray-crowned or Black Rosy-Finches. These might have to wait until December to get added to my Big Year list unless I could find them during the breeding season in Alaska and/or the Great Basin, respectively. In Nathrop, we encountered Pinyon Jay, a highly sought target for the Brits.

April 20 was the final day of the grouse tour. We spent the night of April 19 in Pueblo West. We got an early start hoping for another shot at Dusky Grouse on Highway 78 west of Beulah, in the San Isabel National Forest. The habitat looked perfect but still no grouse. Consolation prizes here included stunning views of three target species for our group: American Three-toed Woodpecker, Williamson's Sapsucker and Northern Pygmy-Owl.

After checking out of our hotel in Pueblo West, finding Scaled Quail was a cinch. There they were, hiding underneath the first ornamental cholla cactus that we could find in the residential town. The final birding stop of the tour, Lake Pueblo State Park, provided numerous new birds and allowed us to surpass my goal of 150 trip species. Highlights here were all three phoebe species, all five swallow species, singing Bewick's Wren, breeding-plumaged Western Sandpiper and Bonaparte's Gull. For the complete list of birds on this tour, see: https://eBird.org/tripreport/120124.

My USA and Territories Biggest Year list was now at 551 species. How was I doing relative to other Big Year birders? For the ABA Area, ABA Continental and Lower 48 competitions, I had 479 species (Puerto Rican species don't count), which was ranked fifth in eBird for all three categories. My next adventure would be a four-day repositioning cruise from San Diego to Vancouver, April 24–27, which I hoped would net me a horde of Pacific Ocean pelagic species for my Biggest Year.

Scaled Quail
20 Apr 2023, Pueblo West, Colorado

CHAPTER 13
Repositioning Cruise

*P*elagic birds are ocean-dwelling creatures that are difficult to see from mainland shores. These birds are not well known by most land-dwelling birders, me included. They are probably the group of species least understood by ornithologists due to their preference for marine regions, their tendency to nest on remote islands, and their cryptic plumages. Most are drably plumaged, making identification challenging. This is especially true for the shearwaters, petrels and storm-petrels, and many of the *alcids* (seabirds in the family Alcidae) as well.

There are roughly 100 species of pelagic birds on the *ABA Checklist* and several more in the Territories that I could find in 2023. I saw some of these from the shore at La Jolla, California on January 8 (e.g., Black-vented Shearwater, Cassin's Auklet, Scripp's Murrelet). Northern Gannet and Black-legged Kittiwake found me during a storm at First Encounter Beach, Cape Cod on March 4. Thick-billed Murre was at Boston Harbor March 5. I added more alcids at Point Pinos near Monterey on March 9 (Common Murre, Rhinoceros Auklet and Pigeon Guillemot) and from the boat ride across the Santa Cruz Channel on March 13 (Ancient Murrelet). But many more pelagic species awaited detection during my Biggest Year.

Of course, I would try to add more pelagic species whenever the opportunity arose. One such opportunity was the *repositioning cruise* from San Diego to Vancouver, British Columbia on board Holland America's *Eurodam* cruise ship, April 24–27. Several times per year, cruise lines around the world send their ships back to starting points to begin a season anew. The trips can be a great value since they sell heavily discounted berths. E. J. Raynor, a birding buddy from Fort Collins, had recommended this cruise for my Biggest Year. When I discovered that several other Big Year birders were planning to take this cruise, I was on board for it.

I arrived in San Diego the evening of Sunday, April 23, with my wife, Maribel. I had invited her to join me on the cruise to celebrate her birthday (and to give her an opportunity to share part of my Biggest Year experience). We checked into the Wyndham Bayside Hotel across from the cruise terminal in downtown San Diego. My Biggest Year list total was 552 species. Since the grouse tour ended four days earlier, I had added Yellow-throated Vireo near my home on April 22, thanks to a tip from Fort Collins birder Brendan Beers. He had found this rare spring migrant along the Cache La Poudre River at Watson Lake State Wildlife Area in LaPorte, Colorado, just 20 minutes from my home.

I opened my BirdsEye app to see what local species may be around in San Diego County that I still needed for my ABA Area year list. BirdsEye is able to access my eBird account to determine needs and target species. Three species popped up: Little Stint, Vaux's Swift and Pacific-slope Flycatcher. I had tried for the overwintering Little Stint twice in January at the south end of San Diego Bay. It would be migrating north any day now. The swift and flycatcher were spring migrants reported to eBird a few days earlier less than a mile away at Balboa Park in downtown San Diego. Our cruise boarding time was 10:20 AM. Maribel planned for us to have breakfast at 8:45 AM with a former teaching colleague from the Colorado State University Foreign Languages Department she had not seen in 20 years. Time was limited in the morning and I was without wheels. I decided to go for the Balboa Park birds.

I was slow getting up on Monday morning. I left the hotel at 8 AM. Heading toward Balboa Park on foot I noticed that Waterfront Park, adjacent to the hotel, was birdy. I focused my effort there instead. In an hour, I racked up 22 species including four species of warbler (Black-throated Gray, Orange-crowned, Yellow and Yellow-rumped Warblers), several Hooded Oriole and two flycatchers (Cassin's Kingbird and Ash-throated Flycatcher). A third species of flycatcher flew before I could definitively identify it as Pacific-slope Flycatcher. I joined the breakfast a little late at 9:15 AM.

After checking in at the cruise terminal and settling into our room on board the *Eurodam*, I realized that we had several hours to kill before the boat would sail. I convinced Maribel to join me on a visit to Balboa Park. We left the ship and took an Uber to the park at 1:30 PM. We strolled for 90 minutes among the dozens of homeless souls that inhabited this large city park. Multiple Pacific-slope Flycatcher were calling. The taxonomists on the North American Classification Committee of the American Ornithological Society voted to lump Pacific-slope Flycatcher with Cordilleran Flycatcher, restoring them both as subspecies of Western Flycatcher later in 2023. Thankfully, ABA Big Year rules would continue to consider them as separate species for the 2023 Big Year season.

The cruise departed the port as scheduled at 4 PM, April 24. I set up my telescope on the third-level deck with David and Tammy McQuade, a renowned birding powerhouse couple from Fort Myers, Florida. I had crossed paths with them already this year in Texas. I would run into them later in 2023 more than once. There were about 50 birders in several groups scattered around the ship, including a WINGS tour. David introduced me to Mandy Talpas, an expert birding guide from Hawaii whom I would meet again in October. I enjoyed meeting Richard Crossley, a well-known bird photographer and author of several photographic field guides. I had spoken with him by phone on several occasions since the previous September about a possible juvenile Kentish Plover that I had audio-recorded at Timnath Reservoir (a bird found by Brendan Beers) which would be a first Colorado record, if confirmed.

Once we left the harbor we began seeing pelagic species. A few Black-vented Shearwater skimmed the waves. A triad of Pomarine Jaeger powered past the ship. Pairs of tiny murrelets began appearing. One pair popped up close enough for us to see white underwings and the face pattern typical of Scripp's Murrelet. Craveri's and Guadalupe Murrelets were undoubtedly present in these warm waters, but I could not find them.

As we passed by some distant Mexican islands to our south, the avifauna changed. Groups of Cassin's Auklet streamed by with smaller numbers of

Rhinoceros Auklet. A few Brown Booby flew by, and Sooty Shearwater were numerous. There was a smaller number of the large and slow-flapping Pink-footed Shearwater. An enormous flock of Black Storm-Petrel appeared out of nowhere. Several groups of migrating Sabine's Gull and Red-necked Phalarope flew by.

The ship sailed westward to a location about 70 miles offshore and then turned to parallel the shoreline lumbering northward at a steady pace of about 22 MPH. The sun set in the west. We all had some time to recharge at one of the many dining options and to rest in our state rooms. We awoke the next morning, April 25, far off shore from Santa Barbara and heading north. Here we saw even more Sooty Shearwater. Sprinkled among them were two species of albatross and three species of *Pterodroma* petrels but these rarer birds were invisible to my untrained eyes. Pelagic birding is an acquired skill, and even more difficult when the boat won't stop to study birds close by. Oceanic birds are the group I know the least, probably because of my fear of seasickness which had kept me away from pelagic birding for four decades.

I tried to take photographs of any bird that passed near to the ship. I photographed flying Rhinoceros Auklet and my first Tufted Puffin of the year. From a review of my photographs later I was able to add a rare spring sighting of Short-tailed Shearwater I had spotted at 3:15 PM. Later in the afternoon I watched a messy brown stiff-winged bird and mistakenly called out Pink-footed Shearwater, which would not be expected at the latitude we had reached. David McQuade looked at my photo and informed me I had photographed a dark-morph Northern Fulmar. I would see several more as well as a couple of the more familiar (for me) light-morph. During the last hour of daylight, I finally saw and photographed a Murphy's Petrel and a Black-footed Albatross.

The morning of April 26, I practiced spotting birds from my eighth-floor balcony before joining the birder throng. We were off the coast of Oregon now. A dark stiff-winged bird appeared straight out from where I was standing. It sped away from the ship without flapping but rather using its wings as sails, arcing up and down over the ten-foot swells. As it disappeared, I noticed white flashes underneath the wings indicating that I had my first Hawaiian Petrel somewhere off the Oregon coast. I had no documentation, however. Not even a witness. I hoped I would see more from a pelagic boat trip off Hawaii in mid-October. I also saw several candidate Cook's Petrel but left them unidentified due to my inexperience with the species.

Murphy's Petrel
25 Apr 2023, off San Francisco, California

Joining the other birders, I discovered that pelagic bird experts on board had estimated over 250 Murphy's Petrel, possibly a new USA record for this species that wanders the Pacific Ocean when it is not breeding in New Zealand. This cruise had encountered particularly strong westerly winds, bringing the petrels a little closer to the North American coast than had been seen in years.

David McQuade pointed out a sprightly Fork-tailed Storm-Petrel skimming away from the ship. Later, Matt Jensen, a young birder from Minnesota, yelled out he had another one heading north with the boat and not too far out. He followed it through his scope for several minutes and then announced that it appeared to cross the bow from starboard to port. I ran forward along the deck and turned left near the bow to check for it on the port side of the ship. When I could find no birds at all, I postulated that it might still be paralleling the boat on the starboard side near the bow. I returned to the most forward position possible on the starboard side but 100 yards forward from where Matt had spotted it through his telescope. Looking closer to the boat than usual I re-spotted it and found that it was indeed flying along with the boat at about 20 MPH. I watched it flicker among the waves as I peered intently through my camera for about 20 minutes, trying desperately to get a documentation photo.

I finally nailed down a photograph and hurried back to the birder throng at midship. David Winkler (retired Cornell University ornithologist) was there. I knew Fork-tailed Storm-Petrel was his most wanted bird on the trip. He rushed back with me to the spot along with Christine and Jim McMillan of Florida. We stared for 10 minutes at the spot where I had seen it. Eventually Christine re-spotted it and I got another good view of this lifer for me. David unfortunately never picked it up. Pelagic birding can be that way; sunrise to sunset staring into fog...and rain...and wind...and waves, waiting for that elusive bird to make a showing. It can be exhausting but exhilarating when that lifer pops into view.

The third morning of the cruise, April 27, we awoke to dense fog in the Strait of Juan de Fuca which divides Canada's Vancouver Island from the

Olympic Peninsula in the USA. Once the fog lifted, ocean birds were gone from the calm waters. A few migrant land birds buzzed the ship including an unidentified hummingbird (probably Rufous Hummingbird) and a pair of American Pipit. As we approached the port of Victoria, the ship entered Canadian waters and my opportunity for USA year-birds came to an end.

I added 12 new species from the cruise ship to my Biggest Year total. Perhaps because of my inexperience with pelagics, or maybe just bad luck, I missed out on adding more than a half dozen species seen by other observers from the cruise. Species missed were Parasitic and Long-tailed Jaegers, Craveri's Murrelet, Ashy and Leach's Storm-Petrels, Cook's Petrel and Laysan Albatross. To be a successful Big Year birder, I would need to spend many more days at sea in 2023. For more details of the species that I observed on this cruise, including photographs taken, see the on-line eBird trip report: https://eBird.org/tripreport/288736.

Ash-throated Flycatcher
24 Apr 2023, San Diego, California

CHAPTER 14
Second Time in Texas

*F*or my second trip to Texas this year, I flew with Maribel directly from Vancouver, British Columbia to Houston, at the conclusion of the repositioning cruise the morning of April 28, 2023. My 29-year-old son, Nick, picked us up at Bush Intercontinental Airport at about 6 PM after driving a few hours from his home in Austin. We headed east toward Louisiana. At dusk we stopped in good habitat for nightjars. We were hoping for Eastern Whip-poor-will or Chuck-will's-widow but settled for an unidentified nighthawk and a distant view of Barred Owl, which had been skillfully spotted by Nick's young eyes.

The next morning, April 29, my targets were birds of the piney woods of East Texas. Northbound migrating songbirds were also plentiful, as we found ourselves in the heart of the Central Flyway at the peak of spring migration. Some of these species I had seen in Puerto Rico in late January and early February. By reencountering them in Texas I could count them for my Lower 48 and ABA Area year-list totals. By 9 AM, in the Angelina National Forest near Boykin Spring, we had added the endangered Red-cockaded Woodpecker, Brown-headed Nuthatch and Bachman's Sparrow.

At Martin Dies, Jr. State Park, we added Swallow-tailed and Mississippi Kites, Red-headed Woodpecker, Acadian and Great Crested Flycatchers, Philadelphia and Red-eyed Vireos, Swainson's and Gray-cheeked Thrushes, Swainson's and Prothonotary Warblers. At the Big Thicket Kirby Nature Trail, we added Yellow-billed Cuckoo and Kentucky, Canada and Golden-winged Warblers. We ended the day at Anahuac National Wildlife Refuge Skillern Tract, where we found more migrants, including Scissor-tailed Flycatcher and Blue Grosbeak.

We had rented an apartment opposite Galveston Beach for four nights. We decided to stay close by on April 30. After breakfast, we visited Galveston Island State Park and found the shrubs along the entrance road crawling with colorful migrants: numerous Baltimore and Orchard Orioles, Indigo Bunting, Summer and Scarlet Tanagers.

After an excellent lunch overlooking the Bay at Waterman's Restaurant, we visited a popular nearby sanctuary called Laffite's Cove Nature Preserve. This small forest grove featured well-maintained trails and water drips to attract thirsty birds, and benches to facilitate observation. Here we found a good variety of species including Worm-eating Warbler and a female Cerulean Warbler.

To celebrate the arrival of May, we headed out early in order to arrive at High Island just after sunrise on May 1. High Island is one of the best-known locations in the USA to see migrating warblers. Along the flyway, on the north edge of the Gulf of Mexico, tired birds can fill the trees and shrubs. Certain weather conditions can produce a *fallout*. Getting there from Galveston Island required a ferry crossing to the Bolivar Peninsula plus almost an hour of driving. Upon arrival, we paid to enter Houston Audubon Society Smith Oaks Sanctuary. Except for the din from nesting waders and cormorants, the trees were quiet. The sanctuary is quite large. As we explored the numerous trails and boardwalks, activity increased. There was no fallout, but by the end of the morning, we had tallied more than 80 species. Year-birds for me were Painted Bunting, Blue-winged Warbler, Olive-sided Flycatcher and a flyover heard-only Upland Sandpiper.

After a picnic lunch, we headed back to the extensive marshlands of Anahuac National Wildlife Refuge in search of rails (King, Yellow and Black Rails). We drove the auto loop around Shoveler Pond. The only marsh birds we found were Sora (a small rail) and Least Bittern. We did see some new shorebirds including Wilson's Phalarope and White-rumped Sandpiper. A mystery sandpiper that I photographed appeared intermediate between Least Sandpiper and Little Stint (from Eurasia). Little Stint has been documented breeding in Alaska. I wondered if this mystery bird was actually a hybrid between these two small sandpipers.

Next, we visited another Houston Audubon Sanctuary at Bolivar Flats. The specialties here are birds of the Gulf Coast beaches and mudflats. There were Gulls (Laughing, Franklin's, Herring), Terns (Least, Common, Black), Plovers (Wilson's, Snowy, Semipalmated, Black-bellied), and assorted sandpipers (Sanderling, Ruddy Turnstone, American Avocet, Willet, Red Knot, Dunlin), many of which were in their beautiful alternate (breeding) plumage.

On May 2, Nick and I left the apartment at sunrise and went a short distance back to Galveston Island State Park hoping to find some sparrow species I still needed for the year list. Instead, we found a locked gate. The park would open at 8 AM. We scurried to a nearby eBird hotspot that should have similar avifauna. Upon arrival, we were thrilled to hear the distinctive *ki-ki-doo* call of the diminutive Black Rail, an endangered species. Because of its tenuous conservation status, eBird masks all reports of the species to help protect it from harassment by overzealous birders and wildlife photographers. This was a species that Nick really wanted to find during this trip. We were very pleased to hear one this morning. I had already observed Black Rail in California in March.

Returning to the Galveston Island State Park at 8 AM, we quickly located our target species, Seaside Sparrow. And Nick caught a brief view of Nelson's Sparrow in the salt marsh grassland they call home. My view however was unsatisfactory. We returned to the apartment where Maribel had prepared a hearty home-cooked breakfast.

During breakfast Nick checked the Galveston County *Rare Bird Alert* in eBird. A new checklist from the previous day reported two American Golden-Plover and three Buff-breasted Sandpiper from the golf driving range adjacent to the Galveston Airport. I needed both species. In spring, these species are found on grassy lawns and fresh-cut fields. Most had already migrated north. We had given up hope for finding them during this trip to the coast. But now hope was renewed. Off the three of us went. Arriving ten minutes later, we scanned the large grass lawn through our binoculars. No shore-birds. Four Western Kingbird and a Yellow-headed Blackbird were noteworthy.

"What do you want to do?" Nick asked me. There was an impatient tone in his voice. He wasn't surprised these early migrants had moved on. He was ready to search for more warblers.

"Let's scope the field," I replied. I pulled my spotting scope from the trunk and assembled the tripod. After several minutes of scanning the far reaches of the field, I saw a plover's head pop up from a concealed dip in some taller grass. "Golden plover," I announced. It took a while to convince Nick that the distant lump was indeed a bird. Eventually the American Golden-Plover moved into the open field. Nick was impressed.

Once we were satisfied that no other shorebirds were lurking in the field, Nick asked again, "What do you want to do?" I wanted to check the vicinity for the missing rarities, so we drove to some nearby sports fields and checked around the runways of Galveston Airport. No luck.

"What do you want to do?" Nick asked a third time.

"Let's check the driving range again." We returned to the original field. Voila! *Buffies!* A flock of five Buff-breasted Sandpiper were right there in the middle of the driving range, foraging like robins among the golf balls strewn across the field. My perseverance had paid off.

"Nice work, Dad."

During the remainder of the day, we visited the East End Lagoon Nature Preserve, Sugar Bean Ponds and Laffite's Cove. Birds were everywhere. But new species were hard to find. Nick spotted a Mourning Warbler and a Black-billed Cuckoo, which flew before I got eyes on it. Back at the apartment after sundown, we could hear migrants chirping overhead. Remarkably, a Chuck-will's-widow sang twice from overhead while migrating north!

Our last day on the coast, May 3, we worked hard to nail down King and Yellow Rails. Just after sunrise, we photographed both Clapper Rail and King Rail at East End Lagoon in Galveston. Then after sunset at Anahuac National Wildlife Refuge, we saw another King Rail and audio-recorded several others. We also visited several locations where birders recently had reported singing Yellow Rail. We had no luck hearing or seeing this elusive rail. It winters in the coastal marshes of Texas and Louisiana. During migration it lurks mostly unseen in wet meadows. It also breeds in wet meadows, mostly in the Canadian prairie provinces. I wasn't too worried about missing it on this trip, as I planned to find it on the breeding grounds in Northern Minnesota in June.

We headed toward Houston and found lodging in the suburb of Mont Belvieu. Before being dropped off at the airport in Houston on May 4, I photographed a family of Black-bellied Whistling-Duck. We headed to White Oak Park and picked up a couple of established exotic species, Scaly-breasted Munia and Red-vented Bulbul. I ended the Texas Coast trip with 221 species on the trip list, and a remarkable 61 additions to my year list, which had reached 626 species for my USA and Territories Biggest Year. I found most of my target species but I found no mega-rarities. See eBird trip report here: https://eBird.org/tripreport/123357. My count for ABA Area year-birds was at 568 which was good for fourth place among eBird's *Top 100* list. Next trip: South Florida, where my goal was to reach the milestone of 600 species for the ABA Area in 2023.

Black-bellied Whistling Duck
4 May 2023, Harris County, Texas

CHAPTER 15
South Florida

*F*lorida plays a big role in any North American Big Year strategy. There are three elements to its importance. First, because of its geography it serves as a bottleneck for bird migration along the Atlantic Flyway. Second, it hosts numerous wind-blown vagrants from the Bahamas and Cuba. Third, an extraordinary number of exotic species have become well-established and they count toward official ABA list totals. An even greater number are counted in eBird list totals, although many of these exotic species are not yet deemed *naturalized* by the ABA and are considered *provisional* by eBird.

I began my Florida adventure with 627 USA and Territories Biggest Year-birds (I had added American Bittern near my home in Fort Collins on May 5). My ABA Area list total was 569. I was accompanied by Cliff Hendrick and Irene Fortune, two familiar Quetzal Tours customers from Colorado. Both had already participated in my Biggest Year project, Irene in South Texas, Cliff in Puerto Rico. I arrived to Miami a couple hours earlier than they did on the afternoon of May 6, 2023. After renting a vehicle I picked them up at Miami's International Airport at 5 PM.

With only a couple hours of daylight left, we decided to track down one of South Florida's introduced species, Spot-breasted Oriole. Using eBird and BirdsEye apps on our cell phones, we located a promising hotspot in the suburb of Kendall, Westwind Lake Park, where a pair was reported to be nesting. At 6 PM on a Saturday, the park was bustling with people picnicking and observing youth sporting events. Muscovy Duck, another Florida exotic that has become countable, and a pair of Gray Kingbird were new for my ABA Area list in eBird. The exotic oriole evaded us, unfortunately.

We found a Cuban hangout in nearby Homestead for dinner. The waitress claimed she had seen me before. I didn't recall ever having visited the establishment and thought maybe my twin brother Oliver had eaten there in the past. We spent our first night at the Floridian Hotel in Homestead.

Our first birding stop on Sunday morning, May 7, was just a few minutes away from our hotel, at Portofino Plaza. A thriving colony of Cave Swallow that was nesting under a highway overpass was worthy of study. One way the Cave Swallow differs from the similar Cliff Swallow is in the construction of their nests. Cliff Swallow builds domed nests with an entrance portal, whereas Cave Swallow builds open cup nests. The Portofino Plaza parking lot was studded with ornamental trees that attracted a variety of transient and resident birds. Here we found a migrating Blackpoll Warbler and an introduced Common Myna. Then, in the agricultural fields adjacent to Homestead Airport, I added Short-tailed Hawk, Bobolink and Palm Warbler, all while tracking down a staked out Smooth-billed Ani (ABA Code 3). Special thanks to Jesse Fagan, a tour guide with Field Guides, Inc. who pointed the ani out to us as well as to his group. Cliff and I had seen this species earlier this year in Puerto Rico, where it is much more common. Along with my brother Oliver Komar, Jesse is co-author of the *Peterson Field Guide to Birds of Northern Central America*.

The next stop was about 20 miles east where another staked-out rarity lurked near the visitor center of Biscayne National Park. This was La Sagra's Flycatcher, an ABA Code 4 vagrant from the Bahamas or Cuba. This diminutive nondescript *Myiarchus* flycatcher (the odd descriptor refers to its scientific genus) preferred to keep to itself in the midday heat. We did enjoy the search and appreciated good views of Black-throated Blue Warbler and Swallow-tailed Kite, but alas, no flycatcher.

After lunch, we headed south across the Bay of Biscayne to Key Largo where we encountered a good flock of migrant warblers as well as biting mosquitoes. White-crowned Pigeon, a large dove of coastal palms and mangroves throughout the Caribbean Basin, was plentiful on the Florida Keys. We ended the birding day at dusk on Marathon Key where we relocated several Antillean Nighthawk that had been reported foraging over the mangroves near the

Marathon Airport, a traditional location for this Caribbean species. This species is virtually identical to Common Nighthawk, but easily distinguished by vocalizations. Both species were present. The Antillean Nighthawk song sounds like a bleating sheep with three to five notes. The Common Nighthawk sounds similar but issues only a single note. We overnighted across the street in a quaint beach spot called the Siesta Motel.

White-crowned Pigeon
7 May 2023, Key Largo, Florida

May 8 was our date for visiting the Dry Tortugas National Park. After an hour drive from Marathon, we arrived at the ferry terminal on Key West and boarded the *Yankee Freedom*. It would take us almost three hours out to sea farther west past a chain of uninhabited mosquito-infested isles known as the Marquesas Keys to a cluster of tiny atolls—the Dry Tortugas. Once a military outpost, it is now a national park. We docked at Garden Key which is just large enough to host the decaying brick walls of Fort Jefferson. Just prior to arrival the boat paused at Hospital Key, a dry sandbar that hosted a small colony of breeding Masked Booby and an even smaller number of

Brown Booby. At Garden Key, the shoreline and sky were dominated by thousands of Sooty Tern nesting among the small bushes that lined the beach. Hundreds of Brown Noddy were also nesting among them. In addition, we spotted four Bridled Tern and two Black Noddy. All these birds are special because they are almost never seen on the mainland. A Magnificent Frigatebird colony in some dead trees on a nearby atoll completed the scene.

Aside from the nesting seabirds, the sparse trees and shrubs inside the hexagonal walls of the fort attracted dozens of passerine migrants. Park personnel set a water drip next to trees inside the walled courtyard of the old fortress. As the sun reached its zenith the air temperature was about 80 degrees Fahrenheit. Birds were coming to the drip to drink water. About a week earlier when Jesse Fagan visited with his Field Guides tour, he spotted and identified a Tricolored Munia at the drip. This exotic finch, originally from India, had been wind-blown from its adopted home in Cuba making it an ABA-countable species. A small flock on the Florida mainland near Lake Okeechobee are not yet countable by ABA standards. Since this was the only Tricolored Munia that I could get for my Big Year, I wanted it badly. We made a plan to check the drip hourly during our three-hour stay on Garden Key. I spent most of my time on the atoll searching the vegetation in the courtyard for the munia. The search yielded numerous other species: Scarlet Tanager, Wood Thrush, Swainson's Thrush, Cape May Warbler, Black-throated Blue Warbler, Palm Warbler, American Redstart, Indigo Bunting, Eastern Wood-Pewee, etc. But no munia.

It was getting late and the ferry would be departing soon, so we climbed to the top of the fort's outer wall for a better view of the tern colony including the two Black Noddy. With the noddies were a small number of Roseate Tern. A Québécois birder named Alain Sylvain met us up there and said he and his wife had just been watching the Tricolored Munia at the drip. *Aargh.* We hustled to the drip but the munia had disappeared again. I waited at the drip until the last call for the ferry forced me to abandon my position. This was a big miss for my Biggest Year effort.

Upon returning to Key West at 6 PM, we explored the best-known birding spot there for the final two hours of daylight, Fort Zachary Taylor Historic State Park. A vagrant Red-legged Honeycreeper had been spotted here a few days earlier. It was very birdy. In addition to free-ranging Red Junglefowl nearby, we observed many migrants in the park including a dozen species of warbler. A late Yellow-rumped Warbler and a Blue Grosbeak were flagged as rare by eBird. Unfortunately, we dipped on the honeycreeper. We headed home to the Siesta Motel in Marathon stopping along the route for a satisfying dinner at a roadhouse called Bahama Mama's.

Wednesday morning, May 9, we slowly birded our way back east through the Florida Keys. The birding was excellent but we saw no new birds. A close encounter with an Eastern Screech-Owl was memorable. Back on the mainland we heard the news that a Fork-tailed Flycatcher—a mega-rarity—had been discovered that morning at Fort Zachary Taylor on Key West. We had birded there until dark the night before! We pondered going back but decided instead to make a concerted effort to re-find the La Sagra's Flycatcher near Homestead. After two hours we gave up. A close encounter with a family of endangered West Indian Manatee, a large aquatic mammal, in the canal along our trail was a consolation.

We ended the day at a city park in Kendall called Pinewoods Park. We had received a tip from a birder we met at Dry Tortugas that we could find both Red-whiskered Bulbul and Spot-breasted Oriole here, two exotics on our target list. We arrived a few minutes before sunset. A soft slurred whistle caught my attention. I recognized this call from Lake Murray Park in San Diego County and from White Oak Park in the Houston suburbs. Scaly-breasted Munia! Cliff and Irene were thrilled to see one of their targets. Moving slowly through the park—a narrow strip of green space in a residential neighborhood—we eventually stumbled upon a Red-whiskered Bulbul carrying food. It posed for photos, probably hesitant to visit its nest with us watching. I saw these gorgeous birds, originally from India, in Los Angeles at the Botanic Gardens. We moved on, looking for the oriole, without success.

On Thursday morning, May 10, we drove north from the Floridian Hotel to the Tamiami Trail where Snail Kite was recently reported. Several hours of searching a 30-mile stretch of canals in Everglades National Park was productive but not for finding the kite. I seemed to be going through a target species slump. So, we turned to the guru of South Florida, the Dalai Lama of Florida exotic bird species. We needed professional assistance from the most distinguished birding guide in South Florida, Larry Manfredi. Larry helped John Vanderpoel during his successful ABA Continental Big Year in 2011 and John let him know I would contact him. Larry agreed to spend one afternoon/evening with us because during the week he worked the morning shift as a wildlife observer at an Army Corps of Engineers construction site. It was no coincidence that a La Sagra's Flycatcher turned up here where Larry could encounter it while working. He probably had seen more La Sagra's Flycatcher in Florida than any other birder.

Larry invited us first to sit down in his backyard. His feeders were popular with all three cowbird species in Florida: Bronzed, Brown-headed and Shiny Cowbird. We quickly spied all three. Next, we visited Dolphin Mall in Sweetwater for a drive-up Gray-headed Swamphen. He then took us to a colony of Red-masked Parakeet at the Biltmore Hotel and Golf Course in Coral Gables. A Yellow-chevroned Parakeet flew by. Egyptian Goose made an appearance. The Baptist Hospital hosted a colony of Mitred Parakeet, the largest of the *Psittacara*-genus parakeets. We then returned to Westwind Lakes Park in Kendall which was again crowded with people. Larry spotted the Spot-breasted Oriole for us. After dining with Larry, Cliff and I drove 20 minutes to the entrance station for Everglades National Park. Several Chuck-will's-widow were singing from all directions around the visitor center.

We began our birding day May 11 at sunrise at the canoe launch area of Black Point Park and Marina near the Biscayne National Park visitor center, acting on a tip from Larry Manfredi that this was a reliable spot to find Mangrove Cuckoo. We played one call on my phone and, voila! One called back immediately from right in front of us. It posed briefly for a photo and promptly disappeared.

This was a target species for Irene. Cliff and I had seen one in Puerto Rico but being able to count it for our ABA Area lists was satisfying.

We arranged to meet Larry at 7 AM at his worksite nearby so that he could show us the La Sagra's Flycatcher. Another out-of-state birder met us as well. To our chagrin, the flycatcher failed to appear. This was our third strike looking for this small vagrant.

We headed north through Miami toward Cape Canaveral, a four-hour drive, to look for an overwintering Bahama Mockingbird. En route, we picked an area to buy supplies in Palm Beach County where Nanday Parakeet had been recently reported in eBird. Bingo! Before we could get back on the highway, I spotted a few Nanday Parakeet perched on a wire. We pulled over for better looks and discovered a nest hole in an ornamental palm in the roadway median strip. Then, we looked for a location along our route where the endemic Florida Scrub-Jay was likely. The Helen & Allan Cruickshank Sanctuary in Indian River County fulfilled our criteria nicely. Within a few minutes of parking our car, we were greeted by three Florida Scrub-Jay.

We arrived at Jetty Park Campground on Merritt Island in Brevard County and quickly found the staked-out Bahama Mockingbird (ABA Code 4) singing in the picnic area. We turned back south and drove until dinner time. We stopped to dine and sleep our final Florida night in Vero Beach West.

The next day, May 12, we arrived at Lake Okeechobee around 7 AM and spent the entire morning exploring the area. We were searching for a few final targets and eventually found two of them at the south end of the giant lake. At Belle Glade Marina/Torry Island, we observed a half dozen Limpkin, an odd wader that looks like a cross between a rail and a heron. It feeds almost exclusively on apple snails. A Snail Kite sailed past us just in the nick of time as we had started moving toward the car to drive the final leg to Miami for our return flight to Colorado.

I really enjoyed this trip. We had 138 species on the eBird trip report which can be viewed on-line here: https://eBird.org/tripreport/129815. I added 21 Biggest Year species bringing my species total to 648 in the USA and Territories. Irene and Cliff were great travel companions. They were both thrilled with the additions to their life lists. I also added more than 30 species to my ABA Area and Lower 48 year lists, which kept me high on the leaderboard for those two categories in eBird.org. My 602 species for the Lower 48 category had surpassed my goal of reaching the coveted 600 landmark. I was still five species shy of David and Tammy McQuade's leading position. The tour added one ABA Code 3+ species (Bahama Mockingbird) but missed a few others (Tricolored Munia, La Sagra's Flycatcher and Fork-tailed Flycatcher).

Black-throated Blue Warbler
8 May 2023, Fort Jefferson National Park, Florida

CHAPTER 16
Catching the McQuades

I returned to Fort Collins with one day to spare before my next scheduled trip to West Texas, May 14–19. I wanted to make the most of it. Spring migration was at its peak in Northern Colorado and coincidentally, May 13 was World Migratory Bird Day and eBird's Global Big Day. I had to go birding. The GroupMe text chain for Larimer County sounded off early. A Kentucky Warbler from a few days earlier had been relocated at Prospect Ponds Natural Area along the Cache La Poudre River in Fort Collins. I saw a couple of these along the Texas coast but still needed a photo. Cliff Hendrick agreed to meet me at Prospect Ponds early in the afternoon. Cliff had been with me in Puerto Rico and also in Florida. He was the CEO of a small biotechnology company who was always interested in an opportunity to score new life birds. He recently looked at his life list and noticed that something like 95% of his lifers the past few years had been observed while on tours I had led or organized.

When I arrived to the parking area, birds were everywhere. Buzzy songs from Clay-colored Sparrow and Western Wood-Pewee were additions to my year lists. After three hours searching, however, I never saw the Kentucky Warbler.

Another rarity announcement text led me to a cooperative Field Sparrow (new), which I observed with Greg Osland. Greg had been with me for the Central California tour. Later in the day, I followed another GroupMe alert to the Nix Natural Area where a Gray Flycatcher had been spotted. This was not new but again I desired better documentation. There I met Alex Smilor, one of the student leaders of Colorado State University Field Ornithologists. Together we tracked down the Gray Flycatcher. I got great photos.

Our phones sounded again with a GroupMe text. Cole Wild reported a rare Piping Plover at Kechter Pit wetland. Alex had never seen one so I invited him to join me in the search. When we arrived, a throng of birders had already gathered. We quickly relocated the endangered plover with assistance from the other birders. It was joined by a Sanderling, another uncommon shorebird for Colorado in May.

Field Sparrow
13 May 2023, Fort Collins, Colorado

It was now late in the day and I realized I needed three more Biggest Year-birds to surpass the McQuades for first place in the Lower 48 and the ABA Area competitions. I invited Alex to join me in a visit to the shortgrass prairie about 15 miles north of Fort Collins. By the time we arrived, the sun had set. But the grassland birds were singing like crazy. Lark Bunting (new) had just arrived from its wintering areas in Northern Mexico. I dropped off Alex at his apartment near campus after 9 PM. Then I called Joe Kipper. He and Archer Silverman, a pre-teen birding phenom from Boulder County, were doing a Big Day. I had told him I would join them for owling in Rist

Canyon, just west of Fort Collins, where I had heard a Northern Saw-whet Owl tooting in March.

I met them at my house on the west side of town about 9:30 PM and figured it might be an interesting evening when we heard a shorebird flight call overhead. Clouds had rolled in. The low ceiling was pushing migrants lower than usual in the sky. I identified the calling shorebird as a Lesser Yellowlegs, a new species for my yard. I've observed over 160 species around my residential yard in my 27 years living there.

When we arrived at our owling spot on the backside of Rist Canyon hill (near the Stove Prairie school), we were amazed to hear more shorebirds migrating low overhead. There was a constant stream of Spotted Sandpipers singing above us. We estimated several hundred birds called overhead while we listened for about an hour. Eventually we also heard the soft hoot of a Flammulated Owl (new) and the repetitive rising hoot of a Long-eared Owl!

Among the shorebirds migrating over Stove Prairie (really a montane valley at 7,500 feet elevation), we heard another Lesser Yellowlegs and a Sora. At roughly 11:00 PM, a shorebird called loudly overhead. I didn't recognize it. It alternated between a single note and a multi note call that reminded me of Upland Sandpiper. Its unfamiliarity piqued my interest. I exclaimed to the others, *Record that call!* I hit the record button in my Merlin app just as it gave its last two notes before going silent. I hoped that those two notes would be sufficient either for Merlin to render an identification or for an identifiable sonogram once uploaded to our checklist at eBird.org. As we drove back to Fort Collins, I played flight calls of unusual shorebirds from the Sibley Guide app and was surprised to find a similar call with the foraging call of Sharp-tailed Sandpiper, which had been recorded in Australia. This was an Australasian species I had never seen or heard and that had been observed in Colorado only twice. Imagine my disappointment when I tried listening to my Merlin recording and discovered that an error prevented the app from creating an audible recording. This might have been *the one that got away.*

I lived to find rare birds but I would have to let this one go. Without a recording to compare with, I did not trust my brain to recall accurately the sound. Was it conceivable that a Mega-rarity really flew over our heads calling? Heck yeah. *Rare birds are common!*

Without the Sharp-tailed Sandpiper to vault me into sole possession of first place, I was content with a three-way tie with the McQuades at 607 species for the ABA Area and Lower 48 lists. Hopefully I would find a stray Sharp-tailed Sandpiper during my upcoming planned travel to Adak Island far out on the Aleutian Island chain of Alaska. I had plans to make this sojourn May 27 to 31 with a group of five others including—you guessed it—David and Tammy McQuade.

Gray Flycatcher
13 May 2023, Fort Collins, Colorado

CHAPTER 17
West Texas Road Trip

*T*he main target of the trip to West Texas was the Colima Warbler which extended its nesting range over the border from Mexico only at Big Bend National Park. On the return I planned to stray to the east several hours in order to visit the western edge of the Edward's Plateau where I could add Golden-cheeked Warbler. Two days before the trip, three people sent me a copy of Todd Easterla's checklist (May 14) from Big Bend. While he was watching Colima Warbler, he discovered a stray from Mexico: Crescent-chested Warbler! This would be just the second record for Texas.

I thought this trip would be more popular but only one person registered for it, my buddy Phil Cafaro. Phil, a Fort Collins resident, was a tenured professor of philosophy and a specialist on environmental ethics. He was fascinated by the big issues that confronted the world such as over-population and immigration problems. When I asked him "Why?" he always had a profound answer no matter what the topic. In contrast, if you asked me "Why?" I replied "Why not?" If you asked me about a bird identification, I would answer you. On the other hand, when it came to birds, Phil would respond, "Ask Nick." I had contracted David Wade to drive for the six-day round trip venture expecting more people would register. Oh well.

We got started at 10 AM on Sunday, May 14, 2023. After a brief stop at Kechter Pit to look for shorebirds, we got on Interstate 25 heading south and didn't get off until the Hanover Road exit south of Colorado Springs in El Paso County. I hoped to pick up two year-birds in the Chihuahuan desert habitat east of the interstate: Cassin's Sparrow and Grasshopper Sparrow. We did not find either, but at the Hanover Road firehouse, we found a small group of migrant passerines, including a female Blackpoll Warbler which posed nicely for photographs. We made a couple other leg-stretching stops south of Trinidad, Colorado and at Maxwell National Wildlife Refuge south of Raton, New Mexico. We quit for the night about 11 PM at Tucumcari, New Mexico.

Our route southbound on May 15 took us on small but fast roads. We turned into a side road at Ragland, New Mexico, following a report in eBird for Cassin's Sparrow. The landscape was recently planted wheat fields on one side of the flat road, and tall wild grass with scattered cholla cactus on the other. Here we found numerous Chihuahuan and Western Meadowlarks, as well as Lark, Cassin's and Grasshopper Sparrows, all singing incessantly to defend their breeding territories. A short distance farther south, we began to encounter Mississippi Kite in each town we passed through.

We rolled into Alpine, Texas, at dusk. After a pleasant dinner at the Three Hearts Steakhouse, we crashed early at the Value Lodge on the outskirts of town. We had arranged to meet another birder, Brandon Nooner of Del Rio, Texas, at the Pinnacles trailhead in Big Bend National Park at 5 AM. Apple Maps estimated a two-hour drive from Alpine.

We started rolling south at 3:15 AM May 16 and soon realized that we lacked sufficient gasoline to reach our destination. Terlingua is the only town between Alpine and the Chisos Basin Visitor Center. We hoped the one gas station in Terlingua would be open. Fortunately, it was open but the pit-stop further delayed us and we rolled into the Apple Maps locale for the trailhead at 5:30 AM. We drove around a bit and discovered two other spots to park for the Pinnacles Trail, one at the visitor center and one at the adjacent campground. Very confusing. Unable to locate Brandon, we began hiking around 6:15 AM.

The dawn chorus was fabulous. The landscape was a transition between healthy Chihuahuan desert vegetation and pinyon-juniper forest. Songs surrounded us from Scott's Oriole, Blue Grosbeak, Black-headed Grosbeak, Ash-throated Flycatcher and Rufous-crowned Sparrow. A distant Mexican Whip-poor-will sang. Shortly after 7 AM, my cell phone registered an incoming text message from Brandon. He was viewing the Crescent-chested Warbler. Brandon must have run the four miles up the hill!

We were moving at a slower pace with a couple hours of stop and go hiking yet ahead of us. At 9:15 AM, we heard a song we didn't recognize.

We didn't believe Merlin's assessment. The top suggestions were Dark-eyed Junco and Orange-crowned Warbler. We would determine later that this was Colima Warbler, one of about seven individuals we would hear along the trail. Then higher along the trail at 9:30 AM we heard the unique buzzy-screechy song of the Crescent-chested Warbler (ABA Code 4), also misidentified by Merlin as Orange-crowned Warbler. We would eventually confirm the identification with brief glimpses of this beautiful Mexican *parulid* that looks like a Tropical Parula with a broad white eye-stripe. But where was Brandon? We continued up the Pinnacle Trail switchbacks to the turnoff for Boot Canyon and followed this trail to Boot Spring. As we approached, Brandon met us on the trail. "There you are," he said. "I was afraid you weren't coming."

Crescent-chested Warbler
16 May 2023, Big Bend National Park, Texas
Photo by Brandon Nooner

Bandon Nooner is tall and lanky and always smiling. I knew him from Fort Collins where he attended graduate school after a stint with the Air Force. He was a birder and got hired as a field biologist for a research study on West Nile virus ecology. I was a collaborator on the study and helped teach him local bird song identification for his avian point counts. After getting his Master's degree in Fisheries and Wildlife, he found employment at the US Air Force base in Del Rio where he worked to prevent bird strikes on Air Force jets at Laughlin Air Force Base. As we hiked along the Boot Spring Trail, we marveled at the beauty of our surroundings—densely forested canyons below cliffs with unique rock formations, in the vast remoteness of Big Bend National Park.

We birded together for a while, getting excellent views of Grace's and Colima Warblers, Painted Redstart (a warbler), Blue-throated Mountain-gem (a hummingbird) and Cordilleran Flycatcher. We headed back down the Pinnacles Trail together around 2:30 PM and found the Crescent-chested Warbler in the same area, singing frequently and giving us better views. It never posed for photos unfortunately as it was frequently chased away from its perch by another warbler, presumably a Colima Warbler. As we ended our hike, we were surprised to find a singing Crissal Thrasher. I recorded many bird songs from this hike which I uploaded to my eBird checklist.

En route to our base camp 110 miles away in Alpine, we paused for an early dinner in Terlingua and a visit at dusk to the Christmas Mountains Oasis, a private eBird hotspot in the desert that was created and owned by Carolyn Ohl. A combination of ponds, a botanical garden and bird feeders, this special place attracts some special birds. Highlights were Varied Bunting, Lucifer Hummingbird and Elf Owl.

On the morning of May 17, Phil slept in while Dave and I explored the Davis Mountains. Just outside the quaint town of Fort Davis we hooted up a pair of Western Screech-Owl. At Madera Canyon Picnic Area, highlights were Summer and Hepatic Tanagers, Plumbeous Vireo, Cassin's Kingbird and Western Bluebird. I was very pleased to get audio documentation of Montezuma Quail and Black-chinned Sparrow, two species I had observed without documentation in Arizona in March. On the way to fetch Phil, Dave spotted his lifer Zone-tailed Hawk.

Heading east from Alpine, we stopped for birding at Marathon, Texas about an hour away. The Marathon Cemetery and Fort Peña Colorado Park were both worthwhile stops. After lunch we bee-lined three hours east to the city of Junction. As the sun waned, we explored South Llano River State Park. Thanks to advice from Jesse Huth, we quickly ticked our two targets here: Black-capped Vireo and Golden-cheeked Warbler, both heard singing. After sunset, Chuck-will's-widow songs were everywhere.

We returned to the state park in the morning of May 18 to better appreciate our target species. We were able to get photos of both and watched a Golden-cheeked Warbler feed fledglings. Then we found other fabulous birds of this park, such as Painted Bunting, Red-headed Woodpecker (rare according to eBird), Black-throated Sparrow, Yellow-throated Vireo and Yellow-throated Warbler. The park provided a rich mix of habitats, making it hospitable to a great variety of species. Ecosystems here included prairie grassland, arid shrub and thorn forest, juniper forest and riparian gallery forest along the South Llanos River.

At lunch we plotted out our route home, hoping for a couple more targets in Southwest Oklahoma. Based on eBird reports filtered through the BirdsEye lens, we targeted a recent sighting of Hudsonian Godwit and an old sighting of Louisiana Waterthrush from a potential breeding location. We drove seven and a half hours, stopping for dinner in Vernon, Texas, and for lodging at a motel in Alva, Oklahoma.

On May 19, we drove 30 minutes east of Alva to the Salt Plains National Wildlife Refuge and hiked the Eagle Roost Nature Trail. Birds were everywhere. Most notable were the Hudsonian Godwit, Least Tern, Glossy Ibis, Eastern Wood-Pewee, Alder Flycatcher (identified by its unique call note that was audio-recorded), Yellow-billed Cuckoo, and Blackburnian, Magnolia, and Prothonotary Warblers. Heavy rain ended our productive hike.

An hour later (around noon) we pulled up to Alabaster Caverns State Park. We hiked down a steep, slippery trail into the canyon—the wet red clay dirt was slick. At the creek, steep banks caused me to slip a few times. Fortunately, I grabbed a branch of a red cedar sapling which prevented me from sliding into the creek. After playing a recording of Louisiana Waterthrush, a bird flew by us that may have been one. A minute later it sang a few times and Merlin confirmed the identity! eBird considers Louisiana Waterthrush as rare in Oklahoma. We departed the park around 3 PM and pulled into Fort Collins close to midnight.

This was a whirlwind tour of West Texas. We accomplished a lot of birding in a short amount of time. Phil and Dave were great travel companions. I was happy to share part of my Big Year adventure with these friends. It was also nice to see Brandon Nooner, whom I knew from his graduate school days in Fort Collins. Brandon will pop up in this story again, in November, with a find of an ABA Code 5 mega-rarity that I would chase successfully. We tallied 184 species, including 15 for my Biggest Year list, now at 668 species. One was Code 4. Details are in the eBird trip report here: https://eBird.org/tripreport/133787.

16 May 2023, Big Bend National Park
Nick Komar with (from left)
Phil Cafaro, Brandon Nooner and David Wade

CHAPTER 18
The Colorado Birding Challenge

*I*n 2018, I joined the Board of Directors of the Colorado Field Ornithologists (CFO), a volunteer-run organization dedicated to the advancement of birds and birding in Colorado. I was nominated by Sue Riffe, owner of She Flew Tours in Lyons, Colorado. A year later, CFO faced a leadership crisis. President David Gillilan was burned out after his first two-year term of volunteering as president. He never quite mastered the art of delegation and had taken on many organizational tasks himself. His vice-president, Christian Nunes, had just become a father and announced his retirement from the Board after six years of service. CFO by-laws required that the new president be someone with board experience or a past president. It appeared no one wanted this thankless job. At first, I did not want it either.

The last thing I needed was an additional source of stress. My full-time job at CDC was stressful enough. And with Parkinson's disease causing me to have difficulty handling stress, I passed over the opportunity to take on the president role. Then I thought about the impact I could have as leader of Colorado's premier birding organization. I changed my mind and told the Board of Directors I would accept the nomination. They were thrilled. Crisis averted. But they were also nervous. Never in CFO's 50-year history had someone been nominated for president with the lack of institutional involvement as I had. I had been on the Board for just one year.

After the rubber stamp vote at the CFO annual meeting, held in May 2019 at the annual convention in Montrose, Colorado I assumed my new role as volunteer president. My vision for the organization was to generate more members through offering more activities than our traditional annual conventions. I also wanted to build the organization to allow for a broader mission than currently offered by the CFO convention which featured four days of field trips, a banquet speaker, a silent auction to raise money for bird research and a workshop or two.

In addition to hosting the annual convention, CFO awarded a small number of research grants each year, published a quarterly journal called *Colorado Birds* and curated reports of rare birds through its Bird Records Committee. However, all four of these areas needed substantial improvements. I felt it was important to add more to CFO's current portfolio of activities. Over the next few years, CFO created a speaker series, offered identification workshops for gulls, raptors, shorebirds and hummingbirds, raised $40,000 for the Joe Roller Research Award, revitalized the Bird Records Committee under Peter Gent's leadership, and revitalized *Colorado Birds* under the direction of editor Peter Burke. We also added a Director of Communications to the Board of Directors and filled the position with Linda Lee who produced a bimonthly newsletter for members.

Despite its mission statement supporting Colorado birds, CFO did not have an active conservation program among its activities. Therefore, one of my first acts as president was recruiting a Conservation Director. My good friend Walter Wehtje took on this role. He had recently become the Executive Director of the Ricketts Foundation for Conservation. Unfortunately, Walter soon moved to Wyoming for his new job leaving a void in the Board and in our conservation program. Eventually, I would ask Chuck Hundertmark, a former president of Denver Field Ornithologists, to take over the role. Under his leadership, CFO developed a solid conservation program. Chuck became vice-president in 2022 and then president, taking over my role when my second two-year term ended in June 2023.

To fund conservation activities, in 2021 CFO created an annual fundraiser called the Colorado Birding Challenge. We challenged birders to collect donations and pledges for every species observed on a chosen date in May within a selected county. Participating teams would be challenged to compete for the most species observed and the most money raised. The challenge required all observations to be entered into eBird. We aimed to have a team competing in all 64 Colorado counties. Because some counties are more birdy and habitat-diverse than others, we established county par values, based on data already collected in eBird and on the population size of counties.

In this way, we evened the playing field for those wanting to compete in a small county. The winning team would not necessarily have the largest number of species but would score the highest relative to its assigned par value.

Band-tailed Pigeon
20 May 2023, Bellvue, Colorado

In 2021, for my first Colorado Birding Challenge event, we raised $40,000 with most of the funds benefiting the Bird Conservancy of the Rockies. They used the funds to improve grassland habitat in Northern Mexico where many Colorado grassland birds winter. I participated on May 9, 2021, in the green category by riding my bicycle about 50 miles in Larimer County from the top of Rist Canyon to Arapahoe Bend Natural Area along the Cache La Poudre River. My team was called the Masked Trogons. My teammate was Greg Osland who was also on the CFO Board of Directors. We tallied 107 species to win the green category, which prohibited motorized vehicles.

In 2022, I followed the same route with a team of four cyclists in the green category. My team was the White-bearded Helmetcrests. We tallied 119 species on May 7, scoring second place. The overall effort raised about $45,000 for Gunnison Sage-Grouse conservation. My teammates were Jay Breidt, Doug Swartz and John Shenot.

In 2023, CFO set a goal of raising $50,000 for Pinyon Jay conservation. The White-bearded Helmetcrests rode again (same route). On May 20, I was joined by Jay Breidt and David Wade, who were both clean shaven. I was the only one sporting a partially white beard. We scored 131 species for a second-place finish in the green category. In all, 26 teams participated and raised about $20,000.

The birding was fun although Dave and I slept only three hours beforehand having arrived in Fort Collins after midnight from our West Texas road trip. In fact, I overslept and ran out the door at 4 AM without a belt and wearing Crocs. Somehow, I managed to get through the day. We began our downhill bike ride in the foothills northwest of Fort Collins. The best birds of the morning were Dusky Grouse and MacGillivray's Warbler (both new for my year list), Band-tailed Pigeon, Northern Goshawk, Red-eyed Vireo, Black Phoebe and Blackpoll Warbler. Later in the day at Fort Collins City Park, thanks to a tip from E. J. Raynor, we had a migratory flock of passerines that included Hooded Warbler, Northern Waterthrush, Swainson's Thrush, Rose-breasted Grosbeak and Plumbeous Vireo. Stilt Sandpiper was at Nix Natural Area. American Bittern was at Running Deer Natural Area. Spring migration was peaking in Northern Colorado.

My next big adventure (Alaska) would begin May 25, 2023. I had almost a week to get ready for the trip. During the waiting period I would remain in first place in the ABA Area year list competition, just one species ahead of the McQuades.

CHAPTER 19
Adak, Alaska

When I began my trip to Adak, I was in first place in the ABA Area competition, leading David and Tammy McQuade by one species on the eBird *Top 100*. For this trip, I would be birding with the McQuades! In January, I had run into David and Tammy in South Texas. They told me about their May Adak trip and asked if I was interested in sharing costs. I jumped at the opportunity. Adak is the westernmost town in the USA, located more than halfway out in the Aleutian archipelago but still 400 miles east of Attu, the westernmost island in the chain. Attu had become off limits to the public. That made Adak a viable alternative locale for finding off-course Asian vagrants during spring and fall. Other locations in Alaska that served this purpose were Nome, St. Lawrence Island (home to the village of Gambell) and the Pribilof Islands, particularly the island of St. Paul.

I first met the famous McQuades in Alaska in 2021 when I was birding in Nome with my 28-year-old son Nick, Cliff Hendrick from Fort Collins and Rob Raker from Littleton, Colorado. We were newbies to Alaskan birding. We encountered Dave and Tammy birding by themselves on the Nome-Council Highway heading toward the sea watch point known as Cape Nome. We had all stopped to get a better look at some snipe we hoped were Common Snipe from Eurasia (they were not, just Wilson's Snipe). We discovered that they were doing a Big Year, aiming for 700+ species in the ABA Area. I had heard their names before, from my friend Walter Wehtje who guided them around Western Wyoming for their 2020 Big Year. "You are doing another Big Year, back-to-back?" I asked David.

"We do one every year. Each year we get better at finding the birds and perfecting our route. I think we can reach 800 species in the ABA area."

I asked lots of questions. Tammy explained, "We got hooked on birding after watching *The Big Year*. We thought, next year, we'll start counting birds."

They made plenty of mistakes at first, but after a couple of years, they had become experts at bird identification, and a competitive force to be reckoned with. Were they independently wealthy? No! They worked for a living. Fortunately, they were able to conform their profession to their newfound passion. They worked in a family business as financial advisors. They developed a network of clients around the country and invested in strong customer service, visiting their clients for in-person advising, and, when possible, coinciding their visits with the migratory movements of birds. They were able to finance their travel through their financial advising business! Brilliant. David joined the Board of Directors of the ABA. I admired the McQuades. They personified my own ethic of *work hard/play hard*.

David and Tammy are super nice people. They had become Big Year experts but they didn't hoard their expertise. On the contrary, they freely shared their knowledge with young and/or inexperienced birders, in the field and in the classroom. They also shared their knowledge with experienced birders. They didn't get caught up with the negative side of competitive birding, as some experienced birders do. They were in it for the fun and joy of birding.

I ran into them again in 2022 near Fort Collins. It was a blustery day in March. One of my birding buddies, Josh Bruening, had spotted a mega-rarity for the Lower 48 states, an adult Slaty-backed Gull, at Boyd Lake, a massive man-made irrigation reservoir that apparently lies on the migration pathway of ocean-dwelling birds from the Arctic Ocean. Other oceanic rarities that have turned up there over the years include multiple Yellow-billed Loon, Black-legged Kittiwake, Long-tailed Jaeger and Arctic Tern. Upon hearing of Josh's report through the local hotline, I called David Wade. We rushed the 10 miles to the outskirts of Loveland, Colorado. We found Josh along the beach. He explained that the bird flew before he could snap a photo but he had to take off due to work or family obligations. We hung out a while perusing the many arctic-breeding gulls that were lounging on a nearby sandbar, including Glaucous Gull and several Iceland Gull. Suddenly out of nowhere, a massive slate-backed and bubblegum-pink-legged bird plopped down on the shoreline as if to say "Look at me." Almost as suddenly it flew off again. My open winged flight shots documented the *string of pearls* pattern of white moons in the primaries (outer wing feathers). The photos corroborated the report and news of the Arctic gull species went viral across the country. Later in the day, it was reported lounging with other gulls at the south end of the lake. I returned the following day in part to try for better photos and in part just to keep tabs on the bird, as I knew many people throughout the state (and beyond) would be looking for it.

The wind was howling that day. I had hiked out on a mud flat to get closer and could barely keep my telescope and tripod from blowing over in the gale. I was surprised when four birders approached me and asked about the gull. They were David and Tammy and the Stoll brothers (Ruben and Victor, from Tennessee). One of them was barefoot! The gull was a no-show. The Stoll brothers went on to establish a new Big Year record for the Lower 48 states with 752 species. Ahh but I digress. Where was I? Oh yes, Adak.

Adak is not really a town. It is an abandoned US Navy base. It was closed in 1997 as part of the Congressional Base Realignment and Closure (BRAC) program. The property was donated to native Alaskans, but fewer than 60 people live there full time today. This includes some entrepreneurs trying to turn Adak into an ecotourism destination. Besides birds and marine mammals, the island offers fishing and hunting opportunities. Most of Adak is protected as part of the sprawling Alaska Maritime National Wildlife Refuge. Adak scenery is spectacular.

Our group was comprised of me, the McQuades plus Sam Buttrick of Florida. Two younger birders joined us as well, Raymond VanBuskirk of New Mexico and Oscar Wilhelmy of Arizona. Our adventure began in Anchorage on Friday, May 26, 2023. My friend Andy Bankert agreed to show David, Tammy and me some birding spots in the local area before we flew out west. Andy is a young ornithologist who has lived and birded in Florida, New Mexico and Colorado. I met him when he was a graduate student at Colorado

State University working on a Master's degree in Civil Engineering. He liked to live off the land, so he fit in well in Alaska. Andy moved to Alaska when his wife Carrie got a job controlling bird populations around the Anchorage Airport. Andy found employment conducting shorebird surveys each summer on the North Slope. He moonlights as a birding guide.

While birding around Anchorage, I added Arctic Tern to my USA and Territories Biggest Year list. White-winged Crossbill was new for the McQuades' Big Year. I was happy for the opportunity to get audio and photo documentation of the crossbill, which I had missed in Minnesota in February. A female Spruce Grouse near the Anchorage Airport was not new for the year list, but it was an awesome experience. It flew past me and landed nearby in a deciduous glade with thick underbrush. It was well concealed by the underbrush. We almost gave up looking for it when I nearly stepped on it. It flew a few feet and froze, allowing us to take stunning photographs.

My daughter Angela and her husband, Asher, also happened to be in Anchorage. I met them for breakfast before our Alaska Airlines flight boarded for Adak on Saturday, May 27. After working all week in Anchorage, they were about to have their own Alaska mini adventure before returning to Colorado.

When we landed on Adak, we were met at the airport by other birders visiting the island, including Frank Haas of Pennsylvania, and a group of four organized by Richard (Rick) Taylor, an acquaintance from the Colorado birding community who now lives in Georgia. (Richard is now my book editor and should not be confused with the well-known guide, of the same name, who lives in Arizona.) Richard's group included his brother Chris Taylor of California, Nathan Farnau of Georgia and Rob Batchelder of Washington, DC. Rob thought he recognized me, but he was mistaken. He had birded with my identical twin brother, Oliver, years earlier in Nicaragua.

Frank Haas had decades of experience birding on Adak, visiting annually sometimes in both spring and fall, for years. There is no other person more knowledgeable on where to find birds on the island. We were lucky that our short trip overlapped with his two weeks. He was able to provide some critical tips on where to find the best birds. Frank pointed out an array of seed feeders he set out all over the drivable portions of the island to facilitate observing vagrants. The groups were using a specific radio channel for sharing info about sightings on the island. We agreed to join their network and share any rare bird intelligence. We were also met by two members of the native community who provided permits to explore the island in exchange for $30 each.

After making ourselves at home in one of the refurbished Navy base houses now managed by Adak Adventures, we set out to find some Asian rarities that Frank and the others reported. We readily found Brambling (ABA Code 3) and Hawfinch (ABA Code 4), along with the local subspecies of Gray-crowned Rosy-Finch near one of Frank's feeding stations. Then we searched a wet meadow at Contractor's Marsh and documented several Eurasian species of shorebirds, including Common Snipe, Wood Sandpiper and Ruff (all ABA Code 3).

Brambling
30 May 2023, Adak, Alaska

Because of our proximity to the Asian mainland, Eurasian shorebirds were numerous. The Common Snipe and the Wood Sandpiper were showing signs of breeding locally, singing and performing territorial courtship display flights. I had already recorded Wood Sandpiper on a winter territory in Southern California in March, so I was not able to add this bird to my Biggest Year list. Furthermore, I had already added Ruff from a winter territory in Puerto Rico. And I had seen yet another Ruff on a winter territory in San Bernardino, California.

As we drove our rented SUV over the few roads around the base, we flushed many Rock Ptarmigan. They often gave themselves away with their odd croaking grumble. At Clam Lagoon, we added Parasitic Jaeger, an adult dark morph that flew past us showing off its pointed central tail feathers. We saw three more perched on mudflats, as well as a dozen or more Eurasian Wigeon, a pair of Rock Sandpiper and several pair of Marbled Murrelet. Thanks to the sharp eyes and fine birding skills of Raymond VanBuskirk, we got eyes on a distant pair of Kittlitz's Murrelet. Raymond was a WINGS tour leader for Alaska. We were fortunate to have him on our team.

The six of us made for a tight squeeze in the SUV, so we avoided long drives. It had been three years since the onset of the COVID-19 pandemic, and we were all vaccinated. Nonetheless, sharing close quarters with others was frowned upon because of the possibility of spreading COVID, especially in Alaska where the native population was especially vulnerable to viruses.

Even in May, Adak has several snow-covered mountains. The rest of the lowlands are covered in grass tussocks dotted with occasional trees planted by residents years ago. Each day we searched the few trees around the naval base for newly-arrived vagrants from Asia. Despite persistent west winds during our visit, we never found any. There were plenty of birds, however.

On Sunday, May 28, a colony of Aleutian Tern near the airport was new. We found a pair of Pacific Golden-Plover on the mudflat at Clam Lagoon. Late in the day on May 28, we got a call on the radio from Richard Taylor. He passed word from Frank Haas who located a Wandering Tattler in a rocky stream near one of the upland quarries. They knew it was a species we had not yet seen on Adak. We were grateful for the heads up and joined their group for a few minutes, appreciating the breeding plumage of this patient and cooperative tattler. During winter the Wandering Tattler is a blasé gray color above and whitish below like the dull coloration of a non-breeding Red Knot, or a Willet. But in spring, the pre-alternate molt replaces the whitish feathers of the breast with brighter white feathers with thick black edges forming an attractive fine black and white barring on the underparts. This breeding plumage trait helps differentiate the Wandering Tattler of North America from its Asian sister species, the Gray-tailed Tattler. The barring in the alternate plumage of the Asian species is restricted to the chest and flanks, with no barring on the lower belly or under the tail. The Wandering Tattler was not new for my Biggest Year list, having made an appearance for me along the beach at Ventura Harbor in California during mid-March. However, I was able to photograph it for the first time this year. I would see many more on the wintering grounds of Hawaii and American Samoa. But I am getting ahead of myself.

After the successful chase to see the tattler, we settled in at our house and enjoyed a delicious salmon filet. There is a very limited restaurant service on Adak, so we had brought all our food with us. We shopped in Anchorage prior to our flight. Andy Bankert had donated a salmon from his freezer for our group. Raymond cooked it. Add chef to Raymond's list of talents.

On Monday, May 29, we drove out on a harrowing road to the old Coast Guard LORAN station where we enjoyed a sea watch that included several thousand Northern Fulmar. They were joined by two species of Albatross, Black-footed and Laysan. The birds were close to shore, down steep cliffs, and foraging among a pod of about a dozen Orca! Also new at this site were Red-faced Cormorant and Horned Puffin. We sat in deep grass, protected from howling winds, on bluffs rising about 800 feet above the water within view of the abandoned LORAN Station. To reach the bluff spot, we parked at the station, and hiked through three-foot-tall grass tussocks. At the bluff, just above the granite cliff face, the grass tussocks emerged from very steep terrain, permitting us to stand with our backs against the tussocks as we peered through our spotting scopes at the great variety of seabirds streaming past our position. We were quite comfortable. The most abundant species was the Northern Fulmar. Tammy counted more than 100 headed west in one minute and extrapolated her census to estimate 4000 fulmar, all of which were dark morphs except for a couple pale individuals. One of the great mysteries of the northern oceans is why Northern Fulmar, a shearwater-like petrel with a heavy whitish bill, seems to prefer to nest in colonies with other fulmars of their same morph. This raises the possibility that the two varieties of Northern Fulmar will someday be split into two or, perhaps, more species.

After the sea watch, we headed back toward civilization at the navy base. Our route took us through narrow rutted roads across some remote grasslands in rolling hills. We were on the lookout for the famous Caribou that had been released on Adak during World War II as an emergency food source in the most extreme survival situation. These days, the locals hope to attract a steady stream of hunters looking for a wilderness experience on the edge of Earth. Instead, we spotted a graceful Short-eared Owl on the prowl for small mammalian prey.

Like many resident species on Adak, the *shorties* here look different from their mainland counterparts. These owls are much paler on the underside of the wing, which is white rather than barred with dark markings. Other local populations on Adak that look markedly different from their continental conspecifics include the Gray-crowned Rosy-Finch, Pacific Wren and Song Sparrow, all of which are noticeably larger. Evolution in action! This made me wonder about the number of taxa I would encounter during 2023 at the subspecies level.

On Tuesday, May 30, we contracted a local fishing boat captain, Scott, to take us out for a closer look at the offshore pelagic species. The boat trip was very productive. We found numerous Auklets: Parakeet, Crested, Whiskered and Cassin's, along with all the species we saw previously from the sea watch including both albatross species, thousands of Northern Fulmar and six more alcid species. Raymond's sharp eyes spotted a Short-tailed

Shearwater and a Leach's Storm-Petrel, both of which I missed. The sea turned rough as we approached the bluffs on the north coast of the island below the LORAN station. The 35-foot fishing skiff handled the choppy six-foot waves brilliantly. I'm sure I would have become seasick if Tammy had not given me a Scopolamine patch adhered to the bare skin behind my ear. This prescription medication does wonders for avoiding motion sickness but also causes drowsiness, which almost got me killed later in the year.

David proposed to the captain that we continue encircling the island of Adak. We had not yet found David's target species—the giant Short-tailed Albatross. This rare monster seabird had been reported a few times from boats passing the north shoreline of the island. However, the captain explained that such a route was not possible given the current rough conditions. I was relieved. My wallet was already strained from the high cost of traveling in Alaska. The cost of this pelagic adventure would have risen from about $800 per person to $2,000 per person had we continued around the island.

As we headed for port at the old navy base, we passed a harem of the enormous Steller's Sea Lion. They all ran to the edge of the rocks from where they were sunning themselves, exhibiting surprising agility, considering their huge size. They seemed awfully excited to see us. I think they were inviting us to stop our boat and join them for lunch, only *we* were on the menu!

Back on solid land, we didn't find any more additions to our year lists despite considerable effort to locate another vagrant from Asia. We packed up and left the island on Wednesday, May 31. I observed 68 bird species at Adak. The full trip report is available on-line through the eBird website here: https://eBird.org/tripreport/135407. Seventeen species were new for my USA and Territories Biggest Year list, including three ABA Code 3+ species.

On Adak, the McQuades had caught up to me and passed me by two species. Their next stop was St. Paul Island in the Pribilofs followed by a couple of days in Nome. I was headed to Nome for three days followed by five nights in the little town of Gambell on St. Lawrence Island.

CHAPTER 20
There's No Place Like Nome

Nome is my favorite birding spot in Alaska. Once a bustling metropolis, the largest city in Alaska during the Gold Rush, this town of just 3,700 inhabitants is located on the south shore of the Seward Peninsula along Alaska's west coast. I first visited Nome in June 2021 with my son Nick, and birding friends Cliff Hendrick and Rob Raker. We spent six long days there. Long because in June, it stays light enough for birding 24 hours a day, and it seems like rarities are everywhere. The phrase *rare birds are common* does not apply to Nome. In Nome, rarities are abundant! Ah yes, there is no place like Nome.

Where there are rare birds there are birders. Mid-May to mid-June is birding season in Nome. Hotels and rental cars are booked a year in advance. All the major birding companies have guided tours there. These companies typically spend three days in Nome en route to another destination like Gambell or Point Barrow. I should have planned to spend more time in Nome in 2023, but I scheduled only two days thinking that Adak and Gambell would supply enough excitement.

Because Nome was not a formal destination of my Adak trip or my Gambell tour, I made reservations for lodging and car rental late. There would be seven of us. I found rooms for us spread all over town. Tom Hall of Colorado and Michael Costello of California shared a room at the Golden Sands Guest House in downtown Nome. My brother and I were in a room down the hall from them. Sue Riffe of Colorado was in the Dredge No. 7 Inn a mile west of downtown on the Nome-Teller Highway. I found a room for Lori Pivonka and Sandy Winkler, both of Colorado, at the Aurora Hotel a mile east on the Nome-Council Highway. Both roads are roughly 75 miles long. A third road heads north from Nome about the same distance to the Kougarok River Bridge. The road system ends at those three spots. From Anchorage, one cannot reach

Nome by road. Only by plane, boat, or dog sled. Nome is the finish line of the famous Iditarod dog sled race that retraces the route of Siberian Husky lead sled dogs, Balto and Togo, who delivered life-saving diphtheria antitoxin to the desperate gold miners of Nome during an epidemic in 1925.

Upon arrival in Nome just before noon on Saturday, June 1, 2023, we discovered that one of the two vehicles we rented was busted. Fortunately, Stampede Car Rental had a second vehicle available for the first of the two days we planned to be in Nome. My brother Oliver was scheduled to arrive the next day, so for our first 24 hours in Nome, we had two vehicles for the six of us. Once settled at our three different lodgings, we met for lunch at the Subway sandwich shop across the street from the Aurora Hotel at 1 PM. At 1:30, we were birding.

My first year-bird, Rusty Blackbird, flew by at Cemetery Pond, which hosted breeding Short-billed Gull, Arctic Tern, Red-necked Grebe and breeding plumaged Long-tailed Duck, Pacific Golden-Plover and Long-tailed Jaeger. The jaeger was also new. We headed east on the Nome-Council Highway in our two rented Jeeps. At East End Park, all the common land birds of Nome were singing from the shrubby willows here: American Robin, Gray-cheeked Thrush, American Tree Sparrow, Fox Sparrow, White-crowned Sparrow, Orange-crowned Warbler, Wilson's Warbler and Northern Waterthrush. Hoary Redpoll was new. On our way to the Nome dump about a mile north, a kiting Long-tailed Jaeger posed for photos. The landfill hosted dozens of pallid Glaucous Gull (the largest and palest of the Glaucous Gulls, subspecies *pallidisimus*) and darker *Siberian* Herring Gull (subspecies *vegae*) and a couple of petite Short-billed Gull. An Eastern Yellow Wagtail foraging in the dirt was novel for my year list.

Our next stop was a short distance to the east along the Nome-Council Highway. We received a text message from Aaron Lang, our Gambell guide who had been on the plane with us that morning, informing us that a Gray-tailed Tattler (ABA Code 3) was foraging on the beach just west of the Nome River mouth. Sure enough, we found the Old World tattler working the same stretch of beach. This bird was a lifer for all of us!

At the Nome River mouth, I added Red Phalarope and another Asian stray, Red-necked Stint (ABA Code 3). Other birds here were Red-necked Phalarope, Western Sandpiper, Semipalmated Plover, Red Knot, Arctic Tern, Aleutian Tern and Short-billed Gull. After dinner at a waterfront restaurant in downtown Nome, we headed east again on the Nome-Council Highway. I suggested that we try to reach a bridge about 45 miles east where Gyrfalcon had nested a couple years earlier. Presumably they used the site annually. This would take us across the Safety Sound bridge where Slaty-backed Gull had been reported recently (about 15 miles east of Nome).

Indeed, after crossing the Safety Sound inlet, we could see dozens of Glaucous Gulls with some dark birds among them near the entrance to the sound. Most were Herring Gull. I began to sort through these darker gulls searching for a Slaty-backed Gull but was frequently distracted. First it was jaegers. All three species were sitting on the ice shelf on the sound. Then it was waterfowl. There was an impressive variety of sea ducks and bay ducks, as well as a large number of Tundra Swan. Then Sue Riffe exclaimed, "Whoa, I've got something good. Nick, come look through my scope, now!" She had her spotting scope trained on a medium-sized plover with an orange breast contrasting with a bright white throat.

"What the heck is this?" she asked.

"That is a Lesser Sand-Plover!" I confirmed. I snapped off some distant documentary photos of the vagrant plover (ABA Code 3, also known as Siberian Sand-Plover). We decided to try to get closer for better photographs. After hiking what seemed like forever through marsh grass to get close to the shoreline near the Asian vagrant, we could not find the bird. It was close to midnight, so we curtailed the Gyrfalcon hunt and retraced our path back to Nome for a few hours of sleep.

The next morning, we assembled for birding around 8 AM. We restarted our track toward the Gyrfalcon knowing we were short on time. The second rental Jeep was due back to Stampede Car Rental at 1 PM and my brother Oliver would be landing in Nome around noon.

Along the highway, actually just a dirt road, we spied a well camouflaged female Willow Ptarmigan hunkered among the dwarf willows along the roadside. At Cape Nome, we added Stejneger's Scoter (ABA Code 3) and a migrating Northern Wheatear. The scoter was a recent taxonomic split from the familiar White-winged Scoter, which were also present. The Stejneger's Scoter is from the Northwest Pacific region and differs most notably in the shape and color of its bill. We pushed eastward but did not get very far, stopping frequently for birds. We never even got beyond Safety Sound when it was time to return to town to pick up Oliver.

Oliver's arrival flight was on time. This was a minor miracle as he originated his flight in the Galápagos Islands of Ecuador where he was on assignment teaching students on tour from Zamorano University in Honduras. Oliver was a professor of ecology and protected areas management at Zamorano for more than 12 years. His flight itinerary took him to Quito (Ecuador), San Salvador (El Salvador), San Francisco (California), Anchorage (Alaska) and finally Nome. After dropping his suitcase, we met the rest of the group for lunch at Subway and learned that we were indeed unable to rent the second vehicle for the second day. We would need to fit seven of us in the one Jeep, a five-seater. We packed in and drove two miles to the Nome dump. No Slaty-backed Gull at the dump. Rather than birding like sardines I suggested that Ollie and I get dropped off at the Nome River mouth while the rest of the group searched for Bluethroat and Arctic Warbler along the Nome-Teller Highway.

Five hours later Ollie and I had tallied five Red-necked Stints and four Red Knots. Then it was our turn to use the vehicle. Tom Hall agreed to show us where they had successfully found their targets several miles west of Nome. Unfortunately, we were unable to re-find these birds. We did find a different Bluethroat.

After we dropped off Tom around 10 PM, we returned to the Nome River Mouth hoping to find more shorebirds at low tide. We found one Bar-tailed Godwit with a small flock of Long-billed Dowitcher. We pushed onward, eastbound. Oliver fell asleep in the front seat. I was determined to

128

reach the Gyrfalcon nest 20 miles beyond Safety Sound. Once I passed the sound, the dim light of the Nome night grew even dimmer when I entered a fog bank. The dirt road was becoming slick with light precipitation. I advanced slowly, imagining the consequences of sliding into a ditch. It was about 2 AM when I reached the bridge. Two ravens had occupied the nest! Disappointed, I returned to Safety Sound where a Wolverine was a welcome sight. That woke Ollie up and he got a great photo with his higher quality camera. A River Otter joined the show. It was now 4:15 AM and we made birding stops along the 15-mile stretch of Safety Sound. The highlight was a flock of a dozen Bar-tailed Godwit. We tried to relocate the Lesser Sand-Plover and Gray-tailed Tattler for Ollie's benefit but failed.

Bluethroat
2 Jun 2023, near Nome, Alaska

By 8 AM on June 3, we had picked up the others and like sardines headed to the sea at Cape Nome for our final Nome sea watch. As we arrived, a tour group was leaving. Colorado birder Edie Israel was in the van. She jumped out to greet us. She reported that they hadn't seen much in an hour at the Cape. We had better luck though as the birds had begun to move. We would call out a variety of flyby alcids (Horned and Tufted Puffins, Common Murre), sea ducks (Common Eider, Harlequin Duck, Long-tailed Duck, Red-breasted Merganser, three species of scoter), as well as numerous Black-legged Kittiwake and Pelagic Cormorant, and four species of loon including Yellow-billed Loon, a year-bird for me. Most exciting for me was a flock of 13 Emperor Goose that floated by the cape on a patch of sea ice!

Our time in Nome was coming to an end. Ollie was on the morning flight to Gambell. He wasn't able to get a seat on our flight in the afternoon. When we dropped him off, we learned that his Bering Air flight was on a weather hold and that our afternoon flight would likely be delayed. We used the delay to track down a White Wagtail (ABA Code 3) in downtown Nome.

When we returned to the airport we met Steve Heinl, one of our guides in Gambell. He lives in Ketchikan, Alaska, and had just arrived from Anchorage. He was scheduled to be on our Bering Air flight as well. He informed us that Ollie had arrived safely in Gambell. Our flight was still delayed due to low cloud cover in Gambell. Then the flight was postponed until 10 AM the next day. Steve arranged for us to have lodging and wheels for our additional night in Nome. While disappointed that our Gambell time would be cut short, I saw this as an opportunity to search for more of the bird species that Nome hosts, such as Arctic Warbler, Gyrfalcon and Slaty-backed Gull. Also, we had heard that the Kougarok Road had just opened beyond mile marker 60 giving us access to the breeding location for Bristle-thighed Curlew at mile marker 72. Over dinner we convinced Steve to take us on a hunt for the curlew. This would also be an opportunity to find Gyrfalcon for the group and for me to add Arctic Warbler to my list.

Again, we were packed like sardines. Steve had a rented double-cabin pickup truck with three people up front and four of us squeezed in the back seat. At 10 PM, we arrived at the Gyrfalcon nest site high above the road in a cliff face. Unfortunately, the only raptor we could find was a Rough-legged

Hawk. A Northern Wheatear on the cliff face was a consolation, but too far for photographs. Additional stops en route to the curlew location yielded Bluethroat and both Rock and Willow Ptarmigans. At mile marker 72, we began our forced march up Coffee Dome. Almost immediately, we heard a distant curlew, but we could only find Whimbrel on the hillside. An hour later, around midnight, a Bristle-thighed Curlew flew over our heads giving its unique flight song which I documented with an audio recording.

Returning to Nome, we were amazed by the high number of Snowshoe Hare along the road. A couple of stops at traditional Arctic Warbler breeding sites confirmed that most had not yet arrived on territories from their East Asian wintering grounds. It was close to 3 AM when we got to bed back in Nome. By 11 AM, June 4, the clouds had lifted over Gambell and we were on our way to our next adventure. During just three days in Nome, I had added 17 species to my year list (705 species in the USA and Territories). The full species list for my Nome visit, along with photos and audio files, can be viewed at https://eBird.org/tripreport/141195.

4 Jun 2023, Gambell, Alaska
Nick Komar with Tom Hall
Photo by Oliver Komar

CHAPTER 21
The Gambell Gamble

G ambell, Alaska, is a small whaling village at the northwest tip of St. Lawrence Island in the Bering Sea. About 600 people live there. A lodge is available for visitors. Our birding guide, Aaron Lang, owner/operator of Wilderness Birding Adventures, arranged a stay for our group of seven. He and his assistant guide Steve Heinl had access to the kitchen area. The tour included preparation of our meals for six days on the island. Both guides were very knowledgeable about all Alaskan birds. Steve was among an elite group of five who had observed more than 400 species of birds in the State of Alaska. Both Aaron and Steve are highly respected in the birding community and both served on the Alaska Bird Checklist Committee. Aaron also served on the ABA Checklist Committee.

Our group included Sue Riffe, Tom Hall, Michael Costello, Sandy Winkler, Lori Pivonka, Oliver Komar and yours truly. We hailed from Colorado except for Michael (California) and Oliver (Honduras). Most of us arrived late morning on June 4, almost a full day later than planned because low cloud cover over Gambell delayed our flight from Nome with Bering Air. Aaron arrived from Homer, Alaska, via Anchorage and Nome, two days earlier. My brother Oliver arrived on a flight from Nome on June 3. The airport at Gambell is a single runway with no terminal or staff. The pilot opened the door. The copilot pulled out the stairway and out we went. Two ATVs were waiting for us. One pulled a wooden cart for our luggage and the other, with Aaron at the wheel, pulled a makeshift trailer with benches for our group to sit on. This was the *birding bus* available exclusively for Aaron's tours.

Within minutes we were settling in at the lodge, a no-frills barracks with about 20 small bedrooms with two single beds each. Showers and bathrooms were communal. Aaron informed us that another visiting birder, Brad Benter (who was on official US Fish and Wildlife Service business) had re-found a Siberian House-Martin (ABA Code 4) that showed up a few days earlier in

Gambell and was waiting for us to arrive at the site to make sure we got it for our checklist.

With Asian vagrants like this swallow, the bird could fly away or perish at any time. We needed to search for it without delay. This species is closely related to the Tree Swallow in North America. Like the Tree Swallow, it is dark iridescent blue above (back, wings, nape and crown) and bright white below (throat, chest and belly). It differed primarily by sporting a large white patch on the rump feathers. Its tail was more deeply forked as well. The Siberian House-Martin survived by hawking small insects in flight, but at Gambell the air temperature rarely exceeded 35 degrees Fahrenheit, and patches of ice and snow still covered the ground. This dramatically reduced the available insect population. We were lucky this bird was still present.

Aaron was excited for us because the wind had been consistently from the west for about a week, so he expected more East Asian vagrants. But sometimes they didn't show up. John Vanderpoel spent ten days at Gambell during the peak of spring migration for his Big Year effort in 2011 and was virtually skunked. So, there were no guarantees. Spending valuable time and funds to be in Gambell was certainly a gamble. And we hoped to strike gold. After being ferried by Aaron's birding cart about a mile from the lodge, we found Brad perched next to the only lake on the island accessible to birders. It was mostly frozen. Brad was between the lake and Gambell's only mountain which featured cliff face, boulders, patches of snow and some seedless grasses. Aaron explained that his land use license allowed access only to the lake area, the town and the seashore. The mountainside was used as a burial ground and hunting zone and it was off limits to birders. The rest of St. Lawrence Island was similarly off limits. The island has almost 2,000 square miles but we birders were restricted to an area of about five square miles.

As I looked around at the ice of the lake and snowfields of the mountainside, I understood Aaron's urgency to find the swallow for us now. *There it is*! exclaimed my brother. A tiny swallow was flying toward us. It seemed to be foraging low over the snowfields perhaps looking for ice gnats in the snow.

We could see the forked tail and the white rump that determined the swallow's identity as the house-martin. Amazing.

Aaron announced, "A Rustic Bunting has been in the circular boneyard the last few days and was seen this morning by the VENT group." Off we went in the open birding bus to a weedy patch near the edge of town. Aaron explained that the four weedy patches dotted around town were historical boneyards where whale bones left over from the community whaling hunts are buried. The nutrients from the bones support the growth of seed-bearing weeds. Furthermore, these weedy patches are full of shallow holes where townspeople have dug for bones that can be recycled for carvings and jewelry and the like. Many of the holes had accumulated fresh water which could also attract birds. We spread out as we moved slowly through the boneyard, to ensure we didn't miss any skulking vagrants. We flushed a few Lapland Longspur and Snow Bunting, both common summer residents. A White Wagtail was also presumed to be a local breeder. It was one of a handful of species that spend the winter in Asia and arrived annually to breed in Alaska. Aaron spotted the female Rustic Bunting, which flushed in front of him and flew a short distance like an *Ammodramus* sparrow. Sparrows in this genus typically are weak flyers. When they land, they scramble like mice through the weeds to avoid detection. This bunting's streaky dark brown and gray plumage provided camouflage against the weeds of the same colors. Eventually we all got decent views of this vagrant Rustic Bunting (ABA Code 3).

While walking back toward the lodge, I snapped off some photos of a small plover with a single black collar that was either a Semipalmated Plover or its Asian cousin Common Ringed Plover. The breeding ranges overlap on St. Lawrence Island. In breeding plumage, the color of the eye-ring is a useful field mark, yellow versus black. This one was black, confirming Common Ringed-Plover (ABA Code 3).

After a lunch break, we searched another boneyard and re-found a Dark-eyed Junco, a vagrant from mainland Alaska. From there, it was a short, but tough hike over mounds of rounded rock to the sea watch point along the beach where another group of birders traveling with Victor Emmanuel

Nature Tours (VENT) had assembled. As we walked toward them, a message came across Aaron's two-way radio. It was from Kevin Zimmer, one of the VENT leaders.

"Just had a flyby Ross's Gull headed in your direction."

Ross's Gull
4 Jun 2023, Gambell, Alaska
Photo by Oliver Komar

There were birds flying by us toward them but nothing in the air moving toward us. Ten minutes passed. Did it fly past us? Had it landed? Yes! There it was, about 100 feet offshore, resting in the calm ocean with a pair of Black-legged Kittiwake which dwarfed the diminutive gull.

Ross's Gull (ABA Code 3) was a small gull from the Arctic Ocean that rarely turned up at Gambell or anywhere else south of the Arctic Circle. Its long narrow wings allowed it to move gracefully, like a tern. Instead of a tern's long forked tail, it had a long diamond or wedge-shaped tail which it used as a rudder to make acrobatic flight maneuvers. At the water's surface it picked up food morsels with its dainty black bill, which resembled that of a bluebird rather than the big heavy beak of a large gull or long beak of a tern. This bird was a year old, so it featured plumage characteristics both immature and adult.

Its wings portrayed the heavy black **M** pattern over a light gray background typical of a juvenile and its breast was bright pink like an adult. Its head was encircled by a thin black line like a necklace which gave the adult Ross's Gull such a unique appearance.

Ross's Gull was my most wanted bird for most of my life, ever since I missed seeing the famous bird at Newburyport Harbor (Massachusetts) in 1975 by a few seconds. I finally caught up to one in Colorado in 2010 that was in non-breeding plumage. This individual was even more beautiful. I was so excited to see the pink Ross's Gull that my arms were shaking more than usual, which made photography quite difficult. I had to get on my belly and prop up my camera with my elbows firmly planted in the pebbles of the beach. The gull was in no rush to leave. I was able to get decent photographs and video of the bird in flight as it foraged in the wave line just offshore.

I took a brief break to photograph a drake and two hen Steller's Eider floating by. The Steller's Eider was a life bird for me, but I was still mesmerized by the Ross's Gull. After about 30 minutes, the gull moved on down the beach and I turned my attention to other birds flying by.

A good variety of species were on the move. I added King Eider, Least Auklet and Black Guillemot to the year lists.

Later that day, we returned to the circular boneyard hoping to find a pipit Aaron had glimpsed earlier. Oliver pointed out a dark-backed gull flying over the north beach. He yelled out "Slaty-backed Gull!" Sure enough, his photos confirmed the identification. Slaty-backed Gull (ABA Code 3) was uncommon but not unexpected at Gambell. It normally nested in Siberia and wintered in Korea and Japan.

That evening at the lodge we were all in a good mood retelling our stories from that day. Brian Gibbons, the VENT tour co-leader who first spotted the Ross's Gull, described a second one he saw later in the day.

Most of the excitement (Asian vagrants and year-birds) occurred that first day in Gambell. During the next five days there, we did find some additional North American vagrants including Golden-crowned Sparrow, Yellow-rumped Warbler and Hermit Thrush. Viewing the array of auklets perched on the steep slopes and rock ledges of the mountain in Gambell was a fabulous experience. Many thousands of pairs of Least, Crested and Parakeet Auklets along with Tufted and Horned Puffins and Pigeon Guillemot was an amazing sight. Unfortunately, we could not find any Dovekie along with them, although a small population of this North Atlantic alcid reportedly persisted near Gambell. A foraging Arctic Fox prowling the mountainside above us, carrying an auklet to its den, made the scene even more interesting.

During most of our time at Gambell, loons were absent. On June 8, the day before our departure, the floodgates for loons finally opened. Over 250 Pacific Loon and 25 Arctic Loon (ABA Code 3) flew by us at the sea watch that afternoon.

On the morning of our departure June 9, we hoped for a surprise at the sea watch. We were not disappointed although the surprise was not a bird but rather a mammal. Aaron was trying to get us onto a high-flying Yellow-billed Loon. Simultaneously Oliver yelled out "Walrus!" A bull Walrus with long pearly tusks was playing in the waves as the loon flew over. Later Aaron spotted a cow Walrus with a pup. In 25 trips to Gambell, Aaron had never seen a Walrus there.

Looking back, the trip to Gambell added 10 species for my USA and Territories Biggest Year (now at 715 species) and launched me back into first place in the eBird ABA Area *Top 100* list for 2023, albeit temporarily. The investment of time and money to visit Gambell paid off. Photos, sound files and checklists can be viewed through the online trip report here: https://eBird.org/tripreport/142935.

CHAPTER 22
Filling the Gaps:
Midwest and New England

I returned home from Alaska on the morning of June 10, 2023, feeling somewhat fatigued. Yes, I had been birding practically nonstop since April and I flew home from Anchorage on a red-eye flight via Salt Lake City. This fatigue felt different from burnout or exhaustion. I had picked up a cold in Gambell. Other than my Parkinson's condition, I had not been sick in years, since before the onset of the COVID-19 pandemic. I tested myself for COVID. The test result came back *positive*. I had COVID! Fortunately, my symptoms were mild and I was already recovered. After informing the Gambell group I learned that two others developed symptoms and tested positive (but not my brother who shared a room with me for a week). Both made full recoveries. It was time to review my progress with my Big Year.

Alaska was quite productive. I added 45 USA and Territories Biggest Year-birds including 15 ABA Code 3+ species! I had now seen 34 of these rarer species, mostly vagrants. My goal was 40 Code 3+ species for the year. This was an excellent accomplishment because unlike Code 1 and Code 2 species, which breed in North America, the frequency of detecting new species as year-birds would not decrease over the course of the year. I figured I would have a good chance to detect 60 by the end of my Big Year!

My USA and Territories total was 715. I was well on my way to my goal of 900 species. Hawaii and the South Pacific Islands should produce at least 100 more species later this year.

My total for the ABA Area was 678, good for third place in the eBird *Top 100*, two species behind the McQuades, who had finished strong in

Alaska with some species in Nome that I had missed, including Spectacled Eider and Arctic Warbler.

In the Lower 48 competition I was in first place, ahead of the McQuades by one species, at 638 species. Spring migration was coming to a close. It was time to take stock of the species I had missed and think about strategic ways to find them.

There were some big misses in Alaska. Gyrfalcon was one of them. It does not breed in the Lower 48. Perhaps I could find one later this summer in Alaska, or on a wintering territory in the northern tier of US States. Red-legged Kittiwake was another miss (although I did not visit the Pribilofs where they are common).

Among warblers, I was still missing Connecticut, Kirtland's, Arctic and Red-faced. Many sparrows had so far evaded me, including Baird's, Nelson's, Saltmarsh, LeConte's, Henslow's, Botteri's and Five-striped. I still needed several flycatchers including Dusky-capped, Brown-crested, Willow, Buff-breasted and Yellow-bellied. Goatsuckers missed included Eastern Whip-poor-will and Buff-collared Nightjar. Many pelagic species were still missing.

I had four tours planned for the summer with the goal of filling these gaps: Wisconsin/Minnesota June 20–25; New England June 25–30; Colorado July 11–15; and finally Arizona during monsoon season Aug 7–12. And spring migration was still happening. In Colorado, recent reports of Willow Flycatcher around Fort Collins were certainly late migrants.

My daily birding in my local patch (Larimer County, Colorado) would focus on finding Willow Flycatcher migrating through riparian habitat near Fort Collins. I searched several local hotspots along the Cache La Poudre River trail, but to no avail.

On June 19, I joined Sue Riffe in Minneapolis, Minnesota. Sue owns She Flew Birding Tours, based in Boulder County, Colorado. She had agreed to serve as driver and co-leader of this tour. Dana Hiatt and Kelly Ormesher would arrive the following morning, from Loveland, Colorado and St. Louis, Missouri, respectively.

Upon our arrival in the afternoon, Sue and I followed an eBird report for Henslow's Sparrow and Willow Flycatcher near Saint Paul at Battle Creek Regional Park. No luck. Sue had led tours to Minnesota previously and had developed an itinerary with my targets in mind.

Once the whole group had assembled, we made a beeline for Eau Claire, Wisconsin. We had heard that a small population of Kirtland's Warbler was thriving in central Wisconsin. Kirtland's Warbler would be a life bird for everyone in the group except Sue. Due to its status as endangered, eBird reports were hidden. Sue used her experience with the species in its core range in Central Michigan to find similar habitat in Wisconsin.

In Michigan the species nested on the ground in dense stands of immature jack pine. The presence of pine boughs a few inches above the ground provided adequate protection from predators. She noticed that her checklists with Kirtland's Warbler in Michigan also contained a couple different species consistently. Using these parameters, she found a large patch of suitable habitat in Wisconsin.

When we arrived, we found a plantation of young pines and a large sign indicating that the habitat was being managed for Kirtland's Warbler conservation. Sue directed us to pines of the right size, not too tall and not too small. And bingo, right away we heard the unique songs of several territorial Kirtland's Warbler. We would return later for the possibility of getting some photos. Later the same evening, we added American Woodcock and Eastern Whip-poor-will.

On June 21, 2023, we returned to the pine plantation early, and very patiently waited for the opportunity to photograph Kirtland's Warbler, a relatively large warbler that sports a blue-gray back and a bright yellow belly. We got the photos! A great morning was had by all in part because the Kirtland's Warbler was so cooperative.

Next, we visited under-birded Petenwell County Park and were pleased to find Blue-winged Warbler. We extended the morning at Necedah National Wildlife Refuge where we found Dickcissel, Least Flycatcher, nesting Bald Eagle, Trumpeter Swan and a nesting family of the endangered Whooping Crane!! Red-headed Woodpecker completed the show. It was fun meeting young local birder Erick Ollie who filled us in on the local birding scene.

After lunch and a siesta, we visited another under-birded eBird hotspot called Buckhorn State Park. We found voracious mosquitoes but also Chestnut-sided Warbler, more American Woodcock and many Eastern Whip-poor-will which began their onomatopoeic serenade just after sundown.

On June 22, we drove northward toward Lake Superior and Northern Minnesota. Our first birding stop was the George W. Mead State Wildlife Area, where we arrived shortly after sunrise. Birds were everywhere: Sandhill Crane and American White Pelican. We parked at the East Honey Island Flowage Area where we encountered Golden-winged Warbler, Yellow-bellied Sapsucker and Black-billed Cuckoo (heard-only, year-bird). Hiking out into the marshes we found Yellow-billed Cuckoo, American Bittern, Sedge Wren, Purple Finch and many nesting Black Tern.

At the headquarters, we met the head biologist, Craig Ziolkowski, who told us how to find Henslow's Sparrow in the preserve and informed us of a pair of resident Whooper Swan with the flock of Trumpeter Swan. We spent considerable time looking for both without success. We did find a territorial singing Mourning Warbler which we speculated was at the southmost edge of the breeding range in Wisconsin.

After lunch we completed our drive to Superior, Wisconsin, on the shore of Lake Superior. We assembled on the beach hoping to relocate a flock of small gulls that contained Bonaparte's and one each of Ross's and Little Gulls. No luck. We spent the night in Duluth, Minnesota, at the west end of Lake Superior.

The next morning, June 23, storm clouds were gathering on the horizon. We headed to the Sax-Zim Bog where I had spent a few days in February in bitter cold and several feet of snow. Arriving on Arkola Road, we detoured to Winterberry Bog, a small property managed by the Friends of Sax-Zim Bog. A birding friend from Colorado (John Malenich) had sent me a message a day earlier that he had seen Connecticut Warbler there. We did not find it. Apparently, the warbler had decided to move on overnight. Consolation was a close encounter with a Black-backed Woodpecker, a singing performance by an extroverted Winter Wren and a good look at the bright black-and-orange face pattern of a Blackburnian Warbler. Back on Arkola Road, we headed toward the Sax-Zim Bog visitor center to get better intel on Connecticut Warbler and any nesting Great Gray Owl. Sue paused at an expansive meadow hoping for LeConte's Sparrow. Instead, we were surprised to find a pair of Dickcissel, a rare species in Northern Minnesota.

At the visitor center, we learned some disturbing news. Rainfall this year had been low, and the drought caused the population of Connecticut Warbler to continue its northbound migration beyond Sax-Zim Bog. However, a couple of Great Gray Owl had been seen recently in the bog. The bog was indeed quiet (except for many singing Nashville Warbler). After a brief and unsuccessful search for the large owls, we decided to head south to McGregor Marsh where we expected to find Willow Flycatcher, LeConte's Sparrow and Yellow Rail. Instead, we found only mosquitoes and a few Savannah Sparrow, Swamp Sparrow and Sedge Wren. After dinner at a local roadhouse, we returned to the marsh under cover of darkness but could not detect any calling Yellow Rail. The rain was picking up, so we called it a night and headed back to Duluth.

On June 24, we began the day birding in Duluth. Along the lake shore, we discovered a couple of eBird rarities—Savannah Sparrow and Sanderling. Several pairs of Common Tern were nesting nearby. Once we got on the road, we aimed for an eBird hotspot called Crex Meadows State Wildlife Area in Central Wisconsin, where Yellow Rail and Henslow's Sparrow had been recently reported to eBird. Fortunately, this spot was along our route toward Minneapolis, Minnesota. No luck finding our targets, but the birding was fabulous. There we found Least Bittern, Golden-winged Warbler, Black Tern and Trumpeter Swan. Afterwards, we successfully chased a locally rare Upland Sandpiper at nearby Fish Lake Wildlife Area. I was happy to upgrade this species from heard-only to seen.

On the final morning of the tour, we saw an eBird alert—Henslow's Sparrow was continuing at Battle Creek Regional Park. We returned there and eventually found a singing Henslow's Sparrow teed up atop a distant forb. It was among several Savannah Sparrow and Bobolink in tall grass prairie habitat. Its song is not much to hear, and barely recognizable as a song. In this regard, we appreciated the Merlin app for its highly functional song identification component. Merlin was certainly helpful in guiding us to the singing bird and corroborating the identification.

I had added four year-birds in Wisconsin and one in Minnesota. A few species were still left on the table and would require more effort later in the year: Connecticut Warbler, LeConte's Sparrow and Yellow Rail. Special thanks to Sue Riffe for driving and planning the route. And to Dana and Kelly for their companionship and support for my Biggest Year effort. Photos and audio files are available online through the eBird trip report, https://eBird.org/tripreport/144004.

I flew from Minneapolis to Boston on Sunday morning, June 25, 2023. I arrived at Boston's Logan Airport at 2:15 PM just as Irene Fortune, Gregg Goodrich and Anna Troth arrived from Colorado. They had signed up for a tour of Northern New England to be led by local guide Eric Hynes.

Eric lives in Central Maine. He grew up in Massachusetts and then moved to Maine where he became a professional birding guide, working for Field Guides, Inc. He recently had been living in Telluride, Colorado, where he established his own guiding company called Box Canyon Birding. I got to know him when we co-led a field trip to San Miguel County during the 2019 Colorado Field Ornithologists annual convention in Montrose. He reminded me that we first met much earlier when his Field Guides grouse tour crossed paths with my Quetzal Tours grouse tour on Rabbit Ears Pass some six years earlier. Eric was now leading tours around the world for Field Guides. He had just returned from guiding in Finland. He picked us up in a rented minivan at 3 PM and off we went.

This was very much a target birding tour. I had informed Eric of my Big Year needs, which included New England specialty species Atlantic Puffin, Razorbill, Bicknell's Thrush, Nelson's and Saltmarsh Sparrows as well as gap species Willow and Yellow-bellied Flycatchers.

We had time to make a couple of birding stops before checking in to our hotel at Scarborough, Maine, just south of Portland. At Wells, Maine, we were unlucky trying to find the Saltmarsh Sparrow that first afternoon, but we did get decent views of Roseate Tern. I had forgotten to photograph this species at the Dry Tortugas in May. I was pleased to have another opportunity and I took advantage of it. In the evening, we visited a unique habitat at Kennebunk Plains. This inland sandy-soiled pine barren hosted Grasshopper Sparrow, Prairie Warbler, American Woodcock and Eastern Whip-poor-will. The whip-poor-will, a nocturnal species in the goatsucker family (Caprimulgidae) put on a magnificent performance for us, flying within feet of me and landing on the road in full view.

The pine barrens at Kennebunk Plains are famous for attracting rarities. We missed a vagrant Loggerhead Shrike (normally found much farther west) that had been reported here earlier in the week. And we let a heard-only, probable Yellow-crowned Night-Heron (normally found much farther south) go unidentified. Its single crow-like call was not enough evidence for us to pull the trigger on identifying such a rare bird in Maine.

On Monday morning, June 26, Scarborough Marsh produced stunning views of both Saltmarsh and Nelson's Sparrows. An old railroad track converted to a recreational trail for bikers, joggers, walkers and birders provided access to the marshes. After the first half mile walking, we had detected no sparrows but were entertained by close views of Willet, the distinctive Eastern form, in breeding plumage. Eric explained that this taxon may one day be split from its larger, grayer cousin, the Western Willet. The dearth of sparrows, Eric suggested, could be due to the late date. The sparrows were wrapping up their breeding season. However, my concern for missing these targets was alleviated when after another half mile, we began hearing the squeaky buzz songs of both sparrow species close to the trail.

After lunching at Eric's brother's successful brew pub in Augusta, we birded in Eric's local patch at Piggery Road. Here we found Swamp Sparrow, Willow Flycatcher (year-bird), Broad-winged Hawk, Virginia Rail, Ruby-throated Hummingbird, Bobolink and Purple Finch. From here we headed *down east* to Bar Harbor. We made brief birding stops around Messalonskee Lake in Kennebec County, where we observed Purple Martin, Black Tern and Sandhill Crane, all of which are unusual in Maine.

Tuesday morning, June 27, we showed up bright and early at the Bar Harbor dock for the Puffins and Lighthouses cruise which we expected to yield several target species plus an unknown number of Atlantic Ocean pelagic species such as shearwaters and storm-petrels. The wind had picked up. The captain was waiting to see if the six-foot waves would settle down. The cruise was scheduled to depart at 9:30 AM. He waited until 9 AM to make the decision to cancel the foray to Machias Seal Island where Atlantic Puffin and Razorbill breed. We were heartbroken. But Eric had a backup plan. We jumped into the minivan and sped off to the southwest to New Harbor, two and a half hours away. We arrived at 11:30, just in time to board the ferry to Eastern Egg Rock for puffin viewing. This would be a shorter cruise with fewer chances for pelagic species. However, this boat runs rain or shine and guarantees views of Atlantic Puffin. Razorbill had been seen on the rock recently. And a vagrant Tufted Puffin from the Pacific Ocean had been spotted in the area as well.

Atlantic Puffin
27 Jun 2023, Eastern Egg Rock, Maine

A basking breeding-plumaged Black Guillemot in the tiny harbor was a good omen. As we left the harbor, several Wilson's Storm-Petrel (year-bird) followed the boat. Then came more pelagic species as we headed out over open water: an impressive number of Sooty Shearwater, a Northern Gannet and several Northern Fulmar. As we approached the island, we began seeing Atlantic Puffin (year-bird) flying by and swimming close to the boat. Common and Roseate Terns were nesting on the island with the puffins. A large alcid flew by encircling the boat. Was it my target Razorbill? No, it was a rarer bird for Maine, a Common Murre! I was excited to see one in Maine waters,

146

although I had seen plenty of these in the Pacific Ocean earlier this year. After 30 minutes along the west side of the island it was time to turn around. The captain didn't want to visit the east side due to the high seas, but I am afraid that was where the Razorbill was hiding. Later we found out that the Tufted Puffin was also using this tiny island as a resting spot, perhaps on the east side. Nevertheless, it was a thrilling ride and we all left very satisfied with the adventure. It was now mid-afternoon and time for a traditional seafood lunch (think fish and chips or lobster roll) followed by a long drive to the Rangeley Lakes region and the boreal forests of Western Maine. We spent the next two nights at Saddleback Mountain Lodge in Rangeley, Maine.

On Wednesday morning, June 28, we delved into the forest atop Quill Hill, a privately owned sanctuary. The dawn chorus featured many species of warblers including Black-and-white, Magnolia, Chestnut-sided, Nashville, Black-throated Blue, Yellow-rumped, and Wilson's and Mourning Warblers. Also, there were Northern Parula and American Redstart. Other songsters included White-throated Sparrow, Rose-breasted Grosbeak, Alder Flycatcher and Indigo Bunting. The next 24 hours of birding this remote region of Western Maine produced a great variety of breeding birds of the northern forests. Additional highlights included Canada, Palm, Blackburnian and Black-throated Green Warblers, Blue-headed Vireo, Yellow-bellied Flycatcher (year-bird), Winter Wren and Boreal Chickadee.

After lunch on Thursday, June 29, we headed southwest toward Mount Washington in New Hampshire. At Grafton Notch State Park, we stopped to appreciate the songs of Philadelphia and Red-eyed Vireos, which conveniently are both present at this location. These vireos look different but sound almost identical. The comparison of songs made a great study. At 4 PM we arrived at the Mount Washington Auto Road in Grafton, New Hampshire. Mount Washington is the highest peak in the Appalachian Mountain Range at 6,288 feet elevation. Here we confirmed our after-hours van tour (cost = $275). Afternoon thunderstorms threatened to put a damper on our plan. However, the van driver Ken agreed to reach tree line regardless of the weather for our quest to find Bicknell's Thrush. In the USA, this species breeds only in the *krummholz* zone of the Northern Appalachian Mountains, including the Adirondacks in New York, Green Mountains of Vermont, and White Mountains of New Hampshire and Maine. The krummholz zone is characterized by elevation-stunted spruce trees. Like many *passerine* bird species (species in the order Passeriformes), Bicknell's Thrush is suffering worrisome population declines and has disappeared from some of its previous breeding areas. I was one of the last to observe the species on Mount Greylock in the Berkshire Range of Western Massachusetts in the late 1970s. As kids, my brother Ollie and I joined an overnight camping trip led by Steve Grinley for the Brookline Bird Club. I don't recall seeing the thrush, only hearing its beautiful haunting melody. We were with my mother Karen Komar and our birding mentor, the late Herman d'Entremont. In those days, the Bicknell's Thrush was considered a subspecies of Gray-cheeked Thrush.

After checking in at our nearby hotel, we returned at 6 PM and drove up the auto road as the last tourists were coming down. We arrived at tree line at 6:45 PM. We listened to the chorus of White-throated Sparrow, Slate-colored Junco and Blackpoll Warbler songs emanating from the stunted vegetation of the krummholz zone for about 30 minutes. No thrushes. In the distance we detected a Swainson's Thrush and a rare Fox Sparrow singing from a presumed breeding territory (they normally breed farther north in Canada). A Black Bear crashed through the brush, running from our presence. Finally, at 7:30 PM we began to hear call notes of Bicknell's Thrush (year-bird). We played a recording of the song and a flurry of songs responded briefly but no thrush dared to show itself. We shifted our location a couple of times. Finally, at 8:30 PM as it was almost too dark to see, Eric spotted our target in the distance singing atop a short spruce tree. He put it in the telescope for decent views by most of us.

Friday, June 30, was the final day of the tour. We had accomplished most of our objectives. We needed to drop off Irene, Gregg and Anna at Logan Airport at 3:00 PM for their return flights to Colorado. Eric chose a route to increase our trip list by several species. The route included a visit to Biddeford Pool on the Maine coast south of Portland. A pair of calling American

Oystercatcher was a pleasant addition. The full trip list of 151 species along with photos and audio files can be found in the online eBird trip report here: https://eBird.org/tripreport/141380.

Once the Northern New England tour ended, I recuperated for a few days at my mother's house in Newton, Massachusetts, in Southern New England. I still went birding during these days. On July 1, I joined Alf Wilson at Winthrop along the coast north of Boston. We took killer photos of Least Tern and Piping Plover at Winthrop Beach. In the adjacent neighborhood he showed me an active Monk Parakeet nest. A block away, at Lewis Lake Park, I spotted a Purple Martin which was flagged as rare in eBird. One town over at Revere Beach, Alf spotted a few Manx Shearwater (year-bird) loafing beyond the surf. These seabirds presumably nested on islands in Boston Harbor. They were reliable off Revere Beach for years and are well known to the local birding community. Because they can be tough to find on pelagic boat trips, I was glad to have seen them now.

With few possibilities for more Biggest Year-birds in New England, I made plans to fly to Miami to chase a couple of rarities. On July 4, my last day in Newton, I invited my mom on a 90-minute drive to Coney Rock Park in Northeast Connecticut. I was chasing an eBird report of a singing Cerulean Warbler. We did not find this warbler, but I thoroughly enjoyed encountering some wonderful birds of the Southern New England forest, including Red-shouldered Hawk, Veery, Wood Thrush, Yellow-throated Vireo, Worm-eating Warbler, Louisiana Waterthrush and Scarlet Tanager, all singing. I was happy to share my Biggest Year adventure with my 87-year-old mother. These opportunities are few and far between.

My USA and Territories year list total was now 728 species.

CHAPTER 23
The Thrill of the Chase

*I*n the middle of May, 2023, an amazing story unfolded in South Florida. Two Large-billed Tern, a South American species, turned up simultaneously on both coasts of Florida. An adult was found in a wildlife management area in Indian River County near Vero Beach on Florida's Atlantic Slope while an immature bird was detected at a canal near Fort Myers on the Gulf Slope.

In years past, I had observed the species in Colombia, Peru and Argentina in its native habitat of tropical inland lagoons and sluggish rivers. How these magnificent terns came to Florida was anyone's guess. I imagined the pair got caught up in bad weather that blew them offshore where they became disoriented and separated. Either that or they were vacationing in Florida and argued about which way to turn on Interstate 75. Remarkably, several weeks later, both birds remained present at or very near to their original discovery locations.

These birds are striking in their plumage and appearance. In flight, they exhibit a wing pattern recalling Sabine's Gull with black, white and gray triangles on the upper side of each wing. They are large birds, the size of Ring-billed Gull or Royal Tern. But the most outstanding feature is the massive yellow bill, which gives them a kingfisher or toucanet vibe. This bill evolved to allow them to catch bigger fish than other species of terns, permitting them to carve out a niche for their survival in a dog-eat-dog world.

My busy tour schedule didn't permit me to make an attempt to chase this ABA Code 5 species until July. Now, having done well on filling my species gaps in the Midwest and New England, I was able to dedicate several days to chasing rare birds in Florida. I arrived early at Miami on the morning of July 5, 2023. For my itinerary, I consulted Bill Kaempfer, a transplanted Coloradoan birder now retired from academia and living near Tampa. He explained to me the access issues for the two terns and advised me on the most accessible locations for several *psittacine* species (species in the order Psittaciformes like parrots, parakeets, macaws, etc.) that evaded me during my Florida tour in May. Bill was also a Big Year birder, trying each year to see 700 species in the USA. I asked him if he would join me but he pointed out the long distances between target locations and convinced me that joining forces during my brief visit was not practical. Little did I know then that our paths would meet later in Hawaii.

I also wanted to try my luck again for an uncooperative La Sagra's Flycatcher which was seen occasionally south of Miami near Biscayne National Park. My efforts to find it in May with Cliff and Irene failed. Larry Manfredi, the grand wizard of South Florida birding, predicted that it would return. He was right. In fact, two days earlier, Alex Lamoreaux (another Big Year birder) had posted to eBird explicit instructions for finding the bird. If once again, I couldn't find that one, another had been discovered at the parking lot of Long Key State Park by Erik Nielsen, whom I knew from my teenage years in Massachusetts. My Colorado friends Kathy Kay and Graham Ray had already chased that one successfully after ticking the immature Large-billed Tern near Fort Myers.

I picked up a trashy, dirt-cheap rental car near the Miami Airport and off I went. First stop was Coral Reef Park in Paradise City south of Miami. Bill Kaempfer told me that a pair of Blue-and-yellow Macaw visits the park each morning at 10 AM. I ticked this species in Puerto Rico earlier in the year, but I hoped to add it to my ABA Area and Lower 48 year lists in eBird, even if not officially countable. The ABA requires documented breeding for 15 consecutive years before it will add an exotic species to the official *ABA Checklist*. The macaw was not yet considered naturalized. I arrived at 11 AM and found no macaws. I did see an apple snail-eating Limpkin and dozens of recently fledged Muscovy Duck, Egyptian Goose and Common Gallinule. It was a great place to be a baby waterfowl! The Muscovy Duck and Egyptian Goose, like the macaw, were exotic species in Florida but were considered naturalized in this locale and therefore were included in the *ABA Checklist*, and were formally countable for my Biggest Year list.

Next stop was Larry Manfredi's worksite to look for the La Sagra's Flycatcher. I arrived about 2 PM on Wednesday afternoon. The environmental remediation work was suspended for the hottest part of the day. I explored the entire area, hiking four miles over four hours with no sign of any *Myiarchus* flycatchers. *Aargh, not again.* This was my fourth attempt to find this bird. The La Sagra's Flycatcher was quickly becoming a leading candidate for my nemesis bird in 2023.

Large-billed Tern
7 Jul 2023, Immokalee, Florida

I hunted too long for the La Sagra's Flycatcher and was not going to have enough daylight to tick the Large-billed Tern before sundown. I eventually arrived at the Ave Maria housing development/golf resort near Fort Myers around 8:30 PM. I searched the area for an hour in the dimming light. No sign of the tern. *Uh oh.* I figured that if I missed it the following morning, I could drive the four hours across the peninsula to Vero Beach and get the adult that same afternoon.

I spent the night in the cheapest, grungiest, most cockroach infested dump I could find in nearby Immokalee, Florida. The cost was $90 which seemed exorbitant to me. The cost of cheap lodging was about double what it was before the COVID-19 outbreak nationwide.

The next morning, I returned to Ave Maria. There were no other birders present. I immediately found the immature Large-billed Tern loitering with a Black Skimmer flock near one of the many man-made lagoons in the development. What a relief that my target species cooperated. This saved me a half-day road trip to the other side of the Florida peninsula to chase the other one, and enabled an opportunity to search for additional target species.

My next target was Tricolored Munia, an exotic species that was believed to have spread to Florida from Cuba where it was originally introduced from South Asia. A small flock had been present over the winter at the south end of Lake Okeechobee in Central Florida. The last detection in eBird was from March. After missing the one at the Fort Jefferson water drip by minutes (seconds?), Cliff, Irene and I failed to find one in the same area of Lake Okeechobee in early May.

The spot was 90 minutes away. When I arrived, the area had been impacted by severe thunderstorms. I made a half-hearted effort to locate one of these tiny *estrildid* finches (of the Estrildidae family) near the lake shore. I found Limpkin, Gray-headed Swamphen and Anhinga but no munia. After 30 minutes of searching, I drove south toward Miami with the aim of watching parrots and macaws arrive to the Brewer Park parrot roost, a hotspot location in eBird. I arrived at sunset but to my disappointment I found few psittacines. One small macaw landed in a distant palm but my attempts to get closer to the tree for better views failed. This was probably a Crimson-fronted Macaw, another exotic species resident in South Florida but not yet established for the required 15 years. This was another species that got away from me. I wasn't too concerned because of its non-naturalized status.

I stayed at a nearby motel intending to return to the parrot roost site in the morning but I overslept, so I went straight to Larry Manfredi's worksite on Friday morning hoping to find the La Sagra's Flycatcher (or Larry himself). I found the latter. Larry seemed happy to see me. This would be his chance to redeem his promise to find me this bird after it failed to show for Irene, Cliff and me with Larry in early May. But alas, it was not in the cards again. My success rate for finding this ABA Code 3 species was now 0 for 5. Larry was a gentleman and drove me to my car parked a mile and a half away, saving me from a second grueling hike in the sweltering heat. Consolation birds included a singing Carolina Wren (rare in eBird), Pileated Woodpecker (I never get tired of this regal species), a flyover Short-tailed Hawk (rare), and killer looks at Common Nighthawk roosting on the ground along the trail.

About noon on my last day in Florida and just one afternoon left for chasing year-birds, my next move was a no-brainer. I could reach Long Key State Park in fewer than two hours of driving. I arrived at 2 PM. The La Sagra's Flycatcher hadn't been reported in three days but I was optimistic. After scouring the trail system, I came up empty again—0 for 6. At 5 PM I headed to Brewer Park for the parrot show but misjudged the time. I arrived after dark.

When I got to the airport for my 6 AM flight I was delighted to learn that it was cancelled and the next available flight was in 24 hours. I rented a car for the day and arrived at the Brewer Park parrot roost at dawn. To my delight I found the parrots: six Orange-winged Parrots perched high in a bare limb. A couple of Yellow-chevroned Parakeets flew by. I decided to return to Coral Reef Park for the Blue-and-yellow Macaw and I am glad I did. I found a dozen roosting in one tree. I also found a pair of White-eyed Parakeet, as well as Mitred and Red-masked Parakeets. I explored this park more fully and was amazed to find an extensive protected patch of piney woods with palmetto understory in the heart of suburban South Miami. After a relaxing morning in the park, I felt energized to try again for the Biscayne La Sagra's Flycatcher. Three hours in the heat of the day was all I could muster. I found a rare Gray Catbird and a panting Great Crested Flycatcher but remarkably no La Sagra's Flycatcher. Zero for 7!

During the afternoon I drove to various parrot locations in South Miami and Miami Beach. I found the motherlode in the heart of Miami Beach, where hundreds of parakeets were staging in preparation to visit a communal roost. Most appeared to be White-eyed Parakeet but I also got photos of a couple Blue-crowned Parakeet.

The extra day enabled me to add several species of exotic psittacines to my eBird totals. However, these were not yet formally accepted as naturalized or established by the ABA and therefore would not be countable for my ABA totals. Audio and photos of these Florida birds can be viewed online within eBird here: https://eBird.org/tripreport/149433. My Biggest Year list for the USA and Territories had reached 732 species.

CHAPTER 24
The Dog Days of Summer

I returned home to Colorado on July 9, 2023, after a short but successful trip to South Florida. Mid-July in Colorado is hot (but not as hot as Florida!). Some years are bone dry and bird nesting activity finishes early. Summer mornings without bird song are eerie. Fortunately, the summer of '23 in Colorado was wet and fields that normally turned brown in July remained green. Daily thundershowers helped keep the insect population high, which in turn allowed for many bird species to attempt to raise second broods. This gave me an opportunity to look for nesting species in Colorado that I still needed for my Biggest Year effort.

I also took advantage of my time in my home county to look for species I needed for my Larimer County year list. I normally finished each year among the top three ranked birders in Larimer County, but this year I was birding mostly away from home. Consequently, I fell behind in the local rankings.

One local species that would be new for my Biggest Year was Baird's Sparrow. In late July 2015, a population of summering Baird's Sparrow was discovered at Soapstone Prairie Natural Area about 20 miles north of Fort Collins near the Colorado-Wyoming border. This was 500 miles south of their normal breeding area in Montana and North Dakota. The following year more territorial males were discovered, and breeding was confirmed in 2017. Since then, Baird's Sparrow returned each year, although not always in places accessible to the public. They were sometimes found along a hiking trail closed to the public until July 15, to protect nesting Mountain Plover and other grassland breeders from human disturbance. In 2023, as of July 10, no Baird's Sparrow had been reported. Official monitoring efforts by the City of Fort Collins and Bird Conservancy of the Rockies (BCR) had been discontinued, so the sparrow's status in off-limits locations was unknown. I made plans with Fort Collins birder Josh Bruening to visit Soapstone Prairie on July 15, the day the closure of the Plover Loop Trail would be lifted.

Upland Sandpiper
23 Jul 2023, Buffalo, South Dakota

Interestingly, new data from research ornithologists at BCR suggested that the Baird's Sparrow population in Colorado becomes active in late summer following breeding in their core territory 500 miles farther north. What if I waited until July 15 and then failed to find any Baird's Sparrow in Colorado? I could search on the wintering grounds in Arizona in December but I've had trouble finding these birds in winter. I looked at my BirdsEye app on my iPhone for recent sightings and found the closest one to be in extreme Northwestern South Dakota near the town of Buffalo. One distant singing bird was heard there, a few days earlier, by a BCR field technician. This detection occurred at the southern edge of the breeding range where the birds are considered rare. I decided it was worth a trip to South Dakota to make sure that Baird's Sparrow was included on my Biggest Year list.

I loaded up my Honda CRV with water, black cherries and peanut M&Ms. I convinced Maribel to keep me company by agreeing to visit Mount Rushmore National Memorial on the return trip. Round trip mileage from

Fort Collins was estimated around 1,300. We started rolling on the morning of July 12 and drove all day through Wyoming, Nebraska and South Dakota. As we approached Baird's Sparrow country that evening, we began to see Upland Sandpiper. I photographed several *uppies* beside the road, documenting this species for the first time in 2023. I had heard one migrating overhead in Galveston, Texas, in early May and had seen one in Wisconsin but was not able to document those records.

The pin for the Baird's Sparrow sighting in eBird was long grass prairie, with no trees as far as the eye could see. As we approached our target destination, I spotted several Short-eared Owl flying around. One came close to me and vocalized, providing an opportunity for me to record audio. Unfortunately, there was no sign of the Baird's Sparrow.

After spending the night at the only motel in Buffalo, South Dakota, we drove up and down a ten-mile stretch of dirt road where the Baird's Sparrow had been reported. Birds were plentiful. A couple of Brewer's Sparrow were flagged as rare in eBird. Chestnut-collared Longspur juveniles were ingesting grit on the dirt road. A family of Sharp-tailed Grouse foraged just off the roadside. Grasshopper Sparrow was ubiquitous. A couple of Bobolink were unexpected. But again, no Baird's Sparrow.

I looked up other locations where Baird's Sparrow had been detected. A parallel road a mile south had numerous pins for sightings, all several years old. After about five miles on that road, I heard the familiar tinkling of the Baird's Sparrow song and audio-recorded it for documentation. I spent 30 minutes trying to see it but never did. Some birds just don't want to be seen.

We followed a scenic route back to Fort Collins, stopping to appreciate Mount Rushmore and the beautiful pine forests of the Black Hills region.

Back in Fort Collins, Josh Bruening arrived at my house at 5:15 AM on Saturday, July 15. He transferred his hybrid mountain/road bike to my bike rack, and we zipped north to Soapstone Prairie Natural Area, arriving at 6

AM. Nine miles of dirt trails, on bicycles mind you, and five hours later, I put my binoculars on a sparrow perched up on a post along the trail and was pleased to see an adult Baird's Sparrow. We watched it fly to the ground, gather several grubs in its bill and bring them to another adult partially concealed by grasses. A nest? Perhaps. Eventually the male sang a few times. Photos and audio from this pair of Baird's Sparrow can be found at: https://eBird.org/checklist/S144654031.

15 Jul 2023, Soapstone Prairie, Colorado
Nick Komar with Josh Bruening

We finished our loop ride several hours later after riding over 20 shadeless miles! Other highlights of this epic ride included dozens of juvenile Thick-billed Longspur and a Prairie Falcon. The falcon was hunting a Lark Bunting which impressively used Josh and me as human shields in order to evade the speedy predator. The falcon came within feet of me and within inches of Josh in its pursuit of the unlucky Lark Bunting. What that bunting lacked in luck it had in smarts, using us to evade the powerful falcon. It would live at least another day in the dog-eat-dog world on the prairie.

Because of the upcoming Colorado Field Ornithologists convention, July 19–23, there was insufficient time for a major out-of-state chase trip, so I focused on local birding opportunities in Colorado. The number of Colorado breeding birds that could be new for my Biggest Year effort was countable on one hand: Black Swift and Yellow Rail.

Yellow Rail did not normally breed in Colorado and until 2022, was not known from Colorado during the breeding season for at least a century. Then in mid-July 2022, Eric DeFonso discovered two singing birds at Monte Vista National Wildlife Refuge in the San Luis Valley. Probable third and fourth birds were reported in the following days suggesting that a small population existed. Normally these birds nested in Central Canada but there was a small satellite population in Northern California. The San Luis Valley was situated on a nearly direct path from the wintering grounds on the Texas coast to the population in California so perhaps these birds discovered the San Luis Valley during their migration. Breeding was never confirmed however.

The Yellow Rail was unreported in 2023 but Cole Wild, Kathy Kay and I decided to explore the area, which was severely under-birded, especially during the dog days of summer. We got started early on July 16, heading first to the Lodgepole Pine forests of Gunnison County near Cottonwood Pass where a few days earlier Eric DeFonso reported Cassia Crossbill. Finding only Red Crossbill, we continued to Monte Vista, arriving after dark. We spent most of the night listening and playing recordings for Yellow Rail without success. Sora and Virginia Rails were abundant. We ended the night at Zapata Falls in the Sangre de Cristo Mountains. We had about two hours to sleep in the car before we could search for Black Swifts at the falls. Cole stretched out on the back seat of Kathy's Mazda. I leaned the front passenger seat back to get comfortable. I glanced at Kathy beside me, eyelids drawn down, in the driver's seat. I wondered what our spouses would think if they saw us now.

Cole and Kathy were compatible birding companions for me. They both had experience with Big Year competitions. Cole established a new Colorado birding record when he reported 412 species for the state in 2010, smashing the previous record of 391 species held by Andrew Spencer, one of Cole's mentors. Cole was just 28 years old in 2010. He started birding in 2003 when he attended a field trip I co-led along with Chris Wood where we tracked down a Kelp Gull that was visiting Larimer County lakes and landfills for the first time. This rare gull is normally found in the southern cone of South America.

In 2010, Cole Wild did so well that I thought his story should be published. Cole was not a writer, nor liked to write, so I offered to co-author a book based on his story. In 2011, we published *Wild Birding Colorado, the Big Year of 2010*. My writing style was straightforward and matter-of-fact based on influences from James Joyce (from my readings in high school) and scientific writing style that I used in publishing more than 100 peer-reviewed journal articles during my work as a federal biologist.

Cole was always willing to drive long distances, sleep in the car and generally bird to the extreme, which fit well within my ethic of *work hard, play hard*. When Cole first broke into birding, we birded together almost every weekend. In 2005, we drove for 36 hours with my son Nick, just 12 years old at the time, in order to bird the cloud forests of Tamaulipas, Mexico for a few days. I also took Cole (and Nick) birding to Northwest Mexico and Ecuador. In March, Cole had accompanied me to Western Nebraska to find the Common Crane for my Biggest Year. My birding time with Cole dropped off when he married in 2011 and fathered three children with wife Heather.

Like Cole, Kathy Kay is a passionate and competitive birder. She inherited the birding bug from her Swedish-born father but she only got serious about competitive birding in recent years since the COVID-19 pandemic. Prior to that she had her hands full with her own career development (Environmental Policy), marriage to a pediatric cardiologist and motherhood. Her daughter Brianna was attending the University of Chicago during 2023.

In 2018, Kathy moved from Gennessee, Colorado, to Denver where she met other birders and quickly became active in the birding community.

She joined my tour to Oaxaca in December 2022, where she also met Sue Riffe, my son Nick and Jay Breidt (from team White-bearded Helmetcrests). It was an intense tour. We recorded over 400 species of birds in eight days including a half-day pelagic boat trip. Birding was like a new sports car for Kathy. She was breaking it in and taking it for a spin to see what it could do for her. So far it had been a wild ride. I think she will keep the car and take it for many more adventures.

Back to mid-July 2023. Dawn was approaching. We hiked the half-mile Zapata Falls Trail and counted about seven Black Swift exiting the falls area a few minutes after dawn. We then returned to eastern Gunnison County where we met up with Adrian Lakin at Taylor Park. He and I searched unsuccessfully for Cassia Crossbill while Cole and Kathy chased and ticked a locally rare Western Gull at Antero Reservoir in Park County that had been found a couple days earlier by Mark Peterson. I returned home late Monday evening with just one day to rest before the Colorado Field Ornithologists annual convention.

Baird's Sparrow and Black Swift were new to my USA and Territories Biggest Year list, which now was at 734 species.

Baird's Sparrow
15 Jul 2023, Soapstone Prairie, Colorado

CHAPTER 25
Duty Calls

I picked up Cliff Hendrick at 6 AM, July 19, 2023. We headed to the Mount Blue Sky (formerly Mount Evans) auto road, a two-hour drive from Fort Collins. This road is the highest paved road in North America, reaching near the peak of Mount Blue Sky above 14,000 feet. We paid $2 for admission, taking advantage of Cliff's senior discount for visits to federally managed parks. We scouted the area around Summit Lake where I would return with a field trip a few days later. Bird diversity is low at high elevation. All we observed were American Pipit, Brown-capped Rosy-Finch and a distant White-tailed Ptarmigan. We also checked the forests at the lower elevations for Cassia Crossbill, without luck.

One of the principal bird targets of the Colorado Field Ornithologists' (CFO) convention field trips was Cassia Crossbill, formerly known as Red Crossbill Type 9. This population was elevated to species status in 2016 after biologists determined that it was sufficiently distinct, genetically, from other crossbill populations. Birders in the field could distinguish it from the other 11 North American crossbill types by its unique flight call. Otherwise, they appear identical. Up until last year, Cassia Crossbill was only known from the lodgepole pine forests of Cassia County and a couple of neighboring counties in Southern Idaho. They were thought to be the only sedentary crossbills in the US. Other crossbills are nomadic, roaming the forests of the continent for consumption of cone crops. Each crossbill subtype is adapted for a different type of cone.

In 2021, Christian Nunes recorded the flight calls of a small group of crossbills in Grand County, Colorado, in the mountains northwest of Denver. He sent the recordings to crossbill vocalization expert Matt Young to determine the types of Red Crossbill present. To Christian's surprise, Matt told him they were Cassia Crossbill, which had never been reported in Colorado.

Wow! It is a special day when you discover a new bird species for your home state. I had been birding avidly in Colorado for close to three decades and never discovered a new state bird.

The next summer, Eric DeFonso was conducting bird surveys in Summit County, Colorado, and found more Cassia Crossbill. This summer, 2023, Eric discovered Cassia Crossbill in Gunnison County. Confirmed reports began turning up throughout the Colorado mountains, all documented by sound recordings. Nathan Pieplow, author of the *Peterson Field Guide to North American Bird Sounds*, reviewed some of his crossbill recordings from Colorado and discovered that Cassia Crossbill had been in Colorado for at least ten years!

On the first day of the CFO convention, Chris Wood led a field trip to the Alfred M. Bailey Bird Nesting Area in Summit County to search for Cassia Crossbill. This was the site where Eric DeFonso detected them in the summer of 2022. The conference organizers, including myself, were thrilled to hear Chris's report that he found the birds in the same spot as 2022! This was great news because several field trips were scheduled to search for the species, but recently reported birds in Gunnison and Chaffee counties were too far away from the convention venue in Summit County. The crossbills found by Chris were less than an hour away.

The convention was four days long and I led or co-led a field trip each morning. On July 20, I led a posse to Park County. Highlights were Mountain Plover, Prairie Falcon and a large flock of Type 4 Red Crossbills. On July 21, I co-led (with Chris Wood) the Mount Blue Sky field trip. Brown-capped Rosy-Finch and mountain goats stole the show. On July 22, it was my turn to search for the Cassia Crossbill for a group of about 20 conventioneers. Unfortunately, we were unsuccessful in our quest. On July 23, I joined co-leader Rebecca Weiss and led a contingent to Jackson County. Highlights included a family of Greater Sage-Grouse, nesting Red-necked Grebe and an unexpected American Bittern. At 3:00 PM, Rebecca led most of the group back to the convention center at Copper Mountain Resort. I continued the field trip a few more hours, exploring the Laramie River valley of Larimer County. Two birders joined me: Cliff Hendrick of Fort Collins, Colorado (who had also birded with me in January in Puerto Rico and South Florida in May) and a visiting Israeli birder, Yaron Charka. Highlights were a pair of White-winged Crossbill (photographed by Yaron; these are very rare in Colorado) and a migrating male Calliope Hummingbird.

American Bittern
23 Jul 2023, Walden, Colorado

This convention was held jointly with Western Field Ornithologists. Chris Wood and Jesse Barry (of the Cornell Laboratory of Ornithology) were invited speakers. They each gave fabulous presentations about community participation in birding and science through the use of eBird and Merlin mobile apps, respectively. Although my second and final two-year term as CFO president had ended in June, I still had numerous responsibilities at the convention.

During the banquet dinner, I asked Chris if eBird could establish a new major region comprising the 50 states and outlying territories of the USA. He said he would pass the suggestion on to the eBird team. Shortly afterward, Marshall Iliff contacted me and said they would consider creating this category. Marshall is eBird's operations manager. Once established, tracking list totals for USA and Territories would be easy using eBird.

The CFO convention was a worthwhile distraction from my Biggest Year project. Although I birded daily during the event, I picked up only one new species, the Calliope Hummingbird, which was USA and Territories Biggest Year-bird 735. With the conference completed, one less distraction impeded my progress.

CHAPTER 26
American Birding Association
Code 3+ Species

I began my USA and Territories Biggest Year effort in January 2023, with a goal of finding 40 ABA Code 3+ birds as part of my quest for 900 species. These are mostly true vagrants to the USA or very rare breeding birds. As July was nearing its end, I had already observed 36 of these, 15 in Alaska alone.

My son Nick was finishing up a vacation in the Florida Panhandle. I invited him to join me in searching for an ABA Code 3 American Flamingo that had taken up residency at St. Marks National Wildlife Refuge south of Tallahassee, Florida. This bird showed up following Hurricane Michael in 2018, was unbanded and presumed to be of wild origin. Birders named it *Pinky*.

Nick picked me up at the Pensacola Airport the morning of July 29. Four hours later, we arrived at the St. Marks National Wildlife Refuge and followed recent eBird reports to locate Pinky. We were lucky, as Pinky stood out like a sore thumb in one of the large bays adjacent to the entrance road. The location also hosted a close encounter with a Bobcat, which crossed the entrance road just in front of our slow-moving vehicle. About an hour after arriving, an afternoon thunderstorm rolled in. We turned the car around and headed toward Nick's home in Austin, Texas.

We would make two birding stops en route. The first was along Florida's Gulf Coast where Nick successfully chased a rare Gray Kingbird for his ABA life list, and then on July 30, in Lee County, Texas, we unsuccessfully chased a vagrant Yellow-green Vireo, a Middle American species that had been summering at a state park there. Yellow-green Vireo is an ABA Code 3 species.

The next morning, Monday, July 31, Nick went back to work in Austin. I rented a car and drove six hours toward Brownsville, Texas, in the Rio Grande Valley. On the way I picked up Brown-crested Flycatcher at Laguna Atascosa National Wildlife Refuge. I arrived at Brownsville's Oliveira Park in time to watch several hundred parrots arriving to roost overnight, including at least 20 White-fronted Parrot, an introduced species that may not be countable by ABA standards.

I stayed in a motel near McAllen Monday night. Tuesday morning, I visited Cannon Road (an eBird hotspot) where another Yellow-green Vireo had been singing all summer, but not this morning. Then I got word that Jim and Brenda Carpenter had reported a pair of Striped Cuckoo (a potential USA first record, if accepted) at the National Butterfly Center. I arrived just as the gate was closing at 5 PM. I played a recording for this Middle American cuckoo species from outside the gate, to no avail. I continued west to Roma for lodging, as I had arranged to meet guide Zach Johnson and the Carpenters nearby at Santa Margarita Ranch at 7 AM the next morning. The guiding fee (required) was $175 each for a morning on the ranch. This was my only chance of seeing Brown Jay, an ABA Code 4 species. A small group had taken up residence earlier this year after a 12-year absence in the United States.

I arrived in Roma at sunset. After checking into a small motel ($60) I wandered over to the boat launch along the Rio Grande River at Salineño. It was too dark to see much but I heard some good night birds here: Lesser Nighthawk, Common Pauraque and Eastern Screech-Owl.

At 7 AM on August 2, we met at the Santa Margarita Ranch house along with another guide (Ryan Rodriguez) and two more clients. I looked forward to meeting the Carpenters, who were among the top ten in the ABA Area year list competition, making them Big Year birders in my book. The Carpenters arrived in a small RV. They explained to me that Jim had recently retired. They were relatively new to birding and were on a mission to visit all of the national parks, birding as they went. I asked them about their Striped Cuckoo observation. They explained that they were not familiar with the species, but noticed that Merlin had picked up the song and identified it. They then saw the pair which flew before they could be photographed. The audio was not recorded either because the cell phone overheated. Lacking confidence without the documentation necessary to support the record, they planned to retract the report from eBird. I encouraged them not to retract the report. I wondered how many records of rarities were lost in similar circumstances. If only birders understood what took me decades to discover—*rare birds are common!*

American Flamingo
29 Jul 2023, St. Mark's NWR, Florida
Photo by Nicholas Alexander Komar

Local guides Ryan and Zach also understood that rare birds are common, at least at the Santa Margarita Ranch. Ryan's eBird checklists from this site along the Rio Grande River often surpassed 100 species, and would typically include five to ten eBird rarities. We climbed into the ranch owner's ATV and drove a dirt track downhill into the lush riparian forest of the Rio Grande Valley. Within minutes a juvenile Brown Jay began screaming as if to say "Where are my oranges?" More jays answered the screams from farther away. Zach broke out the half-oranges, and impaled them on branches in a tree. Soon the gang of four Brown Jay were feeding on the fruits. Zach played the song of Red-billed Pigeon. One sang back once. Other highlights of this guided visit included: Bell's Vireo, four fledgling Muscovy Duck in the river, presumably of wild origin, and three Zone-tailed Hawk (all marked rare in eBird). We ended the morning with more than 50 species. Details can be viewed here: https://eBird.org/checklist/S146299761.

In the afternoon I returned to the Butterfly Center and searched the property along the Rio Grande for more than two hours. The 100+ degree Fahrenheit heat was almost unbearable. There was no sign of the cuckoos but a flock of seven Groove-billed Ani had me wondering why I tried so hard to see one in January. There was also a Northern Beardless-Tyrannulet here.

I would try twice more for the Yellow-green Vireo at Cannon Road unsuccessfully. Heading back to Austin, I picked up singing Botteri's Sparrow at dusk on August 3 and then drove all night to Lee County in hopes of finding that Yellow-green Vireo singing in the dawn chorus. This was my fifth strike despite hearing songs from about 20 other vireos including about a dozen White-eyed, and a few each of Yellow-throated and Red-eyed Vireos. Yellow-green Vireo was competing with La Sagra's Flycatcher for my 2023 nemesis bird. The score was seven misses for La Sagra's Flycatcher versus five for Yellow-green Vireo.

I ended this short but productive trip with two additional ABA Code 3+ species (American Flamingo and Brown Jay), giving me 38 for the year. My USA and Territories Big Year list total was now 743.

CHAPTER 27

Return to Southeastern Arizona

I knew I would have to return to Arizona for Mexican species that only reach the sky islands area of Southeastern Arizona during summer breeding. I gambled and waited until the monsoon season late in the summer to take advantage of post-breeding dispersers from Mexico. I would be accompanied by five tour participants from August 7–12, 2023: Cliff Hendrick of Colorado, Joe Burns of California, Alf Wilson of Massachusetts and Bud Younts of North Carolina. Eric DeFonso of Colorado was our driver. We assembled at Sky Harbor Airport in Phoenix at 8 AM on August 7.

Shortly after sunrise, the temperature was already a scorching hot 95 degrees Fahrenheit. Temperatures in the Phoenix desert had been reaching 115 to 120 degrees by late afternoon. Considering our advanced ages (58 to 78 years old), I didn't want to bird in temperatures over 100 degrees, so we made just one significant birding stop near Phoenix at Red Mountain Park in Mesa, Arizona. In just over an hour here, we found Gambel's Quail, Harris's Hawk, Vermilion Flycatcher, Curve-billed and Bendire's Thrashers. These were all species I saw in March when I birded Arizona with Scott Rashid.

We arrived at our lodging destination in the Santa Rita Mountains south of Tucson by 3 PM. I had reserved three cabins at the Madera Kubo Lodge in Madera Canyon. Almost immediately, I added two USA and Territories Biggest Year-birds: Sulphur-bellied and Dusky-capped Flycatchers. These two flycatchers are Neotropical migrants, wintering in South and Central America, respectively. Southern Arizona represents the northernmost extreme of their breeding ranges. The hummingbird feeders at the lodge were buzzing with the usual cohort of Broad-billed Hummingbird and numerous newly arrived Rufous Hummingbird, which had finished their breeding season far to the north.

A few Black-chinned and Rivoli's Hummingbirds joined the fray, and so did a rare Berylline Hummingbird (ABA Code 3). We spent the late afternoon hiking the upper part of Madera Canyon hoping to find Elegant Trogon. The trogon did not cooperate but we added Red-faced Warbler to my list. During the hike I almost stepped on a Black-tailed Rattlesnake. After dark, we were serenaded by several resident Whiskered Screech-Owl.

On August 8, we began birding in the desert lowlands near Madera Canyon. We had great views of Rufous-winged and Botteri's Sparrows near Arivaca. The breeding ranges of these two species just barely cross over the Mexico border into Arizona. The Botteri's Sparrow in Arizona is a different subspecies from the one found in South Texas. We had hoped to find an ABA Code 3 Ferruginous Pygmy-Owl staked out near Arivaca, but I screwed up and rented a minivan instead of a high clearance SUV. Eric was a sensible, but risk-averse, driver and refused to proceed toward the remote stakeout when the road became steep and rocky. Alf pointed out my poor judgment in rental vehicles to the group. "You really screwed up, Ollie." He regularly called me by my brother's name, a habit left over from the 1980s when he and Ollie were business partners.

Following a tip from John Vanderpoel, we found Black-capped Gnatcatcher (ABA Code 3) at Montosa Canyon later in the morning. That afternoon, we relocated a singing Five-striped Sparrow (ABA Code 3) that had been reported by others at Box Canyon.

We left Madera Canyon August 9 heading south toward Nogales and Patagonia. At Patagonia Lake State Park, we heard numerous Bell's Vireo and Yellow-breasted Chat. We watched Curve-billed Thrasher and Summer Tanager feeding fledglings. We found our first Thick-billed Kingbird and I spotted a White-nosed Coati (a mammal). Nearby at the Paton Hummingbird Center, we added Violet-crowned and Costa's Hummingbirds to the trip list.

Later in the afternoon we arrived at the Ash Canyon Bird Sanctuary, on the eastern flank of the Huachuca Mountain Range. Hundreds of hummers buzzed dozens of feeders. A handful of Lucifer Hummingbird were new for

172

the trip and a rare Plain-capped Starthroat (ABA Code 4) was new for my year list. We ended the day at Miller Canyon and Beatty Guest Ranch where we stayed for the final three nights of the tour. The private hummingbird feeder setup on the ranch property hosted two male White-eared Hummingbird (ABA Code 3) among the more usual species. As the sun set, we hiked about a mile up the canyon hoping to find two recently reported rarities, Rufous-capped Warbler and Flame-colored Tanager. We did not have luck with those but were rewarded with several nocturnal species including Mexican Whip-poor-will, Whiskered Screech-Owl, Northern Pygmy-Owl and a distant call from a Spotted Owl.

10 Aug 2023, Hunter Canyon, Arizona
From Right: Nick Komar, Bud Younts, Joe Burns,
Cliff Hendrick, Eric DeFonso, Alfred Wilson

On August 10 we began the day scouring the Miller Canyon Trail for the two rarities we missed the previous evening. Still nothing. So, we headed to the next canyon to the south: Hunter Canyon. The mile-long hike uphill in 90+ degree heat was strenuous. However, we were rewarded with a pair of Rufous-capped Warbler (ABA Code 3) at the end of the hike. Eric DeFonso spotted a Buff-breasted Flycatcher, a sky island specialty species whose voice I recorded using the Merlin app. Later that afternoon, we visited Ramsey Canyon where we finally found Elegant Trogon, and Carr Canyon, where we ended our day in tall pines with a mixed flock that included Greater Pewee.

On August 11, we drove east across the desert grasslands that separated the Huachuca Mountains from the Chiricahuas. When we stopped for breakfast burritos, we heard the songs of Chihuahuan Meadowlark, a taxon that was recently elevated to full species status rather than a subspecies of Eastern Meadowlark. Entering the Chiricahua National Monument from the west side, we slowly gained elevation. The grassland became studded with juniper trees, creating a pygmy forest. Then tall ponderosa pine became the dominant tree. We detoured to Pine Canyon in search of a reported Slate-throated Redstart (a vagrant from Mexico), which did not appear. Numerous Type 2 Red Crossbill were sampling Arizona's ponderosa pine cones.

Farther up the main road we came to Pinery Canyon Campground. Here we found a pair of calling Buff-breasted Flycatcher harassing a perched Cooper's Hawk that was digesting a recent meal (perhaps a flycatcher nestling). Above Onion Saddle we found a good amount of bird activity but pushed on to Barfoot Park Campground upon hearing from Todd Deininger and Bill Kaempfer, friends from Colorado and Florida, respectively. They were seeing six species of warbler there. Indeed, when we arrived, we found Olive, Grace's, Red-faced, Townsend's, Hermit and Virginia's Warblers. Several Mexican Chickadee, a species that reaches the USA only in the high elevation forests of the Chiricahuas, foraged among the mixed flocks and made all of us happy and satisfied with our visit to the Chiricahuas. Descending through Pinery Canyon, the group was further pleased by a roadside Northern Pygmy-Owl I spotted.

We made a final birding stop in the lowlands at Willcox, Arizona, where a shallow pond known as Lake Cochise hosted hordes of migrant shorebirds, waterfowl and swallows. We scored several dozen Scaled Quail here, new for the trip. We celebrated a successful day (and trip) by grilling steaks back at the ranch. Bud Younts knows how to cook steaks!

The trip wasn't over yet. On the final day, August 12, we had another shot at finding the Spotted Owl and Flame-colored Tanager in Miller Canyon. We failed but I was satisfied with a cooperative Red-faced Warbler that I photographed and audio-recorded. We had time before flying home from Phoenix for a brief foray into the skirts of Mount Lemmon (more Red-faced Warbler and lots of Yellow-eyed Junco) and then two hours later we visited Daley Park in Tempe, Arizona, where I had found Acorn Woodpecker and Rosy-faced Lovebird a year earlier. To my delight, both species were still present. The lovebird is an established exotic that is countable by ABA rules. It was introduced from Africa via the pet trade decades ago. It looks similar to parrotlets of South America. Lovebirds are noisy creatures but quite cute. My family had one as a pet when I was a boy. We called it Peach-faced Lovebird then.

The final species count was 190 for this short trip. The full list, as well as photos and audio files, can be viewed at the eBird online trip report here: https://eBird.org/tripreport/150950. As I suspected, five nights was insufficient to track down all our targets. I planned to return to Arizona in early October to find some of the other species I had missed. Birds I still needed that may be found in Arizona in the fall included Ferruginous Pygmy-Owl, Flame-colored Tanager, Tufted Flycatcher, Buff-collared Nightjar, Eared Quetzal, Northern Jacana, Ruddy Ground-Dove, Rufous-backed Robin and Yellow Grosbeak. As most of these are vagrants or strays, I would be lucky to see three of these.

All the remaining target species listed above are ranked Code 3+ by the American Birding Association. I figured I needed 40 to 50 of these to be competitive in the ABA Area competition this year. Prior to our trip to

Arizona, I was at 38. I added six more bringing my total to 44. These were the Berylline and White-eared Hummingbirds, Plain-capped Starthroat, Black-capped Gnatcatcher, Five-striped Sparrow and Rufous-capped Warbler. At the end of my trip, I was still in third place in the ABA Area competition, with 708 species, just a few species behind David and Tammy McQuade. I was quite pleased that I had reached the 700 species threshold.

Five-striped Sparrow
12 Aug 2023, Box Canyon, Arizona

I wasn't the only one pleased with the results of this tour. Cliff Hendrick scored a handful of lifers. Bud Younts filled in some gaps for his own ABA Area Big Year. He was among the top ten. Eric, Joe and Alf all had lifers, but were on the tour mainly to support me in my Biggest Year quest. I can imagine Alf's heavy North London accent saying, "Don't forget to tell them about the Thick-billed Parrot, Ollie."

I wasn't going to tell you this story, but it is a good one, albeit embarrassing for me. We had just finished the grueling hike into Hunter Canyon, a magical place in my experience. I've only been there twice. Both times I found ABA Code 3+ vagrants and many other sky island specialties. The heat combined with my exhaustion and excitement were practically hallucinogenic. I heard a distant familiar sound coming from the forested ridge high above us. Considering the estimated distance to the ridge line, about a kilometer, I imagined the sound to be very loud. *Parrots?* "Parrots," I blurted out to my companions. Trying to put a specific name to these parrots, I considered that there are no exotic parrot species known from this canyon. And we were in the historic range of a native species of parrot now considered extirpated from the sky islands, the Thick-billed Parrot. As this thought crossed my mind, I recalled a report of a Thick-billed Parrot visiting the Guadelupe Mountains of Southwestern New Mexico about 20 years ago, and realized that these endangered parrots persist in nearby temperate ecosystems in Northern Mexico fewer than 50 miles from where we were standing. "Record those calls," I directed my companions with a tone of urgency. "Scan that ridgeline for parrots." But all we could see were a couple of Acorn Woodpecker. Eric DeFonso was another ear-birder like me. He was very intrigued by the sounds and agreed with me that they reminisced of parrots. Neither he nor I were familiar with the calls made by Thick-billed Parrot.

Seeking to share our discovery of putative parrots at Hunter Canyon, I posted to the Arizona Birds Facebook page. I queried the community about knowledge of parrot sightings in the area. The responses were enlightening. A couple of field ornithologists familiar with the vocalizations of Acorn Woodpecker confirmed that the parrot-like calls we recorded were indeed woodpeckers. Furthermore, a biologist with experience handling Thick-billed Parrot in captivity confirmed that these calls were not a match. But all concurred that birders in the pine forests of Southeastern Arizona should be alert for a possible return of Thick-billed Parrot to its former breeding range in Arizona. They thanked me for bringing the issue to the consciousness of birders in the region.

CHAPTER 28
In Search of the
Elusive Himalayan Snowcock

The Ruby Mountains of Nevada rise dramatically, from the Great Basin Desert to over 12,000 feet above sea level. They are home to one of the most bizarre and exotic species on the North American checklist, the Himalayan Snowcock. This is a peacock-sized gallinaceous bird from the Himalayas of Nepal that was introduced into the Ruby Mountains for hunters in 1963 and has become established there. Seeing it requires a good amount of luck combined with a predawn two-hour uphill hike to a volcanic lake. Viewing these birds from a helicopter is an expensive second option.

On the morning of August 22, 2023, I picked up my one tour participant Dana Hiatt in Loveland, Colorado for the drive west. Dana was a regular Quetzal Tours participant in 2023, having joined me in California, Puerto Rico, Minnesota and now Nevada. Dana had her own target list and especially wanted to see Pinyon Jay and several grouse/quail species. We found our first one, Greater Sage-Grouse, in a field east of Coalmont in Jackson County (North Park), Colorado.

On August 23, at 7 AM we picked up Forrest Luke in Craig, Colorado. Forrest had volunteered to be the official driver for the tour. Forrest had driven for me before and sometimes guides locally in Western Colorado for Quetzal Tours customers. He recently retired from his position as environmental manager at a massive coal mine near Craig. He guided us to nearby Cedar Mountain where, to Dana's delight, a flock of 60 Pinyon Jay streamed by. Then we ascended Black Mountain to about 9,000 feet elevation, where we encountered Townsend's Warbler migrating and Pine Grosbeak. Returning to the valley floor which, in this area, seems more like a sea of sagebrush, we added Willow and Dusky Flycatchers at a marshy area.

We continued northbound along Highway 13. Arriving in Wyoming, we steered westward along Interstate 80. We stopped for a late lunch and birding at the Little America Hotel and rest area near Green River. A Red-necked Phalarope, Yellow-headed Blackbird and American Redstart were all unexpected surprises. After a couple more hours of driving westbound, we rested at a cemetery in Salt Lake City, Utah. This memorial park was an excellent location for finding California Quail which is an introduced species in much of the interior west. We searched for the quail for an hour until sunset without success. We could have rested at this park forever but decided to continue our journey instead, arriving in Elko, Nevada, about 11 PM.

We got a very early start on August 24. We were out the door by 3:30 AM. We arrived at our destination about an hour later, at the end of Canyon Road in the Lamoille Creek Recreation Area at the base of the Ruby Mountains. There was no moon. In the darkness we struggled to find the Island Lake trailhead, but eventually we were on our way up a narrow dirt trail which gradually gained 1,000 feet in elevation as it cut across a frighteningly steep mountainside. After a mile or so, the trail made some switchbacks as it reached the crater lake. On the far side of the small lake, cliffs towered another 1,000 feet above us. Vegetation was sparse and mainly shrubby but there was a significant patch of limber pine. The morning sunshine was just hitting the upper cliffs. A brief rain shower created a magnificent rainbow over the lake.

We waited from shortly after 6:00 AM until about 10:30 AM for a troupe of Himalayan Snowcock to appear in the shrubbery or on the cliff face. We waited in vain. Apparently, they come down to the lake on certain days to forage. They must have several different foraging areas available to them. We noted the ominous presence of both Peregrine Falcon and Golden Eagle this morning and wondered if these predators had affected the snowcocks' decision to forage elsewhere.

The snowcock can also be detected by its vocalizations. We strained to hear something unusual as the morning wore on. At one point around 7:30 AM, I heard a bizarre sound from the distant cliff face. It sounded like a hammer banging against a metal stake. Listening more carefully, I could detect a triplicate structure within each bang. Listening to recordings of the snowcock vocals later, I recognized one of these to be the sound I heard. Unfortunately, we did not record the sound. Forrest was near me when I pointed out the odd sound. He also heard it. Chukar has a similar call. I could not be sure that the sound I had heard did not come from a Chukar. Chukar is a small quail-like bird, also introduced from Asia into the arid Western USA.

24 Aug 2023, Ruby Mountains, near Elko, Nevada

After waiting four hours it was time to retreat back to the trailhead. While the birding was somewhat frustrating this morning in the upper reaches of the Ruby Mountains, we hiked back in good spirits. We all had enjoyed the hunt immensely and felt lucky just to be there in the presence of such majestic beauty and serenity. There were other creatures besides our missing targets to entertain us. Butterflies, wildflowers, a throng of Clark's Nutcrackers to name a few. My highlight of the morning was witnessing a Long-tailed Weasel take a Golden-mantled Ground-Squirrel almost equal to it in size as prey. Nature is full of wonders. This place was as wondrous as anywhere. I looked forward to visiting Elko and the Ruby Mountains again, although not in 2023.

My attention turned to tracking down the Cassia Crossbill for my tour customer, Dana. During July, I searched unsuccessfully several times in

Colorado where they decidedly are not common. Now I would look for them where they should be common, in the lodgepole pine forests of southern Idaho. The historical range of this newest addition to the list of breeding bird species of North America is in Cassia County, Idaho, and also in some neighboring counties. Looking at BirdsEye, we found the closest locations of recent sightings to be in Twin Falls County, just west of Cassia County. We arrived at the site close to 5 PM after the long scenic drive from Elko. The habitat was hilly grasslands. Between the grassy hills, a valley was decorated by a ribbon of thick lodgepole pine forest. This forest was quite birdy. Birds of various species seemed to be everywhere. Among the throng were flycatchers, woodpeckers, chickadees, finches, and...crossbills! A silent flock of foraging crossbills looked identical to Red Crossbill. When the flock flew off, they became noisy, emitting a typical "chip chip chip" flight call that Merlin recognized as Cassia Crossbill.

We began our homeward-bound drive from Twin Falls, Idaho, on August 25. We headed east on Interstate 84 until we reached the outskirts of Salt Lake City, Utah. Here we detoured to Antelope Island National Wildlife Refuge in order to get closer to the shores of Great Salt Lake, a massive water body. The shores were infested with emerging brine flies. The number of birds attracted to this food source was staggering. Thousands of Black-necked Stilt, Green-winged Teal and Ring-billed and California Gulls lined the shorelines along the six-mile causeway leading to the island. I watched a couple of Franklin's Gull run along the shoreline with their mouths wide open through clouds of flies. No wonder gull populations are increasing as many other species are declining. Gulls seem willing to eat just about anything. After hearing a Chukar vocalizing and seeing a Burrowing Owl on the island, we were ready to continue our journey, which led us to another park in Salt Lake City. This time we were able to find a covey of California Quail, which posed for photographs. After more driving, a break for dinner and then more driving yet, we stopped for the night in Green River, Utah.

The first stop of our final tour day, August 26, was in Redlands, Colorado, near the east entrance of the Colorado National Monument. Here we searched for—and readily found—Gambel's Quail, yet another introduced quail species. From Redlands, we continued south to Box Canyon Falls in Ouray, Colorado. A short hike along a paved path leads to the spectacular falls and a small cavern where several pairs of Black Swift nest annually. Lighting was dim but we were able to get some decent photos of several fully grown nestlings. The route we took back to Craig, Colorado, led us over the Grand Mesa, the world's largest flat-top mountain. A short hike through subalpine spruce-fir forest gave us great views of a pair of American Three-toed Woodpecker, another one of Dana's target species. By now, we had run out of birding time, as we all had other commitments to attend the following day, and we still had many hours to go, driving through the mountain parks, passes and canyons between Craig and Loveland/Fort Collins. It was well after midnight by the time we were safely all home with our spouses.

This tour tallied 130 species, none of which were new for my quest. The eBird trip report is available at https://eBird.org/tripreport/153373. I still needed to find 152 species to achieve my personal goal of observing 900 species in the USA and Territories in a single calendar year.

Black Swift
26 Aug 2023, Ouray, Colorado

CHAPTER 29
Happy Hurricane Season

*A*s August came to an end, the fall migration of birds was nearing its peak. And it was the season of tropical storms. At any given moment, I could turn on The Weather Channel and a series of storms were brewing in the equatorial regions of both oceans. Hurricanes in the Atlantic Ocean and typhoons in the Pacific meant trouble for those unlucky to live in their pathway of destruction. But for the rest of us, and especially us birders, these storms brought excitement. Some birds get caught in the powerful winds associated with these storms and get displaced, sometimes by hundreds or even thousands of miles.

The storms are caused by warming of the oceans in the tropics. Hot air above the water rises producing a broad area of low pressure. Warm, moisture-laden air then converges to equalize the pressure. This, in turn, causes broad scale uplifting and adiabatic cooling which causes the water vapor to condense into cumuliform clouds and rain. Condensation releases latent heat directly into the atmosphere and, when conditions are right, a giant heat engine forms intensifying the effect resulting in a tropical storm. These storms can last for weeks and cover thousands of miles directly affecting the migratory patterns of birds caught in the strong winds.

The first of these massive storms to cause havoc in 2023 was named Hillary, a Pacific Ocean typhoon that bore its weight into the American Southwest on August 18, driving seabirds from the ocean and the Gulf of California (Northwest Mexico) into desert lakes such as the Salton Sea. Birders there found Least and Black Storm-Petrels, species that normally forage in deep ocean waters miles away from the seacoasts. Seeing one on an inland lake is a special treat. Numerous lakes were visited briefly by tropical pelagic species such as Wedge-tailed Shearwater and Cook's Petrel. Multiple Magnificent Frigatebird were blown into Arizona. Unfortunately, almost all these lost avian souls perish, unable to find adequate food needed to sustain them in freshwater ecosystems.

The next storm was Hurricane Idalia which wound its way through the Caribbean Sea and into the Gulf of Mexico. It made landfall in Florida's Big Bend area on August 26 not far from where Nick and I had ticked Pinky, the American Flamingo that had been displaced by Hurricane Michael several years earlier. In the aftermath of Hurricane Idalia, small groups of storm-driven flamingos began showing up in a dozen Eastern USA states from Kansas in the west, to Wisconsin in the north and North Carolina in the east. Sightings of flamingos came from over a dozen locations in Florida. One of these birds carried a leg band and proved to have come from the wild population that resides on Mexico's Yucatán Peninsula. Oddly no other species appeared to have been displaced, or so I thought.

During the aftermath of Hurricane Idalia, Adam Pickos visited the white sands of Dune Allen Beach in the town of Santa Rosa Beach on the Florida Panhandle, during the morning of September 3, 2023. I don't know if he was looking for oddities. Nonetheless, he noticed an oddly plumaged gull begging for food scraps from beachgoers. It was just slightly larger than nearby Laughing Gull, with a slightly longer beak and longer legs as well. Its plumage was almost uniformly dark gray. Adam tentatively identified it as Gray Gull, a species restricted to the Pacific Ocean coastline of Chile and Peru. Well-known gull identification experts Alvaro Jaramillo and Amar Ayyash weighed in on Facebook with their support for this identification based on the photographs published in eBird.

I was eager to chase this gull, which once accepted by the appropriate ornithological records committees would represent the first confirmed record of Gray Gull in the USA. But first I needed to make sure it would stick. If it turned out to be a *one-day wonder*, a chase trip would be a terrible waste of time and valuable resources. That part of Florida is not easy to reach. Fortunately, it turned up at the same location on September 4, although it proved to be somewhat unreliable and difficult to track down. I was very happy to receive an email message from the local eBird reviewer, Bruce Purdy, offering assistance if I decided to chase the bird for my Big Year. The next day, I devised a plan. I would fly one-way to Atlanta, Georgia, on September 6, arriving after midnight. Richard (Rick) Taylor, whom I had also run into on Adak Island and is now my book editor, would pick me up at the airport and we would drive six hours overnight, arriving at the stakeout by dawn.

Richard is a retired Air Force meteorologist so I learned a lot about stormy weather during our overnight drive to the Florida Gulf Coast. When we arrived at the beach access, we were quickly joined by another chaser who had driven four hours from Central Florida. His name was Wes Biggs, a well-known birding personality in Florida. As the sun rose, we scoured the beach for the dark gull with no luck. After visiting six other beach access points, we returned to the original stakeout location where about 15 birders were now assembled. A distant juvenile Herring Gull created some excitement because it was unusually uniform in color. We had been searching for about four hours and no sign of the Gray Gull.

Richard and I decided to split up. I hiked west into a secluded area of beach within Topsail State Park. Richard drove into the state park and hiked about a mile to reach the beach. We met on the shore and together hiked west another mile. Unlike farther east, few people but many birds occupied this section of beach. We encountered several hundred Laughing Gull and a good variety of tern species including Royal, Caspian, Sandwich, Forster's, Common, Black and Least Terns. A Snowy Plover was the highlight among shorebird species. A huge number (millions) of dead and dying minnows had washed ashore and provided evidence that the waters of the Gulf of Mexico were especially hot this year. The food supply for any wayward gull was impressive. I felt positive about finding our target bird this day but it was not happening. At about 2 PM we met up with Bruce Purdy, the local eBird reviewer. Still no luck. We spent the last hour of daylight at a spot on the beach with a good-sized gull flock. Richard brought the gulls in with popcorn. By the end of the day, I had been exposed to so much sun and heat I felt like popcorn.

Snowy Plover
7 Sep 2023, Walton County, Florida

I decided it wasn't worth spending more days in Florida searching, but rather I would go a day early to California where I was wait-listed on a San Diego pelagic trip for September 10. Arriving early would allow me to chase a Yellow-footed Gull that had been reported at the Salton Sea. After sundown Richard and I drove his vehicle six hours back to Atlanta arriving in time for me to catch a flight to Ontario (Southern California) via Denver.

I found out later that the Bosler twins (Justin and Devin, well known birders currently residing in Texas and Oklahoma, respectively) also had been searching for the Gray Gull that day. Indeed, they found it at the original stakeout location at daybreak the following day! I hoped for another opportunity to see Gray Gull in 2023. I also wondered what hurricane-displaced bird species might get added to my Big Year list.

CHAPTER 30
West Coast Pelagic Fiasco

*T*he Pacific Ocean still held numerous species for my Big Year quest. John Vanderpoel had warned me that I needed to take some pelagic trips off Southern California during late summer and that they sell out quickly. Indeed, I was too late to reserve a spot but I put myself on the waitlist for a trip from San Diego on Sunday, September 10, 2023. I was 15th on the list so not too hopeful. However, a storm was brewing off Tijuana so I was doubtful the boat would even go.

I landed late Friday morning, September 8, at Ontario (35 miles east of downtown Los Angeles) and was picked up by my friend Joe Burns. After birding with me in Southeastern Arizona a month earlier, Joe had offered to host me in California if I needed to chase a bird there. The typhoon in late August had brought dozens of Yellow-footed Gull from the Gulf of California south of the US-Mexican border to the Salton Sea north of the border and a few had stuck around.

We drove directly from the Ontario airport a couple hours southeast on Interstate 10 to Desert Shores, California, once a thriving marina resort but now a ghost town on the shrinking salty lake. No dark-backed gulls there, so we drove south along the west side of the lake to the south end where thousands of shorebirds and waterfowl had gathered but no sign of the gull! We did find a surprisingly large number of Laughing Gull (dozens) in an agricultural field, along with thousands of Ring-billed Gull, White-faced Ibis and a good variety of shorebirds. I thought I caught glimpses of Ruff and Sharp-tailed Sandpiper, two potential rarities, but could never get confirming views. After baking in the hot SoCal desert all afternoon, we decided to retreat home to the cool montane San Bernardino National Forest where Joe lived with his wife Barbara in the village of Lytle Creek.

Upon later review of my photos of the avian throng in one irrigated field south of the Salton Sea, I noticed that we had overlooked a very rare Glossy Ibis, for which only a handful of prior Southern California eBird records exist. Also later, we heard that Guy McCaskie had spotted a Ruff there the following day, September 9. The same day, Valentina Roumi had spotted a Yellow-footed Gull at the south end of the lake. Valentina was a Big Year birder from Colorado. Our paths had crossed in Minnesota in February, on the repositioning cruise in April, and she was on the manifest for the San Diego pelagic trip. Bill Kaempfer and John Vanderpoel were also signed up for the boat trip.

Yellow-footed Gull
11 Sep 2023, Imperial, California

We could not return to Salton Sea immediately because we had made other plans for Saturday. Joe was busy in the morning and I was in need of extra sleep. We headed out again in search of year-birds on Saturday afternoon. With the storm looming offshore, we decided to try a sea watch from the coast at Point Dume. Indeed, hundreds of Black-vented Shearwater were visible from the rampart above the beach. Then some seemingly good news arrived. A pelagic trip out of Ventura had a last-minute opening for Sunday, September 10, weather permitting. We returned toward Lytle Creek optimistic about finding seabirds the next day. En route, we detoured to downtown

Los Angeles to a well-known Vaux's Swift roost site. Arriving at dusk, I expected to find swifts readily, but apparently, they had other plans for Saturday night. No swifts.

My streak of bad luck continued the next morning, Sunday, September 10. I arrived on time at Ventura Harbor after driving Joe's borrowed car for two hours from Lytle Creek, only to learn that the captain decided to cancel due to rough seas! To add insult to injury, the boat out of San Diego did not cancel that same morning and had one more spot available. Valentina, John and Bill were aboard that boat.

Back at Lytle Creek, Joe took me into the National Forest to look for Spotted Owl. It would not be a year-bird but I wanted a photo. No luck. I did get better photos of White-headed Woodpecker along the Vivian Creek Trail. As the day was winding down, Joe suggested another attempt for roosting Vaux's Swift in nearby San Bernardino. We arrived at a city park at dusk and as we stepped out of the car, a dozen small swifts flew over the park's pond, right on cue. I snapped a photo for documentation. Finally, after a bit of a year-bird drought, I had added USA and Territories Biggest Year-bird 757. A whole month had passed since the last one when I ticked Greater Pewee during the Arizona tour.

I made plans to meet John and Bill at Salton Sea on Monday, September 11. Joe and I arrived first at the south end of the lake and quickly spotted a massive dark-backed heavy-billed adult Yellow-footed Gull (year-bird), as well as a couple of rare Purple Martin and a small flock of Bank Swallow, also rare according to eBird. We headed to the irrigated field where another adult Yellow-footed Gull posed for photos close to the road.

Now that my luck had seemingly changed for the better, I began thinking about my next move. The Gray Gull failure was nagging me. A cheap flight was scheduled to depart John Wayne Airport in Orange County at 6 PM. Joe and I headed back to Lytle Creek to pack my things. The California seabirds would have to wait for another opportunity.

CHAPTER 31
Gull Gone Wild

You may be wondering how I managed to fly wherever I wanted to at a moment's notice. The answer is Frontier Airlines Go-Wild Pass. On September 8, 2023, I purchased a pass for $150 that essentially allowed me to travel almost anywhere for a month for $15 per flight. I would take full advantage of this pass to chase rarities during the remainder of the year. On September 12, I used it on a flight back to Pensacola, where I met another Colorado birder seeking the Gray Gull. My friend Kathy Kay arrived at Pensacola Airport about the same time as I did. The only rental vehicle available to her was a U-Haul truck. I invited her to share my rental car if she would drive.

Off we went on a mission to find the Gray Gull, speeding eastbound on Interstate 10 toward Santa Rosa Beach, Florida. We arrived at the Dune Allen Beach access about 3 PM serendipitously at the same time as Richard Taylor who had, once again, driven six hours from the Atlanta metropolitan area. This time, the three of us quickly located the Gray Gull (USA and Territories Biggest Year-bird 759) which was much more cooperative on this day. It was close to one of the beach access points with a parking lot. It joined a small flock of Laughing Gull, offering us an excellent comparison. Many of its feathers were worn and broken, perhaps having been battered in the recent hurricane. The immature bird was a messy creature, part way through its *pre-basic* molt, looking like a big ugly immature Laughing Gull. We were dazzled by this misfit, thrilled to be in its presence on the steaming hot, sandy beach just a stone's throw away from the nearest beach bathers. I felt awed by its status as the rarest bird in the USA at that moment, a larophile's dream. This would be the first accepted record for the species in the USA. There was a hypothetical record from Louisiana several years earlier. We took hundreds of photographs from every imaginable angle. If you don't appreciate why this bird impressed us, you may not be a larophile (i.e. lover of gulls) like me. Not everybody is. In fact, some birders hate gulls!

Over dinner, the three of us toasted to our success in finding our target Gray Gull. Plenty of birding stories were shared that evening. I enjoyed learning about Richard and Kathy's birding ambitions. They both were as ambitious as me, if not more so. Richard was on a life bird quest. His USA life list was approaching 800 species. Kathy had accomplished her mission to photograph all 19 species of owl in the ABA Area in May, and had expanded her birding goal to see how far she could go in the USA Lower 48 Big Year competition. She was on her way to a top-ten finish. She told me about the pelagic trip off North Carolina the following weekend and encouraged me to join her. I was missing most of the species she expected to see. Richard agreed to drive me to Atlanta the next morning where I had a better chance of finding a Go-Wild flight with Frontier Airlines to my next destination. Kathy agreed to return the rental car to Pensacola on her way to the North Carolina coast.

Gray Gull
12 Sep 2023, Santa Rosa Beach, Florida

191

En route to Atlanta, I spotted a Wood Stork in Alabama, which was convenient because I had neglected to photograph one earlier in the year. At the Atlanta Airport I hopped on the next Frontier flight to Miami and was at Long Key State Park shortly after sunrise on September 14, 2023. After parking my rented car, I quickly heard the call of my nemesis bird, the La Sagra's Flycatcher. As it was my eighth attempt to find this ABA Code 3 species in South Florida, I recognized the call note immediately. I recorded the audio and attached the file to my eBird checklist. You can find it here: https://eBird.org/checklist/S149882557. As a true nemesis would do, it never showed itself despite me searching all morning plus an additional hour in the early afternoon. At 3 PM, I gave up and drove the car two hours back to Miami.

Where to next? I was wait-listed on Captain Brian Patteson's pelagic boat trip off Cape Hatteras on Sunday, September 17. I had time to spend a day in Cape May, New Jersey, where I would have a good chance of finding a migrating Connecticut Warbler. The closest major airport to Cape May is in Philadelphia, Pennsylvania. I booked a flight to Philadelphia via Atlanta. Unfortunately, the plane was late arriving into Atlanta, causing me to miss the connecting flight to Philadelphia. Instead, the following morning I flew from Atlanta to Raleigh where I borrowed my cousin's car—thank you, Zach Anderson! I drove four hours to an Airbnb near Nags Head on North Carolina's Outer Banks where I joined a small group of Colorado birders who were eager to see Atlantic Ocean pelagics with Brian Patteson, captain of the *Stormy Petrel*.

Brian's expeditions to the steamy Gulf Stream waters were famous for regularly finding warm water species such as Band-rumped Storm-Petrel, Black-capped Petrel and Audubon's Shearwater as well as typical cold-water species of the North Atlantic such as Cory's and Great Shearwaters and Leach's Storm-Petrel. All would be Big Year-birds for me. The boat was originally scheduled to sail Saturday, September 16, but Hurricane Lee was heading north from the Bahamas toward Nova Scotia. Rough seas were expected off North Carolina. Brian postponed the trip until the following day when the storm surge would be receding.

The lure of the nearby hurricane potentially catapulting exotic species such as Bermuda and Fea's Petrels and White-faced Storm-Petrel from the Central Atlantic Ocean toward the North Carolina coast created high expectations. These expectations were further heightened by the presence of avian vagrants lingering from Hurricane Idalia a few weeks earlier. For example, a remarkable group of 17 American Flamingo had assembled on the bay side of the Outer Banks at Pea Island National Wildlife Refuge. And a local birder had discovered an Elegant Tern (a Pacific Ocean species) among the Royal Tern flock at Oregon Inlet, representing a first state record for North Carolina.

I was worried that none of the 20 registrants would cancel their trip on the *Stormy Petrel*, and my worries were corroborated when I called Brian Saturday morning to check on the status of my registration. He told me that everyone had confirmed their participation the next day. I told Brian I would come to the dock in the morning just in case space opened up. "Fine, but I don't want any pressure to allow you to join if we are full." No pressure, I agreed. Imagine my relief when Brian called me late Saturday night informing me of a cancellation. Space had opened up for me to board the boat. My excitement for finding unusual species was growing. Would we find a Trindade Petrel? Or a South Polar Skua? A Red-billed Tropicbird or a Yellow-nosed Albatross? So many possibilities and conditions were perfect.

I carpooled on Sunday morning with Kathy Kay. When we arrived at the Nags Head dock, we found nobody there. We had gone to the wrong dock!! Kathy drove like Danica Patrick to reach the departing pelagic trip before it left the Cape Hatteras dock (70 miles away) but we arrived 15 minutes too late. We tried to find another boat to take us out to the *Stormy Petrel* but no dice. Local deep-sea fishermen had either already headed out to the Gulf Stream about 40 miles offshore or were enjoying their Sunday off. Kathy and I looked at each other and wondered how on earth we could have missed this boat. We tried a sea watch from shore at Cape Hatteras and another from the Nags Head pier but saw only a single distant jaeger. We found a fishing boat that was going out the next day for a few hours in the afternoon. We booked passage on that boat but didn't see much as the captain never wandered more than a mile from shore. The sea birds would have to wait for another opportunity to be part of my Biggest Year. I thought about asking Captain Patteson what birds were seen from the boat that day, but frankly, I didn't want to know.

On Monday evening I snagged a late Frontier flight from Raleigh to Philadelphia with one thing on my mind: Connecticut Warbler. I rented a car and was stationed at Higbee Beach (on Cape May, New Jersey) well before daybreak on Tuesday, September 19. I had missed this skulker during spring migration in South Florida and also on its breeding grounds in Northern Minnesota in late June. In the fall, southbound Connecticut Warbler accumulate along the Atlantic Coast between Portland, Maine, and Cape May before making their long migration flights across the Atlantic Ocean to the coastline of Northeast South America. Being a skulker, it is generally difficult to detect during the migration season. Mid-September is their peak period of detection during fall migration at Cape May.

I joined the birding throng at Higbee Beach expecting to locate Connecticut Warbler by its unique chip note. But that never happened. I spent the entire day searching various Cape May hotspots with no luck. It was a scorching hot day, and I fantasized or hallucinated that a distant white-rumped swallow was a vagrant Mangrove Swallow. I couldn't prove it though. My photos only contained Tree Swallow, an expected species with dark rump. I was getting desperate for an addition to my year list.

After searching the thickets of Cape May all day, I found a cheap hotel at Wildwood, New Jersey. The town had a boardwalk along the beach and an Atlantic City vibe. From the hotel balcony that evening, I heard some flight calls I didn't recognize. Could it be Leach's Storm-Petrel heading inland to an obscure nest site? Now that was thinking outside the box—way outside the box. I began to fear that the stress of my Big Year was affecting my judgement.

The next morning, I flew from Philadelphia to Boston. I rode the subway from Logan International Airport to Newton Highlands where my mother still lives in the house where I grew up birding with my twin brother Oliver. It was late in the day and I still needed to submit my daily eBird checklist.

I drove my mom's car to nearby Nahanton Park where the habitat was appropriate for Connecticut Warbler. Nothing. I looked at the BirdsEye app and found a recent report for one near Worcester at Westborough Wildlife Management Area. I made plans to go there with my mom the next morning.

On Thursday, September 21, my mom Karen and I walked into the trail at Westborough WMA. We were about a mile from the Connecticut Warbler sighting but there was excellent habitat all around us. My mom is 87 years old and couldn't go the full distance with me. She is also hard of hearing so I had her use the Merlin app and told her to call me if Connecticut Warbler popped up on her iPhone screen. I speed-walked ahead on the path until I reached the cornfields where Connecticut Warbler had been reported the previous day. I met another birder there as well. After being separated from Karen for 30 minutes or so, she called to say that her Merlin app had detected Connecticut Warbler! I hoofed it back toward her and found…silence. I asked to listen to her recording to confirm that Merlin had correctly detected the warbler's chip note, but her phone battery was low and the recording from Merlin failed to load.

In the afternoon I bought passage on a whale watch expedition to Jeffreys Ledge from Gloucester Harbor. I met two other birders on board who were visiting from Great Britain. Conditions were pristine and the marine mammals cooperated for us: Humpback Whale and Atlantic White-sided Dolphin. Birds were few and far between. Half a dozen Northern Gannet popped in and out of view. One young one was a pale brown color and my imagination got the best of me. I reported a tentative identification on eBird as Red-footed Booby which would be a mega-rarity in Massachusetts, but plausible given the recent passage of Hurricane Lee close by. Once I reviewed the photos on my laptop computer, I felt it was too large and not a perfect plumage match either—a sub-adult Gannet after all. Other identified species included a pair of Bonaparte's Gull, a handful of Great Cormorant among a larger number of Double-crested Cormorant, and several flocks of Common Eider and White-winged Scoter. No shearwaters, storm-petrels, or alcids.

Friday morning, September 22, I met with Marshall Iliff. Marshall is a phenomenal birder and is the operations manager for eBird. I had suggested we meet at his local patch—Millennium Park in West Roxbury. I was eager to update him on the progress of my Biggest Year and encourage him to establish USA and Territories as a major region in eBird so that my followers could track my total species via eBird in real time rather than from my blog. I birded Millennium Park when I lived across the Charles River from it during my final years in graduate school at Harvard University from 1994 to 1997. I also birded adjacent properties in Newton when I was in high school between 1980 and 1983, before the old West Roxbury landfill was converted to Millennium Park.

Marshall offered to help me find a Connecticut Warbler in a weedy section of the park. After an hour he glimpsed a bird fly low over the weeds that fit the bill. He had heard the unique call note as well. Unfortunately, I never got a good look or listen and left it off my list. Connecticut Warbler was now competing with La Sagra's Flycatcher and Yellow-green Vireo for worst nemesis bird of my Biggest Year. To be fair, I should add Yellow Rail and LeConte's Sparrow as contenders. Time will tell which of these five species proved to be the hardest for me to track down in 2023.

In the afternoon, I returned to Gloucester for another whale watch expedition. I had hoped to get better views and documentation of the brownish *sulid* (species in the Sulidae family that includes gannets and boobies) that I had called a Red-footed Booby but was disheartened when I realized the boat captain had steered us away from Jeffreys Ledge. Instead, we visited the northwest corner of Stellwagen Bank, a deep-water fishing ground for whales, seabirds and the Gloucester fishing fleet. This location was not currently productive for fish; hence no pelagic bird species were present. The only whales we found were leaving the unproductive feeding grounds and heading toward Jeffreys Ledge.

On Saturday, September 23, I decided to try a whale watch out of Provincetown, located at the outer tip of Cape Cod. The boat visited the southeast corner of Stellwagen Bank and I finally found seabirds. Dozens of

196

Manx, Sooty and Great Shearwaters surrounded the boat. The latter was species 761 for my Biggest Year list. Also, a Parasitic Jaeger was new for my USA Lower 48 list, which was slowly approaching the 700 species threshold.

On Sunday, September 24, I left Massachusetts but not on Frontier Airlines. Instead, I joined my mother and her companion Peter Schuntermann on an Amtrak passenger train to New Rochelle, New York, where we attended my brother Ned's wedding! I didn't stay long though. I borrowed Ned's wife's car and drove an hour to Jones Beach on Long Island. I was chasing a report of Cory's Shearwater seen from land. However, it was too dark and rainy by the time I arrived. After dark, I drove an hour back to their house in Yonkers, New York. Thanks to Robin Newberger (Ned's wife) for letting me use her car. The following day I borrowed a different car and explored some of the Hudson River valley parkland near Yonkers. This was still prime territory for migrating Connecticut Warbler. Despite the rainy weather, the Connecticut Warbler drought continued for me. There were plenty of reports in eBird however. That Monday evening, Ned dropped me off at LaGuardia Airport for my flight to Miami for a scheduled visit to Puerto Rico the following morning. This was a full-fare costly flight with Delta Airlines, as no Frontier flights were available.

Frontier's Go-Wild Pass was a fun way to chase birds for a couple of weeks. During this period, I took nine flights for a total cost of approximately $285. I added Vaux's Swift, Yellow-footed Gull, Gray Gull, La Sagra's Flycatcher, and Great Shearwater. Three of these new Biggest Year species were ABA Code 3+ species.

What were the McQuades doing during these two weeks? They were in Hawaii racking up another 50+ species for their ABA Area Big Year. Linus Blomqvist was also in Hawaii. As a result, I had fallen to fourth place in the ABA Area competition. I was not worried. This race was a marathon, not a sprint, and I felt positive about my prospects of finishing the year at the top of the totem pole for the ABA Area as well as the USA and Territories.

CHAPTER 32
Return to Puerto Rico

B ecause I had visited Puerto Rico during winter, I knew I had left some Caribbean species on the table and would have to return during the summer months to add them to my Biggest Year list. The two most conspicuous species in this category were Antillean Nighthawk and Caribbean Martin. Both are migratory and disappear from the *Isla del Encanto* (Island of Enchantment) in winter. There may be a few martins that spend the winter (reported in eBird). But I was watching for them throughout my visit in late January and early February. They return to breed in April and remain common to abundant through the end of September, following a pattern that is similar for Antillean Nighthawk.

As it turned out I had already added Antillean Nighthawk at the Marathon Airport in Florida in May so I wasn't worried about that species. If the Caribbean Martin was the only species I could add, then a return trip to Puerto Rico would not have been cost-effective. However, there were several other rarities (Masked Duck, Yellow-breasted Crake, Scarlet Ibis, Lesser Antillean Bullfinch) and some uncommon exotic species (Pin-tailed Wydah, Indian Silverbill, Java Sparrow, Yellow-crowned Bishop, White Cockatoo, Orange-fronted Parakeet, Orange-winged Parrot, Saffron Finch) that could help get me to my goal of 900 species for the USA and Territories. To that end, I scheduled a five-day trip to Puerto Rico, September 26–30, reserving a full fare Frontier Airlines flight from and back to Miami. I left the flights to and from Florida open in case I had an opportunity to chase a new vagrant in Florida.

My friend Manuel Amador offered to host me during my Puerto Rico visit and provide a vehicle for me! Manuel and his wife Mabel had a small house in Guaynabo, a suburb of San Juan. Manuel was a retired medical entomologist with the CDC Dengue Branch in San Juan. I had worked with him when I was at CDC in Fort Collins. We had become great friends.

I arrived in San Juan at 9:30 AM on Tuesday, September 26, 2023, after spending a short night sleeping on the floor in the Miami airport. Manuel picked me up and we were soon heading toward the southwest corner of the island, a three-hour drive. Our targets were Masked Duck and Yellow-breasted Crake at Laguna Cartagena National Wildlife Refuge. The plan was to arrive at the observation tower before dark to try to see these nocturnally active species. If we missed them or arrived too late to see them in the fading light of dusk, we would listen for them singing from the wetlands under cover of darkness. If we didn't hear them, we would spend the night in a hotel nearby and return in the morning before sunrise.

We followed map directions to the eBird hotspot which was a mistake as the route left us a mile from the observation tower. The foot trail was overgrown with dew-laden vegetation. We got thoroughly soaked with dew and sweat trying to reach our destination. When we finally arrived at the observation tower it was already too dark to see. And we could barely hear over the din of the cicadas, coquí tree frogs and other noisy insects and amphibians. We did however hear a couple of nearby Puerto Rican Owl.

On the hike in to the tower we had seen some birds flying silently in the fading light and assumed they were Puerto Rican Nightjar which are common in the region. As we retreated to our vehicle after straining to hear water birds over the amphibian din, we lit up our pathway with the lamps provided by our cell phones. Then we noticed one of the nightjars flying within inches of our phones hawking insects that were attracted to the lights. By now I was exhausted (I had slept only a few hours the night before on the Miami airport floor), uncomfortably sopping wet and unfocused. I did not pay too much attention to the nightjar because I had already audio-recorded the species in February. However, I had not seen the nightjar very well during my previous trip and didn't have a photo so Manuel and I tried to photograph the bird when it came close to the light.

I need some lessons in nocturnal photography as nothing could be seen in my photos. However, during our attempt to photograph this bird, we got better looks. It had long tapered wings, a short, notched tail and no obvious white patches anywhere in the plumage. The lack of white and the short tail ruled out Antillean Nighthawk, Pauraque and the migratory North American nightjars (whip-poor-wills and Chuck-will's-widow) which all have long tails, and males have large white patches in their tails. I could not recall what Puerto Rican Nightjar looked like but I assumed that was this bird.

"Funny," I thought out loud, "the long wings and short tail recall Short-tailed Nighthawk," a species I had seen in Brazil. Several days later I remembered to look up Puerto Rican Nightjar and was dumbfounded when I saw that its tail resembled that of the whip-poor-wills: long with large bright white patches. Now I was cursing myself that I did not have a photo. Manuel had noted a crook in the wing shape, giving the shape a bat-like vibe (similar to Lesser Nighthawk). His description was also consistent with Short-tailed Nighthawk, which would be a new species record for Puerto Rico, if only we had some documentation. Without photographic or audio documentation, it would be considered a hypothetical sight record at best. In the spirit of caution in accepting rare or unsupported sightings of species, I decided not to count Short-tailed Nighthawk for my Biggest Year list. Interestingly, I learned from my brother that Short-tailed Nighthawk has wandered to Belize and the Bay Islands off Honduras. Perusing the eBird database, I could not find any confirmed reports of extralimital Short-tailed Nighthawk in the Caribbean region.

On Wednesday, September 27, we rose before sun-up and this time approached the wetland from the appropriate side. On the entrance road (a private farm road), we stopped to assess an odd-looking long-legged wader that blocked our path. We could not make out plumage details in the darkness, despite illumination by our car headlights. As we approached, it would turn and run a short distance and then face us again, blocking our path. Its large size, overall shape, behavior and habitat (dirt road with puddles in an arid or agricultural setting) reminded me of Double-striped Thick-knee, a large drab-plumaged plover of dry grasslands in Central and South America. I managed to get some poor images from a two-second video of the bird as it flew away from us.

Evaluating the fuzzy video frame by frame in my camera viewfinder I could see a black and white pattern in the wing which a thick-knee would exhibit. If it were a thick-knee, it would again be a first record for Puerto Rico (there is a previous record for the USA in Texas). Thinking outside the box can be dangerous. Sometimes I forget to think inside the box. I reported this large plover to eBird as a rare Double-striped Thick-knee only to discover later that one of the frozen video frames clearly shows the upper wing pattern of non-breeding Black-bellied Plover, a locally common wintering shorebird.

As soon as I made this discovery, I retracted the identification but the damage had already been done. Now I was getting a reputation of having a wild imagination and carelessness in my bird identification practices (at least in Puerto Rico). Given this reputation, how would anyone take my report of Short-tailed Nighthawk seriously? I would need to have rock solid documentary evidence.

The morning visit to Laguna Cartagena was successful. I spotted and photographed a foraging Yellow-breasted Crake (Biggest Year-bird 762) among the water lilies. I also spied a singing male Pin-tailed Wydah perched atop a shrub (763). Several swallows hunted insects over the marshy lake. I thought I had noticed a large one among these swallows, possibly a Caribbean Martin or a rare migrant Cuban Martin. However, all the swallows that I inspected closely were the smaller Cave Swallow.

We made several stops along the route back to San Juan. At one spot along the three-hour drive, I thought I heard the smack of a Connecticut Warbler's chip note through my open window. Yes, Connecticut Warbler sometimes use Puerto Rico as a migratory stopover en route to South America and had even spent the winter there. So, this visit was yet another opportunity to detect this rare warbler which had become another nemesis species for me. Manuel turned the car around and I investigated the chip note on foot. The habitat was an overgrown pasture with lots of weeds and shrubs, appropriate for Connecticut Warbler. Many birds were present. I played a recorded call for Connecticut Warbler and pished. An Indian Silverbill (764) responded, perching briefly on a phone wire but not long enough for me to snap a photo. It was silent so I could not record audio. It quickly returned to its life of foraging among the weeds. This was a weak add to my Biggest Year list and I hoped to encounter another one that I could document.

Another potential add for my Biggest Year list was Ruddy Quail-Dove. Julio Salgado, our guide in February, had told me that he feared that Hurricane Maria had extirpated the species from the island in 2017. Checking BirdsEye for species I still needed to see, this one popped up, indicating several recent observations had been reported to eBird. One of these was close to our route so we headed in that direction. When we arrived, I noted that the habitat was appropriate for quail-dove—steep hillside covered in dense tropical forest.

Puerto Rican Tody
27 Sep 2023, Salinas, Puerto Rico

Manuel parked at the bottom of the hill and I began hiking uphill along a two track. Several Zenaida Dove caught my attention. This similarly-colored dove imitated the appearance of the Ruddy Quail-Dove quite closely and theoretically could be the source of the recent report. My attention quickly turned to some smack-like chip notes from the dense understory. Could these be Connecticut Warbler? I pished and a Puerto Rican Tody popped into view. What a cutie!

We followed another lead from the BirdsEye app to the mangrove-ringed mudflats near Salinas on the south coast where Caribbean Martin had been reported earlier in the week. No sign of martins but migrating shore-birds were everywhere on the mudflats. The sun was setting. I would not have time to identify them all. I quickly snapped some photos of some nearby Wilson's Plover. An hour later we were home in the suburbs of San Juan.

On Thursday, September 28, I dropped Manuel off at his embroidery shop in Rio Piedras and drove an hour east to Ceiba. Here I hiked into the mangrove swamps of the Medio Mundo y Daguao Natural Preserve in search of a resident Scarlet Ibis. The 100-degree Fahrenheit heat combined with 100% humidity was almost unbearable. I could not drink enough water, and soon my stock was depleted. In the extreme heat I would not last long. After three hours of searching, I surrendered. I had not found my target but I did see a loose flock of five adult American Flamingo!

After a break to rehydrate and cool off, I visited the municipal beach at Ceiba. I was surprised to find several Brown Booby foraging close by, as well as a small group of Gull-billed Tern, flagged as rare in eBird. I drove back toward San Juan through the neighborhoods of Fajardo hoping to find Caribbean Martin in this coastal community. I only found Cave Swallow. The sun was setting as I drove into El Yunque National Forest. No martins but I did find several Puerto Rican Owl.

Friday, September 29, I headed back to Laguna Cartagena to try to corroborate my earlier report of Double-striped Thick-knee and look through the swallow flock more carefully to find a Caribbean Martin. Manuel gave me the use of his car again. I left his driveway at 3 AM, hoping to arrive early enough for a chance to re-find the Short-tailed Nighthawk as well.

No sign of thick-knee or nighthawk. I could not conjure up a Masked Duck either, despite perfect habitat (shallow, water-lily choked lake). I found about 100 Cave Swallow but not a single martin. I returned to San Juan via Salinas, again looking for martins without luck.

My son Nick had been following my progress in Puerto Rico. He called me and said that I should look for the Caribbean Martin at Bayamón, a suburb of San Juan. He had done some digging on eBird.org and his research revealed that every checklist submitted from the Parque Lineal in Bayamón during the past week had a martin. I arrived there with an hour of daylight remaining. The beautifully manicured park followed a canal a couple of miles. The riparian habitat along the canal was ideal for swallows and martins. There was a ton of bird activity in the park. I stayed until dark but did not encounter any martins. I scrutinized over 100 Cave Swallow and hiked about three miles.

Saturday, September 30, was my final morning in Puerto Rico. My flight was scheduled for 10:30 AM so I had a couple hours to kill in the morning. I decided to return to Parque Lineal in Bayamón in search of the elusive Caribbean Martin. I found a different trail that was even more productive for birds and after hiking two miles and spending a couple hours searching the fabulous habitat, it was time to catch my flight. As I arrived at my parked car, a bird flew through the periphery of my vision. I turned to view the flying object better and there it was: a female Caribbean Martin (765) was coursing over the canal right by the parking area. Go figure. I snapped off a couple of quick shots with my Nikon Coolpix P950 point-and-shoot camera so I would have the proof I needed to document the sighting.

With the Caribbean Martin, I had added four new birds to my year list. But I had left a bunch of species off the list. I told Manuel that I hoped to return once more before the end of the year. Now I was off to Miami, Florida. I had seen a report of Thick-billed Vireo, an ABA Code 3+ species, from Boca Raton which is about an hour north of Miami. I hoped to arrive in time to find it before dark as my connection to Denver was scheduled for 6 AM Sunday morning.

CHAPTER 33
Another Bahama Mama

$\mathcal{A}$ s I had hoped, a new rarity was discovered in Florida during my stay in Puerto Rico. While birding his local patch, Beto Matheus had discovered a vagrant Thick-billed Vireo at Spanish River Park in Boca Raton. The vireo is a stray from the Bahamas. It is very rare in Florida but seems to occur fairly regularly. I was quite pleased to hear that it was found again the next day in the same spot. If I could find it, the Thick-billed Vireo (ABA Code 4) would be a Biggest Year-bird and also a life bird for me!

Recall that I had not booked my plane ticket from Miami to Denver in order to have flexibility to chase a new bird near Miami. The stars seemed to line up perfectly for the chase. My flight from San Juan was scheduled to arrive just after noon on Saturday, September 30, 2023. Boca Raton is just an hour north of the Miami Airport. My next trip (a road trip to Phoenix) was scheduled to depart Colorado on Sunday afternoon, so I booked a connecting flight for 6:00 AM on Sunday from Miami to Denver. I would have the entire afternoon available for chasing a new bird. I thought, *One afternoon should be adequate for finding this vireo.* Right?

Wrong! First, the flight from San Juan departed two hours late. Then the sales manager at Dollar Car Rental insisted that I wait 30 minutes before being attended because I reserved my vehicle through a third party. "If you just booked through a third party, then the vehicle is not yet ready for you. Please wait over there." And finally (and most importantly), when I arrived at the park with 30 minutes of daylight to spare, the heavens decided that that moment in time and space was the best time to drop several inches of rainfall. I donned my rain parka, but I was still soaking wet within minutes of getting out of the car. And the storm clouds were so thick that no ray of sunlight could get through. It was hopeless. I returned to the airport quite displeased with the turn of events.

I returned the rental at 4:45 AM and then realized that I had forgotten to save the Frontier Airlines confirmation number when I made the reservation. Without this, I could not check in for the flight by 5:15 AM as required. There was only one thing I could do, which was make a new reservation for the next available flight, at 6 AM the following morning. Now with 24 hours to kill, I knew what I had to do. I made a new reservation for the rental vehicle and was at the vireo spot at Spanish River Park just after sunrise on Sunday morning.

Thick-billed Vireo
1 Oct 2023, Boca Raton, Florida

Several other birders were already there. The vireo made us all wait a couple hours before eventually appearing in its customary fig tree. The Thick-billed Vireo was Biggest Year-bird number 766. Coincidentally, while on my way back to Miami in the early evening, my brother Ollie texted me. We realized we would both be in town that night. He was traveling from Honduras to Massachusetts. A late arrival in Miami meant a missed connection, and the airline would put him up in a nearby hotel. That solved my lodging needs for the night. Early the following morning I drove him back to the airport and then dropped off my rental for my own flight to Colorado.

CHAPTER 34
Grand Slam in Arizona

My road trip to Arizona had to be delayed a day because I had missed my flight on October 1 from Miami to Denver. Maribel and I packed up our Honda CRV with munchies and headed south toward Phoenix, Arizona, late in the day on October 2, 2023. For the past several years we have made it a family tradition to play in a father-son baseball tournament on the beautifully manicured fields and stadiums of the Cactus League, used by the Major League teams during spring training. This year, I would use the baseball trip as an opportunity to add a few more bird species to my Biggest Year list!

Before leaving Fort Collins, we stopped at JJ's Country Corner to fill up with fuel and fill the tires with air. One of the tires was low. Then we stopped in Frederick, Colorado, to see my daughter Angela and her husband Asher, who were not attending the baseball tournament this year. They were expecting the birth of our first grandchild in April! We had not even passed Denver when we felt too tired to continue so we stopped for the night. The cheapest motel we could find was $150. A sign of the times.

On October 3, we drove all day headed south on Interstate 25 until a flat tire forced us to stop for the night at Belen, New Mexico, just south of Albuquerque. Fortunately, the local tire repair shop got us back on the road headed south on October 4 for just $20! We entered Arizona at Portal, home of Chiricahua National Monument.

We parked at 2 PM at the trailhead for Cave Creek South Fork Trail. Before I ventured up the trail, Maribel asked me how much time I needed to find the bird I was seeking. I did some quick calculations in my head and told her that I would be at least 45 minutes. "Come with me. You can use the exercise and it is a beautiful trail," I offered, knowing full well that she would decline my invitation, preferring to listen to tunes in the car while she scrolled through her Facebook and Twitter accounts.

Tufted Flycatcher
4 Oct 2023, Cave Creek Canyon, Arizona

I found my target a mile up the trail: a vagrant Tufted Flycatcher (USA and Territories Biggest Year-bird 767). It posed beautifully for photographs but as far as I know other birders who searched for it the same afternoon or later failed to find it. When I reached the car, two hours had passed. I thought Maribel would be happy to see me. I was excited to share with her my success story of how I found my target, an ABA Code 4 species, and show her my photograph. Instead, I found her in tears, livid with me for staying away beyond the 45-minute time frame she was expecting. Returning down the canyon I was sure to check a grove of live oaks where I had seen a vagrant pair of Eared Quetzal a few years earlier. Today, I would not be so lucky.

The next opportunity to chase another vagrant was after the baseball tournament, on Saturday afternoon, October 7. At Glendale Recharge Ponds, I relocated and photographed a female Ruddy Ground-Dove (768, ABA Code 3). There I also added an exotic species that is now free-ranging around Phoenix, Budgerigar (769), and also got photographs of Lesser Nighthawk for the first time this year.

On Sunday, October 8, I arranged for Joe Kipper to join us, take over the driving, and return our vehicle to Fort Collins while we flew home. Before dropping us at Sky Harbor Airport Monday evening we managed to chase and photograph two more Mexican strays in the Tucson area: Rufous-backed Robin (770, ABA Code 3) and Ferruginous Pygmy-Owl (771, ABA Code 3). Four new species classified as ABA Code 3+ was a phenomenal outcome of this family trip.An avian grand slam! Checklists along with photos and audio can be reviewed at https://eBird.org/tripreport/295378.

Back home in Fort Collins, I would have one day to prepare for my departure on October 10, to Hawaii, my home for the next two weeks. The McQuades had just returned from Hawaii with 52 new species for their ABA Area year list (an amazing 792 species). I knew I needed the same success in Hawaii if I hoped to achieve first place in the ABA Area competition or to reach my personal goal of 900 species for the USA and Territories.

CHAPTER 35
Big Year Birding in Hawaii

I arrived in Maui early in the afternoon of Wednesday, October 11, 2023, after an uncomfortable night sleeping on the floor at the airport in Portland, Oregon. I had a half hour break before my commuter flight to Kona on the island of Hawaii, so I walked around the Maui Airport parking lot counting birds for an eBird checklist. The only native species I encountered was Pacific Golden-Plover, a wintering shorebird species. The rest were exotic (introduced) species, including House Sparrow, Red Junglefowl, Common Myna and Scaly-breasted Munia. Only Zebra Dove was new for the list. When I arrived at the airport in Kona, I added two more exotic species: Spotted Dove and Warbling White-eye.

Bill Kaempfer and John Vanderpoel picked me up at Kona Airport and drove me to our house overlooking Kona, where I added Java Sparrow and Saffron Finch. I knew Bill and John from the Colorado birding community. Bill was president of Colorado Field Ornithologists before he retired as Assistant Provost at the University of Colorado (Boulder) and moved to Florida. John produced gull and hummingbird identification videos and did his own ABA Continental Big Year in 2011. They were both doing Big Years in 2023. When they learned that my Hawaii dates were the same as theirs, they invited me to join them. John was sharing the trip with his wife Linda, celebrating an important anniversary.

Hawaii became an important destination for Big Year birders in 2016 when the ABA decided to include Hawaii as part of the ABA Area. You might be wondering why it wasn't included already. The reason is that the native birds there have little connection to the North American continent. But including them was a good decision. As a result, more birders travelled to Hawaii to see these birds, enabling more federal and state dollars to be spent toward their conservation. I hoped that my Biggest Year project would direct attention to the plight of native bird species in the USA territories in a similar way.

There were between 50 and 60 species found regularly within the State of Hawaii that were not found anywhere else within the ABA Area, so any serious Big Year birder needed to plan at least one trip to Hawaii during the year. After 2016, the Big Year competition in the traditional area of the USA and Canada became known as ABA Continental. This term was considered a region by eBird, so Big Year birders and their followers could track their totals in this category and compare numbers with Big Years of the past, such as John Vanderpoel's 744 species in 2011 (which did not include Hawaii).

Birding in Hawaii presented several challenges. First and foremost was the plight of Hawaii's endemic species. Hawaii's four largest islands each had its own set of endemics, mostly honeycreepers with slightly different adaptations for different feeding behaviors. Most of the Hawaiian endemic species known to science were already extinct, primarily due to avian malaria, a parasitic infection carried by the common house mosquito (*Culex pipiens quinquefasciatus*). This mosquito was considered an introduced pest, brought to Hawaii by human settlers within the last couple of centuries. Some of the disease-free areas where remnant populations of endemic bird species persisted were either too difficult for birders to access (e.g. remote areas on Kauai) or restricted for access (e.g. closed preserves on Maui).

Besides the resident endemic species that must be learned by Big Year birders, there was a variety of migratory shorebirds and waterfowl that occurred as vagrants from both North America and Asia. The Hawaiian Islands hosted a horde of nesting seabirds as well, so pelagic birding during a trip to Hawaii was also important. Finally, there were dozens of exotic species with naturalized populations that were originally introduced to the islands by human settlers. These exotics harkened from all over the world and were generally attractive birds with interesting personalities. They were mostly foreign to North American patch birders so they represented yet another group of novel species that Big Year birders must learn to identify.

We began birding as a team on Thursday, October 12. Moving at a relaxed pace we birded several eBird hotspots along the coast north of Kona, including several municipal parks and beaches (Waikōloa Skatepark, Keokea Beach Park, Waimea District Sports Park) and a nature trail through native Hawaiian forest (Kaulana Manu Nature Trail). New species included Gray Francolin, African Silverbill, Eurasian Skylark, Red-footed Booby, Wedge-tailed Shearwater, Great Frigatebird, Yellow-billed Cardinal, Erkel's Spurfowl, Chestnut-bellied Sandgrouse (ABA Code 3), Yellow-fronted Canary, Hawaii Amakihi, Hawaiian Hawk, Apapane, Iiwi and Omao. The last five listed are endemic Hawaiian species. Except for the shearwater, booby and frigatebird which are locally nesting seabirds, the remainder are exotic species that have become established on the Big Island. The sandgrouse is quite rare and beautiful. We were excited to find a flock of these interesting birds from Africa at a previously unknown location for them.

On Friday, October 13, we began our day at the Kealakehe Wastewater Treatment Plant in Kona. Facilities like this one attract a great variety of birds and this was no exception. I added three new species here: Common Waxbill, Hawaiian Coot and Sharp-tailed Sandpiper (ABA Code 3), a migrant from Asia that I had been patiently awaiting my entire birding career. This municipal facility was unusual in that it welcomed birders to view its wildlife. There were several other rarities there in addition to the Sharp-tailed Sandpiper, including Lesser Yellowlegs, Eurasian Wigeon and Least Tern. We ran into the coordinator of the birding program for the facility, Reginald David, a friend of mine from the past. We had each tried contacting each other but had old contact info. Twenty years prior, I hired him to guide me for a day following a work-related trip to the Big Island. We turned it into a Big Day and broke the ABA Big Day record for the island. The next year I hired him to assist me in guiding a grouse tour I led in Colorado. I hoped to have a chance to bird with him again before the year was over.

In the afternoon, Bill and I explored the Pu'u O'o Nature Trail in the native forest (an hour drive from Kona). Here we added the exotic Chinese Hwamei to our trip list. This shy species sang loudly but never made an appearance. At the end of the day, I spotted a pair of free-ranging Helmeted Guineafowl in our neighborhood.

On Saturday, October 14, I added the exotic Kalij Pheasant in our driveway. Bill and I headed to the Palila Discovery Forest hoping to find the critically endangered, endemic Palila. The dry open forest covers the base of the Mauna Kea volcano. We spent several hours on foot and added Black Francolin, Hawaiian Elepaio and Red-billed Leiothryx. We also saw the Hawaiian subspecies of Short-eared Owl here.

On my fourth day of birding in the State of Hawaii (Sunday, October 15), I joined an organized tour on the island of Oahu, led by birding guide Mandy Talpas. To accomplish this, Bill dropped me at Kona airport at 5:00 AM. The commuter flight took off on time at 6:00 AM for a 45-minute flight to Honolulu, Hawaii's capital city on the island of Oahu. An airport taxi took me to Waikiki Beach where I met Mandy and her three other customers at 7:15 AM. I saw several White Tern from the taxi. The first stop of the birding tour was a large tree on a city boulevard where several pairs of these beautiful white birds were nesting and frolicking in the air over traffic, like fairies. Some locals refer to the bird as a *fairy tern*. The second stop of the tour was a tropical forest. The lush rainforest vegetation was impressive, but Mandy explained to us that none of it was native to Hawaii. Here we found many Warbling White-eye, Red-billed Leiothrix, White-rumped Shama, Red-crested Cardinal and Rose-ringed Parakeet, all exotic species. The real attraction was the one endemic honeycreeper, Oahu Amikihi, which I was able to photograph.

Then we went to a narrow canyon near the Diamond Head crater. Mandy had worked in this canyon on a conservation project for the Oahu Elepaio. Elepaios belong to the Old World family of monarch flycatchers. They behave much like the members of the gnatcatcher family, restricted to the New World. While we sorted through the many exotic Red-vented and Red-whiskered Bulbuls, the Oahu Elepaio eventually emerged as if to greet their old friend Mandy!

The last stop of the morning was Honolulu's famous Kapiolani Park where we parked in front of a massive banyan tree. The tree was fruiting, and its food laden branches attracted hordes of hungry birds, all exotic species. We counted 20 species co-mingling in and around the tree. It was a beautiful sight to see such a diversity living together in peace and harmony. In this era of strained relationships among humans, I felt we had something to learn from these exotic birds.

Mandy was an eloquent spokesperson for the plight of the endemic birds of Hawaii. I had first met her earlier in April on the repositioning cruise from San Diego to Vancouver. I asked her if she had any upcoming pelagic trips. In fact, she had one coming up on Tuesday of the next week out of Kona but the boat was full already. She promised to ask the boat captain if she could take one more passenger. If that didn't work, she could organize another pelagic outing in December. I took an afternoon flight back to Kona hopeful that I would have an opportunity to add more seabirds to my Biggest Year list.

On Monday, October 16, Bill, John and I got an early start, driving for an hour to our meeting spot with Jack Jeffrey, a retired US Fish and Wildlife Service biologist who had worked on conservation of Hawaii's endemic honey-creepers. In retirement, he developed a reputation as the premier photographer of Hawaii's endemic birds. His photographs appeared in many high-quality publications including several of his own books on Hawaiian birds. He also was one of a small handful of guides licensed to take clients into the restricted Hakalau Forest National Wildlife Refuge. We hired him to show us the full suite of endemics that the forest offered. Jack's unique experience working on the forest conservation project for decades made him much more than a birding guide. He was a veritable fountain of valuable information. He was also one of the wittiest people I ever met. Almost every other sentence from him contained a pun, witticism, or joke.

We met Jack at the rendezvous point at 6:30 AM. A Hawaiian Short-eared Owl was hunting nearby. We climbed into his high clearance SUV for a slow drive along a two-track toward the Hakalau Forest. As we neared the trailhead, Jack spotted a drab green Hawaii Creeper which posed for photographs. At the trailhead about a dozen pairs of Hawaiian Goose (also known as Nene) staked out their territories fearlessly in a grassy meadow as we parked nearby.

On the hiking trail, we found Hawaii Elepaio, Apapane, Iiwi, Omao, Hawaii Creeper, Hawaii Amikihi, Hawaii Akepa and Akiapolaau. I got quality photos and audio files for most of these species. We also enjoyed a delightful encounter with a curious Khalij Pheasant that decided to join us for our picnic lunch which Jack had prepared for the group.

On the trail, we met another small birding group led by Lance Tanino, also a veteran Hawaiian birding guide. Lance had originally offered to guide me in Hawaii, but his availability changed and he had to cancel. I was glad to finally meet him face to face. He told me that a pelagic boat trip he had organized from Kona the following Saturday still had space. I jumped at the opportunity. John had encouraged me to take as many pelagic boat trips as possible. From reading John's book entitled *Full Chase Mode*, I learned that one can never have too many pelagic opportunities during a Big Year. I was excited about my upcoming pelagic trips. Bill and John also wanted to do a pelagic from either Kona or later in their trip, from Kauai, but were unable to find a reasonably priced charter for two or three people. Instead, they hired a young birding guide named Adrian Burke to lead a land-based sea watch in Kauai. Burke had been recommended by Linus Blomqvist, another 2023 Big Year birder who had recently visited Hawaii.

The next day, we packed up our bags and cleaned up the house, which was graciously on loan to us. We made some birding stops around Kona, adding Lavender Waxbill to the trip list thanks to a tip from Jack Jeffrey. This tiny arboreal *estrildid* finch (Estrildidae family) was one of my favorite birds of the trip, but sadly it was not added to the official *ABA Checklist* until 2024 so would not count for my official ABA-vetted total. Some big misses from the island of Hawaii were Palila, an endemic finch, and Japanese Quail, an exotic species. I had reached the lofty milestone of 800 species in 2023. Bill was on the verge of reaching 700 species in the ABA Area. Over an early dinner, we toasted to our success on the Big Island. We saw almost everything it had to offer us. We boarded the 7 PM flight from Kona to Lihue (Kauai) via Honolulu.

Kauai is the oldest of the seven volcanic Hawaiian Islands. The islands were formed from an underwater volcano that erupted seven times. Shifting continental plates pushed the nascent islands away from the underwater volcano over geologic time. Each eruption formed a new island in the archipelago. Because each island is a different age, its geography is quite distinct from the others. Kauai features jagged mountains that were too steep to support agriculture or human settlement and although they suffered from erosion, these remote ecosystems serve as a refuge for the sensitive endemic species of flora and fauna. Unfortunately, conservation biologists had not found sustainable ways to prevent the proliferation of avian malaria and other bird-threatening plagues such as predation from introduced rats and mongooses. The numbers of most endemic species of birds on Kauai were still in decline. Breeding seabirds which use burrows on mountainsides for raising their young were also threatened by the introduced predators. Still, after the island of Hawaii, Kauai offered the most species of the Hawaiian Islands for the Big Year birder.

John's wife Linda found lovely lodging for us at the Fern Grotto Inn just outside of Lihue on an old plantation property. We arranged for Adrian Burke to help us track down three of the six species of endemic passerines still surviving on Kauai. The other three were found in deep swamps or mountaintops too dangerous to access. Unfortunately, Adrian woke up Wednesday morning, October 18, with a bad case of food poisoning and couldn't help us after all. We headed to Koke'e State Park unassisted. We left a few hours later having identified just one of the three endemic targets, the Kauai Elepaio.

After lunch, we added Chestnut Munia and Red Avadavat to our list. These are exotic estrildid finches that are common in Kauai. Nevertheless, we had to work hard for identifiable photos of these tiny finches.

On Thursday, October 19, we headed to Hanalei National Wildlife Refuge where we found plenty of Hawaiian Duck. Then we visited Kilauea Point National Wildlife Refuge. This was a fabulous place with great views of a variety of nesting seabirds. We saw hundreds of Red-footed Booby and good numbers of Brown Booby, Wedge-tailed Shearwater (including nestlings at our feet), Great Frigatebird and White-tailed Tropicbird. We returned here Friday morning in search of a staked-out Red-tailed Tropicbird, but had no luck.

In the afternoon, Bill and I searched for a Greater Necklaced Laughingthrush, a rare exotic species that is nomadic, so it was no great surprise that we missed that as well. At the end of the day, Bill dropped me at the airport. A few hours later I was back in Kona on the Big Island of Hawaii, excited to take Lance Tanino's pelagic trip in the morning.

At the Kona Airport, I rented a high clearance pickup truck for three days. I figured I would need it to drive the four-mile dirt road to the Palila Discovery Forest on the flank of the Mauna Kea volcano. The Palila, a critically endangered endemic finch, was one of my principal targets. A sign at the entrance to the access road reads *4WD vehicles only*. The other targets for this visit to the Big Island were seabirds. I had signed up for pelagic boat trips on Saturday and Sunday. Four petrel species had been reported to eBird recently that would be new for my Biggest Year quest: Black-winged, Cook's, Mottled and Bulwer's Petrels. I found my rented apartment quickly, just 20 minutes from the airport and 10 minutes from Kona harbor where the boats are docked. I went straight to bed as I wanted to be fully rested for Lance Tanino's half day trip the next morning.

I woke up Saturday, October 21, at 5:30 AM. I prepared and exited the apartment quickly. I stopped by the McDonald's in Kailua for breakfast to go. I rolled into the harbor area at 6:40 AM thinking I was 10 minutes behind schedule but still with plenty of time for a 7 AM departure. After driving around the docks, I approached the only boat with passenger activity. "Are you birders?" I asked. "No, divers." Had I missed the boat? Could this be happening to me again? I called Lance on his cell phone. "Hey Nick, we missed you this morning."

"I'm here at the dock. Is it too late to join you?"

"Yes. We met at 6:15. We are well on our way. Sorry."

I had misremembered the meeting instructions. Once again, I messed up a great opportunity for a pelagic boat trip. I promised myself I would not do the same tomorrow.

I redirected my pickup toward the Mauna Kea volcano and drove an hour to the entrance road for the Palila Discovery Forest, arriving about 8:30 AM. I would spend six hours searching the complex of trails and dirt roads on the skirt of the massive 13,800-foot Mauna Kea volcano, exploring the vast māmane tree forest where Palila once thrived. In recent years, drought reduced the quality of the food supply for the attractive yellow-headed finch. It was feared that only hundreds now remained. I hoped to get lucky, but it wouldn't be today. I did add one bird to my Biggest Year list: Japanese Bush Warbler. As I retreated to my rented apartment in Kona, it dawned on me that the drought pushing the Palila toward extinction was yet another consequence of climate change. Was humanity doing enough to try to reverse the effects of the rising temperature of Earth? Of course not. Was I doing enough? Sadly, no.

The next morning, Sunday, October 22, I arrived at the docks on time and joined Thane Pratt and a half dozen other birders on a sporty speed boat. This pelagic trip had been donated by the boat captain to the Hawaii birding festival being held that weekend. Thane Pratt signed me up for the adventure.

The weather was fabulous and the waters were calm. We sped due south from Kona harbor toward the tsunami beacon 30 miles offshore. *Pterodroma* petrels (mostly Black-winged Petrel) were on the move, also heading south-bound. These stiff-winged seabirds traveled about twice the speed of the larger Wedge-tailed Shearwaters. We covered the distance to the large tsunami buoy in about 45 minutes, and paused at the buoy where flocks of boobies and shearwaters were foraging. We ended up travelling about 75 miles in about 5 hours and tallied 14 species of sea birds: Brown Booby, Red-footed Booby, Masked Booby and Nazca Booby (ABA Code 4); Wedge-tailed Shearwater; Sooty Tern, Brown Noddy and White Tern; Black-winged Petrel (ABA Code 3), Hawaiian Petrel, Stejneger's Petrel (ABA Code 4) and Bulwer's Petrel (ABA Code 3); Leach's Storm-Petrel and the Hawaiian subspecies of Band-rumped Storm-Petrel. The two storm-petrels and the Stejneger's Petrel were identified later from photographs, with the invaluable expert assistance of Peter Pyle. This was a great list, and I felt lucky to have been invited to join the group, at no cost!

Masked Booby (left) and Nazca Booby (right)
22 Oct 2023, Kona, Hawaii

After the boat trip, I followed a tip from Sherman Wing, one of the boat trip passengers, and added Tanimbar Corella, a large white cockatoo that is nesting on the island. Later in the day I chased a vagrant Bonaparte's Gull unsuccessfully, just for fun. I had already seen the species many times, but not in Hawaii. The effort was worthwhile; I was rewarded with stunning views of a pair of wintering Bristle-thighed Curlew.

On Monday, October 23, I returned to the māmane forest and gave the Palila another effort: eight hours. Sadly, I found none. I returned the rental truck at 7 PM and flew back to Lihue (Kauai) as I had left several species on the table there.

Arriving in Kauai for the second time, I used my Hotels.com app to find lodging. I was disappointed to learn that the cheapest hotel available was $300 per night (the Kauai Inn). Fortunately, it was just minutes from the airport. I reserved lodging for two nights.

I was up and out on the road before sunrise on Tuesday, October 24. I headed to Kilauea Point National Wildlife Refuge where Red-tailed Tropicbird was being seen daily. During my four-and-one-half-hour visit, I was able to secure a few brief distant views of a tropicbird flying out over the ocean from the cliff overlook that sported the diagnostic entirely white wings. No photo, no witness. Not very satisfying. Later that afternoon, I met up with Adrian Burke across the island. He showed me his favorite sea watch spot at the Port Allen airstrip. He was able to observe a couple of Newell's Shearwater in fading sunlight that I didn't see.

On Wednesday, October 25, I checked out after breakfast at the Kauai Inn. A family of free-ranging Indian Peafowl and several Red Junglefowl had wandered into the outdoor dining area to eat fruit scraps set out for them. On my last day in Hawaii, I headed to Koke'e State Park for a second opportunity to find some endemic honeycreepers. The weather was much better at the Pihea Trail during this second visit, and I was able to make more progress on the steep muddy trail. I finally got good views of Chinese

Hwamei and Japanese Bush Warbler. I checked every Apapane and Kauai Elepaio carefully and eventually spied a Kauai Amakihi that I was also able to photograph. I had just enough daylight left for a return to the rocky shoreline at Port Allen Airport. There I did get eyes (through my telescope) on the lingering pair of Newell's Shearwater just as the sun was setting.

Returning to the airport, I found a flight that would transport me overnight to the California coast. I had reserved passage on a pelagic trip from Half Moon Bay on Saturday, October 28, organized by Alvaro's Adventures, Alvaro Jaramillo's birding tour company. Kathy Kay (from Denver) was also registered on this pelagic and was arriving early to chase rarities. I arranged with her to be picked up at the San Francisco Airport late Thursday morning. She was arriving about the same time at the Oakland Airport and would have a rental car. We crossed the Golden Gate Bridge by noon, headed to Arcata Marsh & Wildlife Sanctuary (a four-hour drive) in search of a staked out Garganey, a vagrant duck from Asia.

I was happy to see Kathy again. I was glad she was driving, as I was in no condition to be behind the wheel after flying all night from Kauai. She offered to buy me lunch in exchange for my Big Year stories from Hawaii. I graciously accepted. Kathy's Lower 48 Big Year was in good shape. She had risen in the ranks and was firmly among the top 25 in eBird.

In Hawaii, I observed 96 species of birds. Of these, 54 species were new for my USA and Territories Biggest Year list, now 825 species strong. I felt like I was on top of the world. Checklists, photos and sonograms are viewable at https://eBird.org/tripreport/295542. My ABA Area year list was at 772 species, which was good for third place behind the McQuades.

CHAPTER 36
A Marathon or a Sprint?

Kathy Kay and I made a valiant effort to chase the Garganey at Arcata Marsh on Thursday, October 26, 2023. The Garganey, a small duck that had strayed from Asia, didn't show but Kathy picked out a drake Eurasian Wigeon among the many hundreds of waterfowl present. On Friday, we drove even farther north, almost reaching the Oregon border in Del Norte County. We chased another Asian vagrant, Common Greenshank, at Lake Tolowa, without success. The greenshank is a large sandpiper similar to our Greater Yellowlegs, but with greenish legs. A close encounter with a Barred Owl was a consolation for missing the greenshank. And the scenery was spectacular. The chase for these two potential year-birds required many hours of driving, and Kathy was up to the task. The next day we joined a pelagic birding trip from Half Moon Bay south of San Francisco.

"Given your bad luck with joining pelagic birding trips, I will make sure we get to the dock on time," Kathy told me.

We arrived at the harbor at Half Moon Bay at 6 AM Saturday, October 28, in plenty of time to board Alvaro Jaramillo's organized pelagic. I was looking forward to meeting Alvaro for the first time but it turned out he was guiding in Chile or somewhere else. Instead, he had arranged for several experts in sea bird identification to accompany us and serve as leaders for the group of 20+ birders. Among the experts were luminaries Steve Howell and Peter Pyle, published authorities on seabird identification. I introduced myself to them and was surprised to learn that they had both spent time with my brother Oliver birding in Central America a couple of decades ago. This pelagic boat trip was quite productive, adding two year-birds to the list. I learned a lot from the guides on board, especially with regard to identification of Short-tailed and Sooty Shearwaters, which are quite similar in appearance. Other species observed included Black Storm-Petrel, Ashy Storm-Petrel

(USA and Territories Biggest Year-bird 826), Pink-footed Shearwater, Buller's Shearwater (827) and Northern Fulmar.

Barred Owl
27 Oct 2023, Del Norte, California

The boat returned to the dock with about an hour of daylight to spare so Kathy and I headed a few miles up the coast where we successfully chased Pacific Golden-Plover. I saw plenty of these in Alaska and Hawaii, but I still needed it for my Lower 48 year list in order to be competitive with the McQuades, who were leading me in this category by about 15 species.

Kathy got a *rare bird alert* on her iPhone. "Northern Jacana was seen all day in Phoenix, Arizona," she reported. So, I made Phoenix my next destination, hoping the jacana, a stray from the marshes farther south in Mexico, would stick around long enough for me to see it. Kathy dropped me at the San Francisco Airport. I was in Phoenix with a rental car by 11 PM. I rented the car for a week with an ambitious plan to drive a 2,000-mile loop through Arizona, New Mexico and Texas. My targets were Northern Jacana, Nutting's Flycatcher, Golden-crowned Warbler, LeConte's Sparrow, Yellow Rail, Smith's Longspur and Black Rosy-Finch. In a week, I was scheduled on an east coast pelagic from Pompano Beach, Florida. This race to 900 species was no longer a marathon. With two months to go, it was now a sprint!

223

CHAPTER 37
Risking Everything

I spent all day Monday, October 30, 2023, at Tres Rios Overbank Wetlands, an impressive riparian preserve in Maricopa County, on the outskirts of Phoenix, Arizona. Equally impressive was the cloud of mosquitoes that chased me away from the site at the end of the day. The Northern Jacana had moved on from its favorite patch of water cress. Consolation for missing another staked-out target vagrant was a Brown Pelican (rare in eBird) loafing on a sand bar with cormorants on the principal water retention pond near the entrance to the facility. I also enjoyed meeting local Phoenix-area birder Tommy DeBardeleben.

I left Tres Rios about 6 PM and began my long 2,000-mile sprint. My next destination was Big Bend National Park in Texas. Nolan Walker, a young birding guide from Arizona, had stumbled upon a Nutting's Flycatcher at the Santa Elena Canyon Overlook along the Rio Grande River a couple weeks earlier. It was still being reported almost daily. Most observations were from the morning when it vocalized. I wanted to arrive early Tuesday, October 31, but driving during the night with rest breaks only got me as far as Las Cruces, New Mexico, when the sun began to rise. I arrived at the canyon late in the afternoon hoping to detect the Mexican vagrant by its vocalizations during the dusk pulse of bird activity. Not hearing any song from the overlook, I drove a mile farther to the canyon trailhead. Here the 1,000-foot cliffs on the Mexico side of the Rio Grande served effectively as a border wall. At the trailhead I was able to photograph Canyon Wren for the first time this year, aiding my effort to document every species on my Biggest Year list of birds for the USA and Territories. But alas, the Nutting's Flycatcher was missing in action. Yet another staked-out vagrant failed to cooperate for my quest.

The next vagrant on my list of targets was Golden-crowned Warbler in the lower Rio Grande Valley. To take advantage of daylight, I opted to take the most direct route along US 90 which follows the Rio Grande River from Del Rio to Laredo, Texas. I figured that if I could reach Laredo around dawn, I could snag a photo of Red-billed Pigeon on my way south. Traffic was light during the night, mostly truck traffic. The speed limit was 75 MPH on the two-lane highway. I found myself drifting off to sleep on several occasions. Once I even crossed the center yellow line and found myself face to face with a semi before careening back into my lane just in time to avoid a head on collision. I wondered if driving during the night two nights in a row was worth risking my life. At 4 AM I pulled off the road to sleep at Laredo near the international bridge to Mexico. I decided I did not have time to wait for dawn and resumed driving at 6 AM, taking great care not to enter the bridge itself. I stopped for birding at Salineño Wildlife Preserve just after sunrise at 7:30 AM hoping to find a Red-billed Pigeon I could photograph. No luck. I had heard one sing in July at Santa Margarita Ranch but had not yet documented the species.

I arrived in the lower Rio Grande Valley about mid-day, on Wednesday, November 1. In McAllen, I chased a new report of a female Blue Bunting, another Mexican vagrant, at Estero Llano Grande State Park. This is a big area. Not knowing where to look for the bird within the park, I was surprised to hear several loud chip notes that resembled the call notes of this species as I approached the visitor center. Unfortunately, I could not find it during several hours of searching. I spent the rest of the afternoon at Hugh Ramsey Nature Park near Harlingen where the Golden-crowned Warbler, yet another Mexican vagrant, had established a winter territory. The spot was very birdy, but I didn't find the warbler. I joined forces with a group of Colorado birders (Kathy Kay, Adrian Lakin, Graham Ray, Kenna Sue Trickey and Kelly Ormesher). Kathy spotted the warbler in a tangle and incredibly, everyone got decent views except me. Was I losing my birding touch? Maybe just too tired? I joined my Colorado friends for dinner. Somehow, I weaseled an invitation from them to crash for one night free in the Airbnb they had rented for the week. Kathy offered me the bed and the shower in the master bedroom which I graciously accepted. I suppose after two sleepless nights and several days without washing, I must have appeared and smelled awful. I used her shower. She slept on the couch.

The next day, Thursday, November 2, I returned to Estero Llano Grande State Park. I heard another loud chip note near the entrance, but it turned out to be a Swamp Sparrow (rare in eBird), which sounds quite similar to a Blue Bunting. Several hours later, I eventually glimpsed the female Blue Bunting (USA and Territories Biggest Year-bird 828, ABA Code 4). Unfortunately, the sighting was not witnessed, and I failed to get any type of documentary photo or audio. I finally caught up to the Golden-crowned Warbler too (829, ABA Code 3) and photographed it (barely identifiable) on the morning of Friday, November 3.

It was time to turn my sights northward and look for Yellow Rail. This tiny nocturnal marsh bird avoided all my efforts to find it earlier in the year along the Texas coast in April, and then at potential breeding locations in Wisconsin, Minnesota and Colorado in June and July. It breeds in moist meadows in the boreal forest zone mostly in Canada but winters in the extensive marsh system along the gulf coast in Texas and Louisiana. During the breeding season it vocalizes frequently. I had hoped to track one down by its unique Morse-code-like song. During fall and winter, they go silent and become very difficult to detect. However, before arriving at their winter territories in December, they tend to congregate in flooded rice fields. The best way to see one is to attend the October Yellow Rail Festival in Louisiana. Birders stand by during rice harvesting operations and watch the rails as they are flushed from the pastures by the giant combines used to harvest the rice crop. However, while many of my Big Year competitors, including the McQuades, visited the festival, I was still in Hawaii.

I did not expect to still be looking for Yellow Rail in November. The creature was competing with a handful of other species for the dubious honor of being the most difficult nemesis species of my Biggest Year. Other top contenders were La Sagra's Flycatcher, Yellow-green Vireo, Connecticut Warbler and LeConte's Sparrow.

The rice harvest season near Houston was wrapping up and reports of Yellow Rail sightings on eBird gave me hope in finding one before they disappeared into the extensive mosquito-infested marshes along the coast. I based myself at my son's house in Austin for three nights while visiting several promising locations. Unfortunately, I never found the right situation, a rice field being actively cultivated. I did add one new species: LeConte's Sparrow (830) at Attwater Prairie Chicken National Wildlife Refuge on November 6. There I also found a confiding Short-eared Owl that posed for photographs, numerous Sprague's Pipit and a Lark Bunting, which was flagged rare in eBird. The Yellow Rail continued to avoid me.

Short-eared Owl
6 Nov 2023, Attwater Prairie Chicken NWR, Colorado

My original ambitious plan involved searching for Smith's Longspur near Dallas and a stop for Black Rosy-Finch near Albuquerque, New Mexico, before closing my driving loop in Phoenix. However, these two species had not been reported this far south yet this winter. The prospect of driving another thousand plus miles by myself to return the rental car in Phoenix was daunting, so I plotted a new plan. I would return the rental in Austin for a $500 fee and find a willing co-conspirator to drive back to West Texas to search again for Nutting's Flycatcher, before I flew to Florida for the pelagic boat trip scheduled for November 11.

This new plan changed abruptly when I received news from Nick of a vagrant Roadside Hawk in Brownsville. I was finishing my birding day near Corpus Christi on November 7. Instead of returning to Austin, I headed south to Brownsville. My Colorado friends had one more night at their Airbnb and allowed me to crash there once again, this time on the couch. The next morning, they were gone before I awoke. I arrived at Resaca de La Palma State Park shortly after the gate opened on November 8. Word spread quickly that the hawk had been re-spotted in the same area at daybreak. I encountered a group of birders looking for it. David Chartier (a veteran birder from Colorado Springs) spotted it and pointed out the Roadside Hawk (831, ABA Code 4). Soon thereafter, a horde of dozens of birders arrived from the Rio Grande Valley Birding Festival, just in time to see it perched before it flew and disappeared until dusk.

Within 24 hours, Resaca de la Palma State Park went from being under-birded to being overrun with birders. This was a perfect scenario for the *Patagonia picnic table effect*. After just one day, birders had already discovered more rarities there including Tropical Parula and Blue Bunting. Later Rose-throated and Gray-collared Becards were found there as well. These are all ABA Code 3+ species.

I spent the whole day at Resaca de la Palma and saw the hawk again at the end of the day with another batch of birders including luminaries from the festival such as Nathan Pieplow from Colorado and Jon Dunn from California, both well-known field guide authors. Kathy Kay had joined me (after dropping her birding friends off at the airport in San Antonio, she made a beeline back to Brownsville, a four-hour drive) in hopes of getting the Roadside Hawk. She actually spotted it for the assembled throng of birders. I told her of my plan to re-chase the Nutting's Flycatcher at Big Bend National Park and invited her to be my co-conspirator for the chase. I had already been turned down by my son Nick and Justin Bosler. I was thrilled when she said, "Yes."

The first step involved a four-hour race to San Antonio Airport to drop off my rental by 11 PM. Then it was a seven-hour race to get to the Santa Elena Canyon Overlook by sunrise. We had two hours to find the flycatcher before having to race to Midland-Odessa Airport three hours away to return Kathy's car on time and make our respective flights. When a race is involved, Kathy always rises to the occasion. When she was in race mode, I called her *Danica* (after Danica Patrick, the Formula One race car driver).

The plan was a bit extreme but we executed it perfectly. Once we were on Interstate 10 streaming westward through the darkness, Kathy was tempted to put the pedal to the metal to make up time. I warned her that the Texas Highway Patrol probably patrolled this major thoroughfare during the night. She reluctantly set her cruise control to 82 MPH, just two MPH over the speed limit. We were amazed that she still got pulled over and warned to reduce her speed.

The night and the road seemed to stretch on forever. I tried to make conversation to help keep Kathy alert while she drove. "Tell me something about yourself I don't know," I challenged her.

"I'm a rescuer," she said.

"A rescuer?"

"Yes, when I see a wounded animal, I go into rescue mode. I've had turtles, lizards, raccoons, squirrels and even skunks in my home while I tried to rehabilitate them..."

"*Ahhhhh.*" I secretly wondered if I was one of Kathy's rescue subjects. I tried to liven up the long night with stories of bird rescues, including the time a Ring-billed Gull spent the night in my bathtub, and when I hosted a starving Long-tailed Jaeger in my Fort Collins garage.

When we finally arrived at the Santa Elena Canyon Overlook, we found Colby Watkins and his wife Lauren Stokes, a young couple from Austin whom I had met previously and who knew my son Nick. Soon, the group of assembled birders grew to eight, all there for the same purpose. Finally, we heard a single unique call note, "*wheek,*" a call attributed to Nutting's Flycatcher (832, ABA Code 4). Adding a new species to my list based on a single call note was not very satisfying. Fortunately, Colby audio-recorded it and added the sonogram to our shared eBird checklist.

Consolation was detection of two additional vagrants, a distant singing Crescent-chested Warbler (ABA Code 4) and a chirping Yellow-eyed Junco which only Kathy saw. In both cases, the identity was corroborated by the Merlin sound identification app. These observations represent probable third and second state records, respectively, if accepted by the Texas State Record Committee. The second record of Crescent-chested Warbler in Texas occurred earlier in 2023 when one singing bird was seen and photographed for several days along a hiking trail where Colima Warbler nests. I had successfully chased that bird (see Chapter 17). That spot was more than ten miles from Santa Elena Canyon and several thousand feet higher in elevation. Could this be the same individual? It seemed odd for a warbler to be singing in November yet there were several examples available in eBird of this species singing during the winter months. Unfortunately, these birds were not reported by anyone else at this location.

From Midland, I flew on Southwest Airlines to Fort Lauderdale, Florida, via Dallas–Fort Worth, Texas. I would join my friend Beto Matheus the following day on an ocean voyage in search of seabirds.

During this week of sprinting to chase ABA Code 3+ birds, I added five species for my Biggest Year, including four ABA Code 3+ species, all in

Texas near its border with Mexico. I was 68 species from my lofty goal of 900 in the USA and Territories without having yet visited the South Pacific territories of American Samoa, Guam and the Commonwealth of the Northern Mariana Islands. I was looking forward to my visit to Floridian waters as I still had four or five species to pick up in the Atlantic Ocean.

Kathy also had a great week adding numerous lifers and year-birds for her Big Year. She was climbing in the USA Lower 48 standings, approaching the top ten. I thanked her profusely for being my co-conspirator for the Nutting's Flycatcher chase trip. She said, "Nick I can be your driver anytime. If you need something, just ask. I can't seem to say no to you." She was becoming a great friend and supporter for me. I would call on her again before the end of my Biggest Year.

Rio Grande River at Santa Elena Canyon
31 Oct 2023, Brewster County, Texas

CHAPTER 38
More Pelagic Troubles

*P*elagics and me—we don't mix well. We are like fish-oil and sea water. The trouble started when I was 17 years old and got unbearably seasick off Cape Hatteras, North Carolina. In 2023, I had already missed two boat trips by arriving late to the dock, in North Carolina and Hawaii. Two trips, one in California and one in Maine, were cancelled at the last minute due to rough seas. I wish I could tell you it got better from there.

I arrived at Fort Lauderdale Airport at about 11 PM on Thursday, November 9, 2023, after an exhausting whirlwind overnight road trip to West Texas. Using Hotels.com, I booked a cheap hotel in Pompano Beach and booked an Uber. The Uber dropped me off at a condo in Fort Lauderdale with the same name and address as the hotel. Wrong place. The Uber driver was confused. I was confused. The condo reception clerk was confused. A couple hours later, I rolled up to the correct spot in another Uber. It was 2 AM and the hotel reception was closed. No one answered the phone number on the locked office door. I hitched a ride with the Uber driver to a Marriott about a block away. Fortunately, they had space for a couple of nights.

Beto Matheus had reserved a 21-foot boat from his boat club for Saturday morning, November 11. Based on his experience taking the boat out just a few miles offshore from West Palm Beach earlier in the year, he expected to find some decent pelagic species. My targets were Cory's Shearwater and Black-capped Petrel.

My early arrival gave me an extra day to chase any rarities that may have been discovered in Florida. In fact, a Fork-tailed Flycatcher had just shown up near Apalachicola east of Panama City Beach. Unfortunately, at more than 500 miles, the distance was too great for a one-day road trip. Beto texted me to say he had also reserved a boat for Friday, as he had the day off from work for the Veteran's Day holiday. I told him I would join him on Friday morning as well. His birder parents, Jorge and Ana, were visiting from Minnesota (originally from Venezuela). They joined us. When I didn't show up at the boat, he called and found me still sleeping after the long travel night. I was glad that he was patient and was able to pick me up at the Marriott.

Before leaving the slip, I adhered a Scopolamine patch behind my ear. This would ward off seasickness for three full days. I planned to be on the water Friday, Saturday and Sunday. We tooled around off-shore from Pompano Beach for four hours but the only seabirds around were a few Northern Gannet and a couple Magnificent Frigatebird.

I hoped that our luck would improve on Saturday. We were joined by two Tampa birders (John Swenfurth and Ann Ruben). We got an earlier start and powered out to 20 miles off-shore. The birdlife we encountered was the same as on Friday. Apparently, the location and season were not ideal for finding my target species. Or maybe I was just unlucky. Perhaps if we had put out some chum (fish guts and oil), we could have attracted some oceanic birds. Unfortunately, we inadvertently left the chum container on the dock. *Easy oversight,* you may be thinking. I think it was my anti-pelagic karma.

The wind picked up and the sea surface became quite choppy with four-foot swells. I was glad for the Scopolamine patch. We headed back toward shore. Looking behind us, I glimpsed a stiff-winged bird speeding across the water surface. It quickly disappeared behind a wave crest.

"I may have a petrel, distant, about halfway to the horizon, heading south, crossing the stern," I announced. Beto turned the boat around abruptly, and went full throttle. The boat lurched forward and slammed into a wave.

The jolt knocked our hats off and Beto's sunglasses flew into the ocean. The chase was short-lived. The candidate Black-capped Petrel got away from us. We returned to the docks with no new birds for the year list. I was nonetheless grateful to Beto for reaching out to me with the offer of trying for pelagic species. John and Ann dropped me in Fort Lauderdale on Saturday afternoon, in time for my 6 PM flight to San Francisco, California.

In San Fran, I rented a Toyota Corolla at 11 PM and headed north across the Golden Gate Bridge toward Bodega Bay. I had signed up for Lucas Corneliussen's Deepwater Pelagic. His plan was to carry 20 birders about 60 miles offshore, twice as far as usual and way past the continental shelf where the regular species hang out. To accomplish this feat, we were to assemble at 2:30 AM and depart by 3 AM. We were to tolerate up to 18 hours at sea and swells as large as 12 feet. I didn't remove the seasickness patch knowing that the effect can last for three days. I forgot that a potential side effect is drowsiness!

To make sure I would not arrive late (and risk missing a potentially very successful pelagic experience) I planned to drive straight to the dock, arriving one or two hours early. I would sleep in my rental car and then on the boat as best as I could before daylight. I killed some time stopping for dinner and at a grocery to stock up on snacks. I was 20 miles from the dock and getting sleepy. The road was empty, a two-lane country road that connected Bodega Bay to US101.

I dozed off briefly and found myself driving 50 MPH in the roadside ditch on the left side of the road. I veered right, pushing the vehicle back onto the empty road. JOLT, SMASH, CRUNCH! I hit something, maybe a fence post. As I pulled the car to a stop, the airbags deployed with a smoky bang. I assessed my situation. I was unscathed. The vehicle was not. A voice from Toyota's OnStar service asked if I was injured and informed me that 911 had been called. EMTs arrived and checked me for damages—none. The fire department arrived and checked the vehicle for explosion hazard—none. The police department arrived and prepared an accident report.

"Have you been drinking? Your speech is slurred." I could understand the cop's concern. The paramedic showed the cop my medication for Parkinson's disease. That assuaged his interest.

A tow truck arrived. I called an Uber hoping to still make the pelagic. It was now past 2 AM. The Uber did not arrive. A passing car pulled up and the passenger window lowered.

"Need a ride to the pelagic?" It was Thomas Ford-Hutchinson. We had emailed each other in the past. I grabbed my bags from the trunk of the damaged Toyota just as the tow truck was ready to take it away. Miraculously, Tom and I pulled up to the dock at 2:30 AM sharp. Thank you, Tom!!

Laysan Albatross
12 Nov 2023, Sonoma County, California

As for the pelagic, it was a success. No Pacific petrel species, unfortunately, but numerous other exciting pelagic species, including: Flesh-footed Shearwater (USA and Territories Biggest Year-bird 833, ABA Code 3); Black-footed and Laysan Albatrosses; Sooty, Short-tailed, Buller's, Pink-footed, and Great

Shearwaters; Ashy Storm-Petrel, Northern Fulmar, Red Phalarope, South Polar Skua (834), Pomarine Jaeger, Black-legged Kittiwake, Tufted Puffin, Rhinoceros and Cassin's Auklets and Common Murre. The rarest bird of the day was the Great Shearwater, a stray from the Atlantic Ocean with about 20 prior records for the North Pacific Ocean. The 12-foot swell was unlike anything I had ever experienced. Several passengers were down with seasickness. Fortunately, my Scopolamine patch worked well against seasickness, but not well against drowsiness while driving.

Thanks again to Tom who made the pelagic possible for me. He also drove me to the airport at San Jose, California, on the evening of November 12 for my flight home to Colorado.

Seabirds Offshore
12 Nov 2023, Off Bodega Bay, California

CHAPTER 39
Planning the End Game

I hadn't been home to Colorado in more than a month. My flight from San Jose to Denver on Southwest Airlines arrived at 1 AM on Monday, November 13, 2023. The next shuttle to Fort Collins was not until 5 AM so it would be another uncomfortable night in an airport. I had time to check my status in the competition categories that are tracked in eBird and ponder my next moves.

My primary competition category was USA and Territories. Marshall Iliff had told me that his team of eBird programmers would eventually create this category but that it would not happen soon. I couldn't track my progress in that category compared to other eBird users but I assumed that I was at the top of the ranking by at least 25 species. My species count of 834 was well on my way to my goal of 900 species for my Biggest Year. I still had trips to American Samoa, Guam and the Commonwealth of the Northern Mariana Islands planned for December. I had pushed these trips back from October to enable my brother Oliver to join me in American Samoa in mid-December. My son Nick would join me in the Marianas in late December. I expected to collect 50 new species in the South Pacific. The remaining species needed would have to be tagged in Hawaii, Alaska, the Lower 48 states and the other USA territories (Puerto Rico and US Virgin Islands). Unfortunately, the chain of islands northwest of the Hawaiian Islands, such as Midway, Laysan, Nihoa and the minor outlying islands (including Wake Atoll) were off limits, inaccessible to me.

I needed a plan to find at least 16 more species. Opportunities to chase vagrants would be limited with the dwindling number of available travel days remaining during the busy holiday season. I should focus on visiting locations where multiple resident species can be expected, rather than rely on vagrants to cooperate during the narrow time frames and geographic spaces that I would be able to visit for staked-out birds.

I also wanted to consider secondary priorities. For the ABA Area and the ABA Continental competitions, I was around 20 species behind David and Tammy McQuade in both competitions. With limited days available for chasing vagrants and based on my recent whiffs (unsuccessful chases of Garganey, Common Greenshank, Northern Jacana, Yellow Rail) I didn't think this gap could be overcome. Therefore, a possible three-day trip to Nome to pick up McKay's Bunting, Spectacled Eider and Gyrfalcon was probably not in the cards.

The Lower 48 competition was different. I was also in third place, about 12 species behind the McQuades. Twelve was a gap I could overcome, I thought, especially considering that several species that I had already seen in Alaska and Hawaii could be added to my Lower 48 list if I also observed them in the contiguous mainland states. Species in this category that were still possible to find included Rock Sandpiper, Bar-tailed Godwit, Red-necked Stint, Sharp-tailed Sandpiper, Rusty Blackbird, Gray-crowned Rosy Finch, Slaty-backed Gull, Ross's Gull and King Eider. I could probably knock off two or three of these while chasing new rarities.

Puerto Rico was the destination with the most birds I could add to my Biggest Year list. A dozen possible new species there included Masked Duck, Ruddy Quail-Dove, Scarlet Ibis, Connecticut Warbler, Red-billed Tropicbird, Cory's Shearwater, Black-capped Petrel, Orange-fronted Parakeet, White Cockatoo, Yellow-crowned Bishop and Lesser Antillean Bullfinch. I would be lucky to score four of these during another trip to the Isla del Encanto. I made plans to visit November 29–December 3.

Massachusetts also held a decent list of potential year-birds. I came up with seven possibles: Pink-footed Goose, Dovekie, Razorbill, Cory's Shearwater,

Little Gull, Great Skua and Gyrfalcon. I made plans to spend two days in Massachusetts November 27–28. I would be lucky to score two of these.

Texas still offered a few opportunities. Bare-throated Tiger-Heron was reported almost daily at the Santa Margarita Ranch. Yellow Rail was still possible. And a Cattle Tyrant was just discovered near the shipping port in Corpus Christi. This provisional first state record (and first USA record) was probably a ship-assisted bird. My brother Oliver suggested that it might have boarded a cargo ship in the Panama Canal. I made plans to visit Austin, Texas, for 36 hours, November 17–18. My son Nick would drive me to the coast (Corpus Christi area) and possibly also to the Rio Grande Valley if we could get access to the Santa Margarita Ranch near Salineño for the tiger-heron. I would be lucky to get one of these three targets.

Kansas had a bird that was low hanging fruit (Smith's Longspur). I reserved November 15–16 for a road trip to Kansas. Another fruity species was Black Rosy-Finch reported from Horsetooth Mountain Park just a few miles from my house in Fort Collins.

Hawaii held several additional species I could try to track down between trips to American Samoa (December 7–13) and The Marianas/Guam (December 17–27). These included three endemics on Maui, several endemic species on Kauai, one endemic species (Palila) on the Big Island and one or two exotic species on each of those islands as well (such as Greater Necklaced Laughingthrush on Kauai and Japanese Quail on Hawaii). These birds would count toward my Biggest Year and the ABA Area Big Year competition. I would be in Maui anyway Dec 14–16, so I might as well try for some of those species. Also, I scheduled a pelagic boat trip off Kona on December 15, which might produce one or two more species.

This plan would use up all my birding days through December except for December 4–6 and December 28–31. Also, November 19–26 was free but I had agreed to spend the Thanksgiving break with my wife and kids in

El Salvador visiting my wife's family. Maribel was already in El Salvador so the house in Fort Collins was quiet. Nonetheless I was eager to get on the road and begin executing my end-game plan.

On November 14, my friend from Fort Collins, Phil Cafaro, and I whiffed trying to find Black Rosy-Finch. It was a beautiful day for a hike to Horsetooth Rock and that was the problem. Hopefully the next time I visited Colorado (December 4?) it would be snowing. During snowstorms, flocks of rosy-finches come to backyard feeders in Estes Park and other montane towns. They also can turn up on the plains where they voraciously consume sunflower seeds. Roadside sunflowers grow like weeds on the Colorado plains.

On November 15, I embarked on a two-day 1,000-mile loop east to Lincoln (Nebraska), south to Wichita (Kansas), west to Denver, and finally north back to Fort Collins. My friend, David Wade, was in the driver's seat. We made birding stops on the way in Northeast Colorado (at Timnath Reservoir and Jumbo Reservoir) and Southwest Nebraska (Lake McConaughy) hoping to stumble upon a Gyrfalcon or Little Gull. No luck finding rare year-birds but we found plenty of eBird rarities, especially shorebirds that had lingered much farther north than normal, taking advantage of the mild climate this fall. Rarities included American Golden-Plover, Dunlin, Long-billed Dowitcher and Least Sandpiper at Timnath Reservoir (Timnath, Colorado) and Baird's Sandpiper at Jumbo Reservoir (near Julesburg, Colorado).

The next day, November 16, we visited Spring Creek Prairie Audubon Center (in Southeast Nebraska) hoping for Smith's Longspur. Again, whiff. We finally found gold at the end of the rainbow at a hay field in Eastern Kansas called *Smith's Longspur Field* in eBird. Smith's Longspur (USA and Territories Biggest Year-bird 835) had a very limited range in North America. Their core breeding area in Northwest Canada and wintering area in the Central Great Plains occupied a narrow swath of long grass prairie habitat. Ironically, they seemed to prefer patches of short green grass within this ecosystem, at least during winter.

240

I was happy to share this moment with Dave. We enjoyed the same pace, shared a similar skill level and had similar birding goals. We both were dedicated to using eBird to add scientific value to our birding obsession. In 2015, the year after I first met Dave, we competed for the number one spot in Larimer County. We were tied with 298 species each. On the last day of the year, I added a 299th with a county lifer, a rare Snowy Owl in Loveland. I decided to keep my discovery secret for 24 hours, fearing that a crowd of gawkers might displace the owl from its perch. I wanted the owl to stick until the next day for the Loveland Christmas Bird Count. I called just two birders to share it with them, Cole Wild who lived nearby and Dave. Dave and I ended the year tied with 299 species.

Cattle Tyrant
17 Nov 2023, Corpus Christi, Texas

On Friday, November 17, I flew to Austin, Texas, where my son Nick picked me up at noon. We bee-lined to Corpus Christi where we added the vagrant Cattle Tyrant (836, provisional ABA Code 5). This species was considered provisional because it was not yet on the official *ABA Checklist*. In a case like this, the *ABA Checklist* committee generally would accept the status determined by the State bird records committee. This committee would have to vote on whether the bird could be assumed to have arrived in the ABA Area unassisted by human intervention. This bird acted wild but its occurrence in an urban habitat two blocks from a major shipping port suggested otherwise. The vote from the committee failed 5–4. The Cattle Tyrant spent the entire winter of 2023–2024 in the waterfront area of downtown Corpus Christi. It disappeared in the spring of 2024. When it returned in November 2024, the question of its provenance reemerged. For now, it will remain provisional.

The next morning, we could not get access to the Santa Margarita Ranch to look for the Bare-throated Tiger-Heron. The one scheduled guided tour was filled to capacity. Instead, we visited San Bernard National Wildlife Refuge where we whiffed, again, on Yellow Rail, which is a strong candidate for worst nemesis bird of the year. Nick dropped me off at the airport and I flew back to Denver. I stayed with my daughter Angela in Frederick. The next morning, she and her husband Asher and I took a flight to Dallas–Fort Worth where we met Nick and flew on to El Salvador for a well-deserved vacation from my Biggest Year project. Of course, Nick and I birded daily in El Salvador, spotting about 180 species. Think Turquoise-browed Motmot, Cinnamon-bellied Saltator, Yellow-winged Tanager and many other species that would not count toward the Biggest Year project.

CHAPTER 40
Twitching in Texas and Another Hunt for Yellow Rail
Contributed by Nicholas Alexander Komar

1 was closely monitoring my dad's Biggest Year progress. Every morning, I logged into eBird, found my dad's profile page, and looked through his newly submitted checklists from the previous day. This allowed me to bird vicariously at all the amazing places his journey took him, while also making sure my dad had not succumbed to his crazy ambitions. At this stage in Dad's Biggest Year, I knew he had to grind for every new species. Six weeks remained in 2023. The list of available targets was dwindling.

Living in Texas the past five years, I learned that winter is a good time for Mexican vagrants to show up along the southern border. As part of my morning eBird stalking ritual, I checked the Texas *Rare Bird Alert*. You never know what will show up in Texas. When I read Cattle Tyrant and Bare-throated Tiger Heron, my "holy s—t" moment reached a new level. "How was that even possible??" I hollered from the bathroom.

"Everything OK in there?" my girlfriend asked.

"No, not really. A bird from South America just showed up at a downtown intersection in Corpus Christi, catching bugs around a dumpster …plus another mega-rarity that's the third record for the ABA." My girlfriend put her headphones back on and went back to work. I texted Dad.

Four days later, I picked Dad up at Austin-Bergstrom International Airport and we bee-lined to Corpus. Another target bird had been hanging around the area for the last few weeks, Bar-tailed Godwit. My dad already had seen this bird in Alaska, but not in the Lower 48. We decided to quickly look for the godwit on the way to downtown Corpus, but after checking the two most reliable locations with no luck, we refocused on the main target.

We pulled up to the intersection of Chaparral Street and Schatzell Street around 3:45 PM and saw three other birders pointing their cameras at a tree. Chasing an ABA first record species should never be this easy. We got out of the car and walked over calmly. One of the bird photographers started screaming with joy. An understandable response for any lister who probably made a big effort to be here, but in my head, I thought, *Jesus, lady, don't scare this bird back to Venezuela.* The flycatcher was unfazed and continued posing for photos for all to enjoy. We snapped off a few shots, submitted the most bizarre incidental checklist to eBird.org and carried on. Cattle Tyrant was year-bird 836 for my Dad's Biggest Year in the USA and Territories.

Bar-tailed Godwit
17 Nov 2023, Portland, Texas

We directed our attention back to the godwit. Again, we searched the areas it was last seen. I looked closely at every Marbled Godwit, squinting and un-focusing my binoculars trying to make them look more pale and slightly smaller, but it wasn't working. Finally, with just 20 minutes of daylight left, we returned to Sunset Lake Park in San Patricio County and decided to check out a part of the park we hadn't searched yet. I parked next to a red truck and could see a man holding a large camera walking the shoreline. I got out of the car and said, "You haven't seen the godwit, have you?"

His facial expression turned to dismay. "I was just taking photos of it right here. It flew off as you guys pulled in!"

A classic Code-3 move. We laughed and complimented all the incredible photos the guy had just taken, while internally distraught. "Did you happen to notice which direction the bird flew off to?" He pointed down the shoreline as he continued to marvel at the wonderful sighting he just had. Dad and I sneaked off in the same direction. Able to express our panic freely again, we frantically searched the shoreline at various access points, but no luck. Daylight was running out.

"Why don't you go back and pull the car up and I'll keep checking the shoreline?" My dad directed. I ran back to get the car, shared a few more false pleasantries with the man in the red truck, knowing we only had minutes to spare to find the bird. Then my phone rang. Dad's caller ID. I knew what this meant. I drove up the road and saw my dad holding his camera up to his eye. I crept up to his position slowly. He moved the camera away from his face and gave me a wink.

It was 5:45 PM now and the sun had set. We decided to grab dinner and mull over our options. The tiger-heron was another three-plus hour drive south at the Santa Margarita Ranch, which required permission to access. We had both reached out a couple days prior for access, but only managed to get on the waiting list for the next morning. We only had 24 hours left in Texas before we both were leaving the country for Thanksgiving break, and without guarantee of access to the tiger-heron spot, we decided not to make the drive. Instead, we would try to squeeze one more target bird out of the Texas coast. Introducing our harrowing effort to find the elusive, the cunning, Yellow Rail.

The result of delving into eBird historical data for Yellow Rail along the coast of Texas in November led us to San Bernard National Wildlife Refuge in Brazoria County. The refuge encompassed hundreds of square miles of freshwater and brackish marshes on the coastal plain. We got there at 8:30 AM on Saturday morning. Yellow Rail wintered along the Texas coast but was seldom reported in November. Checklists with large numbers of Yellow Rail get submitted almost every December in this area, but almost always as part of a banding project, or Christmas Bird Count nocturnal surveys where participants are granted special access to take all-terrain vehicles through the marsh to flush up and count birds for population studies. With some reports tallying over 30 individuals, we thought: *Surely, we'd be able to get just one bird during the day, right?*

As we entered the wildlife refuge, I rolled down the windows as I normally do to indicate that we had entered the birding zone. I slowed way down and Dad and I started listening for birds. However, within seconds, a fear we both had before getting there was confirmed. Mosquitoes. Lots of mosquitoes. Luckily, this was not our first rodeo. We came prepared with heavy-duty, long-lasting, mosquito-choking repellent that was about to be tested like never before.

We got to the auto-loop around Moccasin Pond. Our plan was to stay on the road and play a recording near good habitat. We drove by a 12-foot alligator resting calmly on the marsh's edge, seemingly satisfied by its last meal. We got to our first spot and stopped the car. Mosquitos bombarded the windows like blood-thirsty kamikaze pilots. Dad and I looked at each other. "We'll wait until they calm down. They are probably attracted to the movement or exhaust of the car," Dad said as I was already layering up in every piece of clothing I had trying to hide all potential points of entry to my skin and its underlying capillaries. Finally, we got out of the car, bathed ourselves in DEET and started listening for rails. Dad and I have birded from Argentina to Alaska and experienced plenty of buggy situations. So far, the mosquitoes here were bad, but manageable. *So far* being the key words.

Our idea of playing a recording from the road was not yielding any results. We had to come up with a new plan if we were going to get this bird. We noticed a wet grassy track leading away from the road toward a larger swath of short grass marsh, which appeared to be suitable habitat for flushing a rail. We changed our shoes to waterproof boots and started to march. As we walked through the vegetation, it seemed as though more and more mosquitoes began to take notice. We took turns reapplying each other with DEET, figuring this was our only shot to get this bird so we just got to keep moving. We turned off the wet grassy track and fully plunged into the marsh. *There's no way we don't flush up a Yellow Rail now!* We marched through the sawgrass reeds and murky water.

"Hey Dad, do you think they call it Moccasin Pond because of the Water Moccasins found here?"

But Dad didn't acknowledge. He needed this year-bird. We pushed forth. With every step the sawgrass stabbed my shins. My wet socks revealed that my *waterproof* boots were just water resistant. But worse yet, the buzzing around my ears was intensifying. With every movement we were awakening more and more mosquitoes, and now the whole swamp was aware of our stupidity. I looked down. Every inch of my body had a mosquito perched and trying to feed. I looked over at Dad. He was about 20 feet away and was wearing a green shirt. His shirt looked brown now, as I noticed the swarm of mosquitoes on his back. I twisted my neck to try to look at my own back. I could see mosquitoes landing on each other because there was no more room on my back. We walked about 75 yards into the marsh and stirred up millions of mosquitoes.

How did others manage to flush this bird without getting eaten alive? I wondered. Then I remembered the satisfied gator. I yelled out, "DAD WE GOTTA GO!"

He yelled back, "YEP!"

Accepting defeat, we ran out of that marsh as fast as we could, arms flailing around our heads trying to keep the mosquitoes from going in our mouths on each breath. With every swipe of my arm my hand would cut through the curtain of insects. We eventually made it back to the car and spent the entire drive back to Austin swatting the hundreds of mosquitoes that managed their way inside.

The madness in the marsh flushed up several Wilson Snipe, Seaside Sparrow and Sedge Wren, but no rails. Perhaps the Yellow Rail, unlike us, was wise enough to stay clear of the mosquito-infested coast until colder temperatures drive the insect activity down. This nemesis bird remained at large.

18 Nov 2023, Brazoria, Texas
Nicholas Alexander Komar
Searching for Yellow Rail

CHAPTER 41
One Bird at a Time

W e returned home from Thanksgiving vacation in El Salvador on Sunday, November 26, 2023. I was ready to continue my sprint to the finish line. Angela's mother-in-law, Tammara, picked us up at the Denver Airport and dropped us at Angela and Asher's house in Frederick. I borrowed Angela's car, drove an hour to Fort Collins where I grabbed a few items that I needed from home. Then I picked up a *Hot-N-Ready* pizza at Little Caeser's and drove the hour back to Angela's house. She drove me back to the airport where I took a red-eye flight with Frontier Airlines to Philadelphia, connecting to Boston.

Alf Wilson offered to drive me during my two days of birding in Eastern Massachusetts, November 27–28. Alf, who lives in Marblehead on the North Shore, had joined me on several earlier trips in the year, such as Arizona in early August. He picked me up mid-morning on November 27 at Logan Airport. We tooled around nearby Winthrop and Lynn before lunching at a Salvadoran restaurant where Alf tried *pupusas* for the first time. We spent all afternoon at Cape Ann looking for alcids. No luck. One consolation was a female King Eider at Andrew's Point (which I needed for my Lower 48 list).

On November 28, we continued the search for alcids (specifically Razorbill and Dovekie) as well as shearwaters at Corporation Beach on Cape Cod. Three of my target species had been seen there in recent days (Dovekie, Razorbill and Cory's Shearwater). Immediately upon arriving in the morning we spotted dozens of Razorbill, but never confirmed any Dovekie. A Cory's Shearwater photographed the day before was a no-show. Remarkably, a different, dark-plumaged shearwater did pass close to shore and I snapped off some photos. The underwing pattern seemed to support an identification as Sooty Shearwater, whereas the bird seemed to be structured more like a Short-tailed Shearwater. Either one would be considered a vagrant in Massachusetts in late November. I uploaded photos to my eBird checklist under Sooty/Short-tailed Shearwater. Another noteworthy bird there was Pacific Loon. Unfortunately, neither was new for my quest. Details about these sightings are available at https://eBird.org/tripreport/285465. The following morning, Alf and I met at Logan Airport and traveled together to Puerto Rico for the next chapter of the end game.

We had found an inexpensive flight through Orlando to Aguadilla, at the northwest corner of the island. We spent the first two nights in the Hotel Colonial in downtown Mayagüez on the west coast. Birding visits to the Rio Abajo State Forest and the Laguna Cartagena National Wildlife Refuge scored Alf dozens of lifers, but no year-birds for me. I finally scored a new bird for my Biggest Year in the USA and Territories, Ruddy Quail-Dove, singing at Bosque Estatal Sosúa in Sabana Grande, on the third day of the four-day trip. We spent the final night in Viejo San Juan and visited El Yunque National Park on the final morning. Here I photographed Louisiana Waterthrush for the first time in 2023.

I had hoped for a dozen year-birds during my four days in Puerto Rico. But I would leave with just one new species for my list. Full details of bird observations can be found online at https://eBird.org/tripreport/285482. Special thanks to Alf Wilson who drove me around for a week. We had some special moments. The most memorable was speeding out to sea in a two-seat jet ski to check out a group of Brown Booby perched on a buoy several miles off Cabo Rojo. As we rode the plane back to Orlando on Sunday evening, December 3, I pondered my next move.

My South Pacific adventure would begin on December 6. I had an opportunity to score some more Lower 48 species on Monday and Tuesday, December 4 and 5. I was just six species away from the 700 species landmark in the Lower 48 contiguous United States this year. I considered my options. If I could score three in these two days, I might be able to get the remaining three at the end of the month when I returned from the South Pacific. Little Gull was showing well in Buffalo and Cleveland. A Pink-footed Goose was sticking around in New York. The Gray-collared Becard in Brownsville beckoned.

Other needs in the Rio Grande Valley were Mottled Owl and Bare-throated Tiger-Heron at Santa Margarita Ranch (but access was restricted). Little Stint and Yellow-green Vireo were on winter territories in Southern California. Florida still hosted Fork-tailed Flycatcher five hours northwest of Orlando (driving) and now also a Yellow-headed Caracara (breaking news) was somewhere in Biscayne Bay a similar distance south of Orlando. And stormy weather earlier today had grounded thousands of rosy finches in Colorado including two species I still needed for the Lower 48 list. Oh boy. Decisions, decisions, decisions.

Little Gull
4 Dec 2023, Cleveland, Ohio

I decided to leave the Colorado rosy-finches for chasing on Tuesday. My telescope and dirty clothes bag were checked through to Denver on Monday morning. But I could chase one or two more species if I could arrange transportation and fly to Denver Monday night. Kathy Kay offered to drive in Buffalo for Little Gull. Frontier offered the free flight (with my Go-Wild Pass) from Orlando to Buffalo but not from Buffalo to Denver.

The invitation to visit Buffalo for Little Gull was enticing. While not common by any means, this smallest of all gull species was dependable near Niagara Falls in winter. In North America, a small population bred in Hudson Bay and scattered far and wide for winter. I expected to encounter it along the coast of Massachusetts in March, or perhaps a dispersing juvenile at a reservoir in Eastern Colorado in August or September. The year had flown by and no Little Gull had crossed my path. Less than a month to go in my quest for 900 species in the USA and Territories, I would have to make some time in my busy birding schedule to go track one down.

Using my iPhone, I searched for recent sightings of Little Gull in my BirdsEye app. Buffalo and Cleveland had several sightings. Most others were on the Canadian side of the Great Lakes. I opened my Frontier Airlines app to see if there were free flights to and from Cleveland and Buffalo. Cleveland was more accommodating, because a free flight was available to Denver via Las Vegas. I messaged Chuck Slusarczyk, a fellow *larophile* (lover of gulls) who lived in Cleveland. We both frequently contributed to the *North American Gulls* discussion group on Facebook. He agreed to meet me at Waterfront Park on the south shore of Lake Erie.

I passed on boarding my Denver connecting flight in Orlando on Monday morning, December 4, and boarded the Frontier Airlines flight to Cleveland instead. The ticket cost just $15 for the sales tax using the Go-Wild Pass. I arrived mid-morning, rented a car (for $75), bee-lined for Waterfront Park stopping just for a ready-made pepperoni pizza at Little Caesar's.

I found a sizable flock of small tern-like Bonaparte's Gull at the marina and immediately spotted a darker bird which turned out to be a diminutive juvenile Franklin's Gull, a rare species in Ohio. When Chuck arrived, we searched another part of the park with no luck. After splitting up to widen the search, Chuck called with good news. He had located the juvenile Little Gull among the original flock of Bonaparte's Gull. A chain-link fence hindered our view so we both climbed on top of a four-foot-high metal box to clear the fence for the auto focus feature on our cameras to work correctly.

I took as many photos as my bare, frozen fingers would permit. I had left my gloves in Boston.

Several birders had assembled to appreciate the tiny Little Gull which was putting on a great show flying back and forth just over the fence as if trying to impress its human audience. At 11 inches in length, this petite gull is the smallest in the world, smaller than a pigeon. Its plumage features impressed me—wings with a bold black **M** tattooed across them, a thick black band across the tip of the tail and a pinkish wash to the breast and head, reminiscent of the yearling Ross's Gull I had seen at Gambell, before this Little Gull was born! I hung out at this park a while appreciating the enormous flocks with thousands of Ring-billed Gull. Chuck explained that larger gulls arrive to this area in the early spring. I wondered where they were in the winter.

I was surprised to find another rarity, a Harlequin Duck feeding beneath the pier. Full details of the birds observed at Waterfront Park, including photos, may be found on-line at: https://eBird.org/checklist/S155831642.

To get home to Denver, I connected through Las Vegas and finally arrived at 4 AM. Dave Wade met me at the airport and on the way back to Fort Collins we detoured through the Rocky Mountain villages of Silverthorne and Estes Park in search of rosy finches. We found a handful of Gray-crowned Rosy-Finch. The weather was too nice. The Black Rosy-Finch continued to evade me. I slogged through my front door around 2 PM. I hit the sack. The next adventure would start in 16 hours, just enough time to regain strength after several intense days of birding.

The two flights on Frontier, from Cleveland to Denver, had been discounted. I paid just $25. As with the last two forays to Massachusetts and Puerto Rico, I was able to add a single new species to my USA and Territories Biggest Year total, which now was 839 species, but this time at a fraction of the cost. My next trip would be to the South Pacific (Hawaii, American Samoa and Guam) with much loftier expectations.

CHAPTER 42
A Morning in Maui

I had been in Maui in October 2023 but just for a few minutes. I had not done any birding away from the Kahului Airport. Maui hosts several species that would be new for my Biggest Year. Six species of endemic honeycreepers have survived in the native forest on the flanks of the Haleakalā Volcano. These include the Crested Honeycreeper or Maui Akohekohe, the Maui Parrotbill and the Maui Alahuahio which are only found in Maui and are all critically endangered. The other three (Hawaii Amakihi, Apapane and Iiwi) are more widespread and seem to be adapting to new habitats at lower elevation. There is even evidence that they have developed some resistance to avian malaria, the principal cause of population declines for Hawaii's endemic honeycreepers.

My twin brother Oliver joined me for the second time this year. We landed in Maui at 5 PM on Wednesday, December 6, 2023, after meeting the previous night in Fort Collins. Twelve hours later we were trucking up the Haleakalā Highway in our rented Jeep Cherokee. After rising about 6,500 feet above sea level, we turned off toward Hosmer's Grove. Arriving at a small Haleakalā National Park campground, we hiked a short nature trail until we reached a couple of benches overlooking a small canyon of native forest dominated by ohia and māmane trees. Colorful forest birds were buzzing all around. After a couple of hours here we tallied about 15 Apapane, 12 Hawaii Amakihi, eight Iiwi and two Maui Alauahio (USA and Territories Biggest Year-bird 840).

The morning was successful. The other two Maui endemic honey-creepers require special access to a Nature Conservancy property that was closed to the public. To cap off the morning, we noted some interesting exotic species on the mountainside, including Eurasian Skylark, Red-crested Cardinal, Northern Cardinal, House Sparrow and Japanese Bush Warbler.

We had 15 minutes available before checking in for our 1 PM flight to Honolulu, the first leg of our trip to American Samoa. Kanaha Pond State Wildlife Sanctuary abuts the airport. A brief stop there was productive: Laughing Gull, Hawaiian Coot, Wandering Tattler, Sanderling, Ruddy Turnstone, Pacific Golden-Plover and numerous Hawaiian Stilt (an endemic subspecies of Black-necked Stilt).

We ran into some bumps en route to American Samoa. That is a topic for another chapter.

Maui Alauahio
7 Dec 2023, Haleakalā National Park, Maui

CHAPTER 43
Bumps in the Road
Contributed by Oliver Komar

W ith all of my brother Nick's focus on birding in the last few weeks and months of 2023, organizing the logistics for the jaunt to Samoa kind of took a back seat, and well, never really got organized. Several weeks before heading to the South Pacific, he invited me to join him, and after I confirmed I could take the vacation time, I didn't hear much more. At some point I inquired about the travel plans and soon heard back he had purchased those tickets. But several days later, and just a week before the trip, when I asked again about tickets and itineraries, Nick responded that he couldn't find the details in his email. He finally found one email from United Airlines with a confirmation number for my trip from Honduras to Colorado, where I would meet up with him for the travel to American Samoa via Hawaii.

I checked the info and alarm bells went off. The departure was from San Pedro Sula, near the north coast of Honduras, a five- or six-hour drive from my home at Zamorano University; it is not the nearest international airport. The other red flag was that the email did not mention a ticket number, just a confirmed reservation—could it be that the tickets had not yet been purchased? It turns out Nick didn't realize that San Pedro Sula was a different airport from the one I requested at Comayagua, known as Palmerola International Airport (the closest to my home but still a three-hour drive).

The solution turned out to be simple. Get a one-way ticket on a commuter plane from Tegucigalpa to San Pedro Sula. Seats were available. The drive to Tegucigalpa would be just one hour. And the flight was 45 minutes. We were able to confirm the United flight had indeed been purchased. I trusted Nick, an experienced traveler, had the details for the Colorado to American Samoa travel under control.

On Tuesday, December 5, 2023, I traveled all day from Honduras to Denver, where I rented a car for one day and drove north to Fort Collins, arriving around 11 PM. I knocked on Nick's door, then let myself in. No sign of him or anyone else. I found him, exhausted from his travels, fully clothed and sprawled on his bed, asleep. Earlier in the day he had returned from his Puerto Rico trip, having detoured en route to Cleveland, Ohio, for Little Gull, and then to Estes Park for rosy-finches.

Nick went into action mode. First order of business, defrost a delicious dinner prepared some days earlier by his wife Maribel who was still visiting her mother in El Salvador. Then, confirm travel plans for tomorrow.

Nick still had not found the email confirmation for travel to Hawaii and on to American Samoa. It didn't take long to confirm my flight to Hawaii and back to Denver on United. After a bit of a struggle with his email system and its archiving protocols, Nick finally confirmed he had indeed bought his own ticket and our tickets to American Samoa on Hawaiian Airlines.

Next order of business: lodging and vehicles, and of course birding plan for the next morning, which would be Wednesday, December 6. The flight to Hawaii was near midday. Our plan was to leave Fort Collins in my rental, drive through Loveland in search of anything interesting (perhaps a Gyrfalcon— one had wintered there for three years in a row a few years back). We would leave home by 7 AM and have an hour for birding en route to Denver International Airport.

For lodging and a vehicle, Nick had not yet made any arrangements! So, near midnight, we jumped on the internet to see what could be arranged. First, set up a one-day car rental at the airport in Maui. We could use it to drive to a lodge and then to the Haleakalā National Park for birding on Thursday morning. Nick asked me to do the driving throughout the trip. We would have until noon to get back to the airport for the 10-hour travel to Pago Pago in American Samoa (flying with a transfer in Honolulu).

Next order of business, lodging near the airport in Maui. Done. Then a search on Hotels.com for something comfortable and not too expensive in Samoa. It was last minute and Nick wasn't picky (me even less so).

257

There were few options. The first, a *beach fale,* was cheap, but the marketing photos just showed some hammocks under a thatched roof on a beach! Another photo showed a large mattress under thatch, with mosquito netting for walls. "Hmmm, not much privacy," I warned him.

The next option, a beach resort, featured pretty rooms and a swimming pool. Pricier but not out of this world. We took it! Reserving online was a little confusing as the payment form gave a price in the thousands, not the hundreds, but the currency was WST. What is the currency in American Samoa? We had no idea. Surely not a problem.

Finally, we were able to reserve a vehicle at the Pago Pago Airport for six days. We finally collapsed in the wee hours, exhausted but well fed, on Nick's comfortable bed, still fully clothed from the day's long journeys.

Maybe it's time to cut to the chase and make this long story a short one. After birding in Maui (and ten new species for my life list), we grabbed the short, first leg of the flights. Then we waited to board the Samoa flight in Honolulu. While waiting we remembered to contact the lodge to alert them that we would be checking in very late, probably close to midnight, which was due to the normal flight itinerary (the flight from Honolulu to Pago Pago is six and a half hours). And that's when we noticed that the lovely beach resort we reserved wasn't on the same island as the airport! It wasn't even in American Samoa. It was in Western Samoa, a different country! No wonder the currency was WST$ and not American dollars. WST$ is the Samoan Tala, the Western Samoan Tala.

Nick worked on canceling the lodging in Western Samoa, and I worked on finding lodging near Pago Pago International Airport in American Samoa. We got that worked out just in time to board the big bird from Hawaiian Airlines. In his chapter about Maui, Nick mentioned a bumpy ride to Samoa. Actually, the flight on the Airbus 320 was pretty smooth. But the passengers were sweating. The air conditioning wasn't working. The pilot announced it would cool off once we were at altitude (I wondered if the plan was to open a window at high altitude). After a couple hours on the flight, and nearly

1,000 miles across the Pacific, I felt fine. Perhaps they did open a window (just kidding—not actually an option). The pilot came on the intercom with an important announcement. Parts of the plane had cooled off, but other parts were warmer. Some passengers were feeling ill from the heat. She had already turned the plane around and in another 90 minutes we would be landing back in Honolulu!

Several hours later, close to midnight, we boarded a second Airbus, with a new crew. We finally arrived in Pago Pago at dawn on December 8. Nick didn't sleep a wink on the plane. I did, but I still felt exhausted. It was time to settle into Samoa (American Samoa, to be clear), get some rest and find a few dozen species of birds somewhere in the middle of the South Pacific Ocean.

In fairness to Nick, his seemingly lackadaisical approach to organizing logistics had some upside benefits too. In fact, as he correctly pointed out to me, keeping the logistics flexible helped him adjust his Biggest Year strategy up until the last minute. It turned out that one could indeed travel without always having destinations and services reserved in advance.

Gray-crowned Rosy-Finch
5 Dec 2023, Silverthorne, Colorado

CHAPTER 44
Birding Samoa

I did not really know what to expect when Oliver and I arrived in American Samoa on the morning of December 8, 2023, after flying all night from Honolulu. Reviewing data on eBird, it appeared that no birders lived on the islands. This US Territory was severely under-birded. In eBird, the bird list for American Samoa was just 62 species, derived from a few hundred checklists. And the number of species reported in December was markedly fewer. About half the species present would be new for my USA and Territories Biggest Year bird list. I hoped to find 20 new ones in American Samoa for my quest to observe 900 species in one year.

The main island of American Samoa where we stayed, Tutuila, was ridiculously gorgeous. The scenery was spectacular. Amazingly there was almost no tourism here. We heard rumors of occasional cruise ships, but we did not see any during our stay. Of the several hundred passengers on our flight, only a couple appeared to be non-locals. One was on her way to Western Samoa for a wedding. The other was a businessman from Atlanta on business travel. We found the local Samoans incredibly friendly and hospitable. The downside was the high cost of living on Tutuila. We spent about $350 a day for lodging, transportation and food. Oh, if you enjoyed life in the fast lane, you might be very uncomfortable here. The speed limit was 25 miles per hour and passing was not permitted.

Birds were plentiful. As we deplaned directly onto the tarmac, we noticed several White-tailed Tropicbird flying high overhead. Plenty of Common Myna and Red-vented Bulbul flitted around the terminal buildings. Several Buff-banded Rail strutted about on the green lawn in front of the buildings.

We rented a car from the airport and drove slowly along the seacoast a few miles to the capital city, Pago Pago (pronounced *pango-pango* by the locals). We added a Pacific Reef-Heron foraging in the rocky surf. Our hotel, one of only two on the island, was quaint. It featured a secluded beach on a calm harbor and a nice indoor/outdoor restaurant. We found Pacific Imperial-Pigeon in the trees outside our second-floor room. For our first birding outing, we drove along the coast road heading east, which skirted the harbor. At pullouts, we found Lesser and Great Frigatebirds, Red-footed Booby, White Tern, Brown and Blue-gray Noddies, White-rumped Swiftlet, Pacific Kingfisher, Samoan Starling and Eastern Wattled Honeyeater.

Blue-gray Noddy
10 Dec 2023, American Samoa

The following day, we drove west from the hotel, birding the bays and coves near the airport, and around the one golf course on the island. New species added included Black-naped Tern, Pacific Golden-Plover, Sanderling, Ruddy Turnstone, Wandering Tattler, Crimson-fronted Fruit-Dove, Jungle Myna, Australasian Swamphen and Samoan Myzomela. The myzomela is a beautiful black and crimson honeycreeper reminiscent of the Apapane from Hawaii.

By the end of our first day, I had added nine new species. And five more the second day, bringing my total number of species to 854. We had four more days here before returning to Hawaii on December 14.

On Sunday, December 10, Oliver and I rose early to appreciate the dawn chorus in the rainforest. A steady rain was falling. All we heard was Eastern Wattled Honeyeater which seemed to be all around us at Afono Pass (elevation about 1,000 feet). We continued to Afono, a quiet village on the north coast of Tutuila. An eBird checklist from four years earlier reported three species here we were still looking for: Polynesian Starling, Many-colored Fruit-Dove and Fiji Shrikebill. We did not find any of these.

Next, we drove to the east end of Tutuila. The rain had stopped. We found an overlook facing north and tried a sea watch. Bingo! We saw distant shearwater species (probably Wedge-tailed) and a flyby Gray-backed Tern (855). We spent the rest of the day wandering the forest roads of the east end of the island in search of new species. We found a pair at the end of the day: a probable Peregrine Falcon and Polynesian Starling (856). Our trip list for American Samoa was approaching 30 species. After three days on Tutuila, I had added 16 species to my Biggest Year.

Nick Birding in Tutuila
8 Dec 2023, American Samoa

Photo by Oliver Komar

CHAPTER 45
The Bird that Almost Got Away
Contributed by Oliver Komar

Monday, December 11, was a fairly slow day, but it finished with a bang. We woke before dawn, sleep-deprived. The plan was to get into the nearby rainforest on the island's central ridge in time for the pre-dawn avian chorus. Early morning rain dampened that plan and we went back to sleep. We would wait out the rain over breakfast in the hotel restaurant.

We adapted to the rain and decided to start the day's activities focusing on logistics, rather than birds. How could we get on a boat to visit the shearwaters, petrels and storm-petrels that we imagined must be foraging just a few kilometers offshore? Yesterday we could see a handful from the north shore, about half a mile out to sea, maybe more. We stopped at the office of the national marine sanctuary, almost next door to our hotel, to inquire.

A very friendly receptionist named Belle was happy to help us figure out a plan. She gave us several contacts, names and numbers, and even made a few calls to set us up. Soon we had a boat captain on the line. He was talking to us from his boat offshore and promised to help us organize a pelagic trip for the following day.

Next, we needed to get to the airport to change the destinations for our return flights on Hawaiian Airlines (from Maui to Kona, on the Big Island). And we needed information for a day trip (by air) to the Manu'a Islands, which are smaller islands within the territory of American Samoa. On the way to the airport, we stopped briefly at the Pala Lagoon, to see if we could get better photos of Black-naped Tern and documentary photos of the two Sanderling Nick had spotted two days before on Saturday. One of the terns was there but Nick missed getting photos. No sign of Sanderling but today there were a dozen Ruddy Turnstone.

It was almost noon by the time we parked at the airport. Hawaiian Airlines quickly obliged with our itinerary changes. The Samoa Airlines office also provided the info we needed to plan a visit to Manu'a (where we hoped to be able to see Blue-crowned Lorikeet and maybe Fiji Shrikebill). Unfortunately, the flights to either one of the two islands in the Manu'a group ran every other day, so a trip tomorrow (Tuesday) meant returning to the main island (Tutuila, where the capital Pago Pago is located) on Thursday. Our flight to Honolulu was Wednesday night, so the trip was out of the question. We would be better off channeling the funds for the two flights into a pelagic boat trip the next day.

By 12:30 PM we were leaving the airport. Our next plan was to explore the road through the high plateau on the west side of Tutuila. We expected the rainforest to be more extensive there and offer good or even better chances to find forest birds like the Shy Ground Dove and Many-colored Fruit-Dove which so far had eluded us.

We explored the road. Unlike other roads on Tutuila that crossed the mountains, this one did not offer any forest access. Most of the road was lined with homes and gardens, with manicured lawns. The high road was cooler than the coast roads, and among the numerous Christmas decorations on display, we passed a large one that read *Welcome to the North Pole*! It seems some of Santa's elves may be living in American Samoa, at least for the winter. High on the plateau, several Pacific Golden-Plover foraged on the manicured lawns, seemingly happy to share the space with their Samoan neighbors. But no sign of forest birds. We did not even submit an eBird list.

We returned earlier than expected and had time to explore the rest of the roads on the southwest side of Tutuila. We located a beautiful spot to make a south shore sea watch, but after 20 minutes saw nothing more than a few boobies and noddies so we decided to head back east and check out Pago Pago harbor, near our hotel. It was raining again by the time we got there. It wasn't too late though (about 3:30 PM). We checked all the docks in the harbor in case a rare tern might be hanging out, but we found nothing.

The rain let up even though the cloudiness didn't. I suggested we call it a day and rest up well for tomorrow's boat trip. Nick wouldn't hear of it, though. Remember, Nick was obsessed with finding 900 species for his Biggest Year. With just 20 days to go, he still needed 44.

Pacific Kingfisher
10 Dec 2023, American Samoa

We decided to finish the daylight with a hike along the forested ridge above the port city. We could get to the trailhead parking lot in just ten minutes. It seemed a good place to look for the two doves and the Fiji Shrikebill. Or even the large honeyeater called the Mao, which we understood had not been seen on Tutuila for 45 years. We parked at the trailhead parking area. No rain, despite the low hanging cloud cover. The highest peaks on the island were fogged in, but we were lower and still had good visibility. We immediately located a Polynesian Starling singing in a tree at the edge of the small parking lot—a good omen.

265

A few hundred meters up the trail, we listened to the late afternoon bird song chorus, dominated by the loud calls of the abundant and densely populated Eastern Wattled Honeyeater. Nick was straining to hear one of, any of, his target birds. He had Merlin open on his iPhone. He had already recorded the chatter of the White-rumped Swiftlet which coursed the forest track near eye level, especially at breaks in the forest cover.

Near one of these breaks, as we listened, suddenly we heard a frantic piping call, reminiscent of a kestrel (a small falcon that should not be found far from a continent and was not known from Samoa). Nick went into action by hitting the record button on Merlin. I went into action by moving a few steps up the trail into the clearing where there was a much better view. I could tell the calling bird was flying so I scanned the clouds and the airspace above the valley to the northwest. I quickly located the source, a most surprising scene. Far out over the valley, a large dark bird was flying to the left (west). It had long, pointed wings and an exceptionally long tail. It seemed to be struggling (flapping hard) to get away from another much smaller bird (which I never focused on, but if I had to hazard a guess, it might have been a swiftlet). The profile of this bird was raptor-like but the tail was longer than any falcon I had ever seen. The flight style was more like a grackle or a cuckoo. This was a bird I had never seen before and was certainly not expecting. I called to Nick who ran up to see the bird himself but missed it. I only saw it for a couple of seconds or less before it disappeared behind trees in the foreground.

This odd bird was a Long-tailed Koel, a large bird in the cuckoo family that was known to visit Samoa and other Polynesian islands. Its plumage was similar to a hawk, dark brown upperparts with streaked brown breast and barred tail. I did not realize it would appear as large as a hawk in real life but with a spectacularly long tail. We did not expect to see the koel because we believed that the visitors to Samoa would have left for their breeding grounds by November. They breed exclusively in New Zealand. A crazy life history. Since we thought none would be present in December, we had not investigated possible locations or even how they used the habitats. In other words, we were not looking for this species and did not expect to find it on the ridge trail. But it was indeed a new species for both Nick and me. His Biggest Year-bird 857. This was a bird that almost got away.

I only saw the koel for a second or so. Not enough time to even turn on my camera. Nick never saw it. He heard it though. And he managed to get part of its alarm call recorded, which turned out to be critical. In the field, he thought it sounded like a falcon, such as the Eurasian Kestrel, which would be an accidental vagrant if it were so. My description in the field also did not convince Nick. After all, there are raptors with long tails. I had no prior experience with the koel, did not get a photo, and the sighting was fleeting. I can't blame him.

Fortunately, however, Nick had a recording of the bird. Without that, and without access to dozens or hundreds of reference voice recordings of the same species on websites like eBird.org and Xeno-canto.org, the koel would have been the bird that got away without ever being identified. As it was, it *almost* got away.

CHAPTER 46
Final days in American Samoa

December 12, 2023, was our fifth day on Tutuila. We arrived 15 minutes early to the pelagic meeting place at Auasi Harbor, a small but functioning facility built by the US Army Corps of Engineers decades ago. Our boat captain arrived a few minutes later *sans* boat. He had arranged to use a family member's 31-foot pontoon boat. However, the boat was needed to transport materials to the village on Aunu'u, a small island just off the eastern coast of Tutuila. Pelagic karma?

I was relieved that the boat was postponed as the surf was rough and waves were more than four feet high. The boat captain, Peter Taliva'a, invited us to his home in a nearby village for coffee. Peter spoke fluent English and was very knowledgeable about Samoan history and culture. He regularly led tours of Aunu'u Island for cruise ship passengers who dock at the port of Pago Pago. He mentioned having collaborated with birding tours years earlier, as a local guide, when a couple of the large tour companies used to bring birders to the island.

Peter offered for his deckhand, Mike Levi, to accompany us to Aunu'u for the remainder of the morning, particularly to look for Pacific Black Duck. We boarded the next passenger ferry (also a 31-foot pontoon motor boat) for Aunu'u with Mike, a native Samoan who spoke little English.

We spent four hours on this remote island. The island featured five principal ecosystems: village, rocky shoreline (exposing a coral reef at low tide), mangrove swamp, rainforest and a marshy, freshwater volcanic caldera. The diversity of ecosystems provided habitat for most of the bird species of American Samoa. We observed 23 species of birds there, including some noteworthy ones, such as Long-tailed Koel in the mangrove swamp, White-tailed Tropicbird on a nest in the rainforest, Pacific Black Duck (USA and

Territories Biggest Year-bird 858) in the caldera, and finally, in a taro farm outside the village, Australasian Swamphen and Buff-banded Rail. We also had a sighting of two flyby curlews that seemed smaller than Whimbrel. We left them as unidentified but I suspected these were Little Curlew, a migrant from the Asian continent. Little Curlew may be a bird that *did* get away!

The small population of Pacific Black Duck (also known as Australian Grey Duck) on Aunu'u was noteworthy for being the easternmost outpost of the species. We heard there were fewer than 20 present. We counted 10. They were apparently absent from other locations in American Samoa.

We returned to mainland Tutuila with Mike via ferry and joined Peter at his house for a late lunch. We made plans for Peter to take us out to sea the following day (which was our final day in American Samoa). After lunch, we tried for better views of the large falcon we had seen earlier in the week. Instead, we found a colony of Masked Booby!

On the morning of Wednesday, December 13, we met Peter and Mike at the Fagatogo Marina in Pago Pago Harbor which was very close to our hotel. The pontoon motorboat chugged through the harbor and picked up speed at the mouth of the harbor. The seas were much calmer today, but occasional six-foot swells knocked the boat around. I was happy to have a Scopolamine patch behind my ear to ward off seasickness.

As for birds, we saw mostly Brown, Red-footed and Masked Boobies, White Tern, Brown, Black and Blue-gray Noddies. We got close to a White-tailed Tropicbird resting on the water. We eventually observed two Wedge-tailed Shearwater (both dark morph) and a small black-and-white shearwater, Tropical Shearwater (859), which would be the last new bird I would add from American Samoa. No storm-petrels or petrels. Hiring the boat for four hours was an expensive way to add one more bird to my list. The cost was $500 not including tip. At this stage of my year-long quest for 900 species, new ones did not come cheap.

Looking back at my time in American Samoa, I recorded 19 new species for the USA and Territories Biggest Year. Pretty much on target. The scenery at Tutuila Island was breathtaking and although bird diversity was low, it was fun to bird there. In all, I reported 36 species among 38 checklists, putting me within the top ten contributors of eBird reports for the Territory (for all years combined). This probably reflected lack of local contributors to eBird, more than anything else. We felt like we saw most of what was possible. You can visit the list of species seen along with photos and audio files in the eBird trip report accessible here: https://eBird.org/tripreport/206106.

White-tailed Tropicbird
13 Dec 2023, American Samoa

At 859 species I may yet reach 900 species by December 31, but it would not be easy. I was hoping for 30 new species during my scheduled ten-day tour of Guam and the Northern Mariana Islands, where I would be accompanied by my sharp-eyed son, Nick. That left me with four days in Hawaii and three days on the US mainland to find 12 more. Challenging but doable with a little luck and a little help from my friends.

CHAPTER 47
Return to Hawaii
and Arrival in Guam

*E*xpecting to take a Hawaiian pelagic trip from Kona, Oliver and I had redirected our flight from Pago Pago to Kona (was originally to Kahului, Maui). We arrived in Kona (on the island of Hawaii) the morning of December 14, 2023, after flying all night to Honolulu. First stop for birding was the Kona Wastewater Treatment Facility near the Kona Airport. I hoped to find the wintering Sharp-tailed Sandpiper I had seen here in October, as Ollie had never seen one. Rare birds here included Pectoral Sandpiper, Lesser Yellowlegs, Greater Scaup, all of which were present in October as well, but alas, no Sharp-tailed Sandpiper.

I found out that Mandy Talpas's pelagic boat trip from Kona on December 16 was canceled. This was disappointing because the biggest source of new species for me within the ABA Area was indeed sea birds.

I reviewed the species reported within 50 miles in the last two weeks using the BirdsEye app on my iPhone. The app told me that just one species had been seen nearby that I still needed for my ABA Area year list, Palila! Recall that in October I had roamed the māmane forest of the Mauna Kea volcano for a total of 16 hours looking for Palila. Unfortunately, the long-standing drought severely impacted their highly specialized food supply, and the population took a huge hit. Japanese Quail was also possible on the same mountainside. So, there were two species to chase. Several pelagic species were also theoretically possible, such as Cook's, Mottled and Bonin Petrels, so I took Ollie to the northwest corner of the island for an afternoon sea watch. All we found flying beyond the surf were Brown Booby and Black Noddy. By the time we arrived at the Palila Discovery Forest, it was dark.

To be in place at dawn we decided to sleep in our rental vehicle (which saved us driving time and more importantly, about $300 for a hotel room).

Sleeping in the car turned out to be very uncomfortable. The air temperature dipped to 35 degrees Fahrenheit where we were, at 7,000 feet elevation. It was hard to sleep, but we made it through the night without freezing to death. Shortly after sunrise on December 15, we glimpsed a candidate Palila as it flew away from us. Unfortunately, we didn't get enough of a view to count it on my list. After four hours of searching, we gave up. We could not raise a Japanese Quail either. We did spot several Chestnut-bellied Sandgrouse (ABA Code 3) nearby in Waimea. We returned to the sea watch location but again found only boobies and noddies, no petrels.

Chestnut-bellied Sandgrouse,
15 Dec 2023, Waimea, Hawaii

On Saturday, December 16, we joined the annual Christmas Bird Count for North Kona. Compiler Lance Tanino assigned us five residential neighborhoods. A pair of beautiful Lavender Waxbill was our reward. This scarce exotic species from India had lurked around Kona for decades but was not yet in the *ABA Checklist* as a naturalized species. It was added in 2024. Go figure.

At 3 PM, we returned our rental car and boarded a plane to Honolulu. Ollie connected to Maui, and onward to Denver and Honduras. I stayed at the Airport Honolulu Hotel and waited for my connecting flight Sunday afternoon for Guam.

I had spent four days in Hawaii and failed to score any new species for my Biggest Year. That spelled trouble. To reach my goal of 900 species, I would need to capitalize on every opportunity. Also troubling was that Nick's flight from Houston left five hours late and he would miss connecting with the flight to Guam. I departed for Guam on December 17, traveling alone and still at 859 species.

The Marianas are a chain of islands stretching northward from Guam. They comprise two USA territories, Guam and the Commonwealth of the Northern Mariana Islands (CNMI). The flight from Honolulu departed at 3:30 PM on December 17 and arrived about seven and a half hours later at 7 PM on December 18, after crossing several time zones, the International Date Line and more than 3,000 miles. For US citizens, a passport is not required to enter Guam. However, we did have to go through customs inspection, which was quick and painless. I picked up my rental car, drove a few miles to my hotel, checked in, grabbed dinner at a nearby Chinese restaurant, strolled along the beach counting shorebirds for my daily eBird checklist, and went to bed. Although shorebirds are often active at night, my count was zero. My first day in the Marianas had passed and my Biggest Year list was stalled at 859.

On the morning of December 19, I left the hotel at 6:30 AM, grabbed breakfast at McDonald's and planned my birding day. I had all day available until I would pick Nick up at the airport at 7:30 PM, about two hours after sunset. I started off the day visiting beach parks along the west side of the island.

I had lunch at Jeff's Pirate Cove along the eastern shore. This is a popular birding hotspot; I explored the grounds thoroughly after downing a fine burger. I then visited the interior of the south side of Guam at the Layon Landfill. I finished the birding day along the southeast coastline. Avian diversity was low. My day list was just 18 species, but a third of those were new for my year list: Black Drongo, Philippine Collared-Dove, Yellow Bittern, Micronesian Starling, Common Sandpiper and Little Egret. For the full list of species from Guam on December 19, here is my eBird trip report: https://eBird.org/tripreport/184095.

I was now at 865 species for my Biggest Year list. Nick arrived safely and on schedule (well, a full day late) but nursing a cold. He had spent his extra morning in Honolulu birding in the rain and his Canon camera had malfunctioned, which was a bummer. He would have to wait until the end of his trip to bird on Guam, as our flight to Saipan, the largest of the islands in the Commonwealth of the Northern Mariana Islands (CNMI) was early the next morning.

Urban Park
18 Dec 2023, Guam

CHAPTER 48
The Commonwealth of the Northern Mariana Islands

The Commonwealth of the Northern Mariana Islands (CNMI) was a tiny country that found itself unable to sustain its economy after World War II. It toggled back and forth between military domination by the Japanese and Allied Forces. When Japan surrendered to the USA in 1945, CNMI requested assistance from the USA in managing its affairs. But even now, as a USA territory, US citizens are required to show their passports at customs upon arriving at any airport in the CNMI.

Nick and I arrived on Saipan early on Wednesday, December 20, 2023, on a United Airlines flight. The trip from Guam was less than an hour. In Saipan, we rented a car from Enterprise (Nick drove) and began birding immediately. Nick had done quite a bit of research at eBird.org and had determined the important hotspots we would need to visit. My list of target birds on Saipan was about 20 species long. The top two hotspots were the airport catchment pond and the nearby Coral Ocean Resort. We tried to find the pond, but it seemed to be overgrown with weedy vegetation. We could not get decent views of the water. Similarly, a drive-by at the resort yielded no useful views. We tried another shorebird hotspot at a golf driving range close to the airport. We entered the parking lot and found no golfers there. I asked permission to walk the perimeter and was obliged.

We spent an hour there and found no shorebirds or shorebird habitat but the birding was great nonetheless. A couple of large trees filled with dozens of nests of Black Noddy was particularly impressive. I added five year-birds: Mariana Kingfisher, White-throated Ground Dove, Mariana Fruit-Dove, Bridled White-eye and Micronesian Rufous Fantail.

Mariana Fruit-Dove
22 Dec 2023, Tinian, Commonwealth of the Northern Mariana Islands

We then drove to the opposite (northern) end of the small island, to the World War II memorial where we also found good birds. There, I added three year-birds: Micronesian Myzomela, Golden White-eye and Mariana Swiftlet. We also found the massive Brown Noddy colony at Bird Island and had incredible views of flying Red-tailed Tropicbird at Suicide Cliff. We ended the day in American Memorial Park at Garapan, where we found plenty of birds but no new species. We checked in at our hotel in downtown Garapan. We were staying on the second floor. The first floor doubled as a Japanese massage parlor. It seemed that the principal economic commodity of Garapan was Japanese massage.

On Thursday, December 21, Nick and I returned to the north end of Saipan. It is a small island. We arrived in 20 minutes, just before sunrise. Here we first heard and then saw our target, the Micronesian Megapode, a terrestrial forest bird named for its large feet. eBird uses the name Micronesian Scrubfowl. These awkward birds are rarely seen on Saipan. Our luck continued with a singing Saipan Reed-Warbler near Suicide Cliff. Then at the nearby landfill we found a good variety of shorebirds at the settling pond: Wood, Sharp-tailed and Common Sandpipers. I had seen all three earlier in the year. Eurasian Moorhen was new for my year list.

We then birded our way back to the airport at the south end of the island. We were determined to find a better view of the catchment pond. Eventually we found one. A Whiskered Tern foraged over the pond. Not only a year-bird but also a life-bird for both of us! We ended our birding day at Garapan Harbor where we located an overwintering Siberian Sand-plover (Lesser Sand-plover) perched on a dock. I had already seen this beauty on May 31 at Nome, Alaska. I pondered whether it could be the same individual bird, now molted into *basic* (non-breeding) plumage.

We had dinner with Nathan Johnson, a biologist and eBirder who had lived in Saipan for 21 years. We enjoyed learning about the tricks to finding the local birds, while he enjoyed hearing about my Biggest Year project.

On Friday, December 22, Nick and I caught a commuter flight to the island of Tinian, via S.T.A.R. Marianas Air. But first we checked out a couple of spots around the Saipan Airport. The most productive was a pond on the golf course at Coral Ocean Resort. Nick used his charm to convince the resort manager to provide a golf cart free of charge for us to view both ponds on the property. The ponds had emergent vegetation. The west pond had a good variety of birds. Our checklist included Northern Pintail, Green-winged Teal, Garganey, Wood Sandpiper, Black-winged Stilt and Whiskered Tern. The Garganey and stilt were Asian species new for the list.

The flight to Tinian was a short ten-minute jaunt in a tiny four-passenger plane. The pilot was a young man from Colorado. Tinian was a small island but big enough to rent cars at the airport. We rented one and drove to the town harbor where we found Gray-tailed Tattler, a gray mid-sized sandpiper that prefers rocky shoreline. There were few birds out and about and even fewer people. However, what the island lacked in population, it made up with history. Tinian was once occupied by the Japanese. During World War II, the US Navy fought for and conquered it. Later in the war, Tinian served as the base where the Enola Gay loaded its cargo of a single atom bomb destined for the city of Hiroshima, Japan. The military was for the most part long gone now.

We found our target species, the tiny Tinian Monarch, an Old World flycatcher related to the elepaios from Hawaii. It was foraging at eye level in scrub forest near some limestone caves where Japanese soldiers had made their last defensive stand against the American invading force.

Despite the somewhat ugly history, the island was beautiful. Nick and I found a secluded beach we had all to ourselves. We took a break from birding to swim in the ocean. When the break was over, we headed back to the airport with an eye open for Asian bird species that might have settled on the island.

We were looking mainly for raptors and egrets. There were no ponds or mudflats available for shorebirds. Most of the island was secondary forest scrub. We flushed numerous flocks (>100 individuals per flock) of Orange-cheeked Waxbill, a tiny introduced species of estrildid finch. I thought these would make great snacks for a Japanese Sparrowhawk. When we came to an area of cattle pasture, our search became focused on finding cattle-egrets. The Asian subspecies had recently been elevated to full species status, now called Eastern Cattle-Egret. It is longer necked, longer legged and darker legged than its yellow-legged *western* counterpart. In breeding plumage, it sports an orange neck and head rather than a yellow-orange patch limited to the nape and crown. Time was running out on us when I spotted a white egret fluttering near a small group of cattle. Then there were four. Soon we spotted a tree full of them—15 birds in all. We confirmed the field marks for *basic* (non-breeding) plumaged Eastern Cattle-Egret.

I was pleased we found an Asian visitor (Eastern Cattle-Egret) in addition to the resident endemic Tinian Monarch for my Biggest Year list, now at 881 bird species. We arrived back on Saipan at dusk. Next stop—the island of Rota.

CHAPTER 49
Three days on Rota
Contributed by Nicholas Alexander Komar

We arrived on the island of Rota on December 23, 2023. The flight from Saipan took about 30 minutes in a dual-engine jumper plane that fit up to eight people (including the pilot). You could really feel the air in a plane that small, which was troubling considering nothing was in your control. The pilots for S.T.A.R. (Saipan, Tinian, Aguijan, Rota) Marianas Airline were all young, professional and interesting people. One was a 22-year-old guy from Colorado Springs who studied at the Air Force Academy. Another was a 23-year-old Indian woman who grew up in Maine and had been involved in aviation since she was six years old. I found it fascinating to learn how each of them ended up flying these tiny planes way out here in the middle of the Pacific Ocean.

The birding goal on Rota was to find Mariana Crow and Rota White-eye, both critically endangered species endemic to this island. We were given suggestions by locals on how to find both, so we felt confident about our ability to get those two species quickly and spend the rest of the 48 hours checking vagrant traps that have a history of hosting wintering Asian birds.

Our first birding stop was at the Rota Resort Golf Club near the airport. We parked the car and stepped out to look at a pond hoping for a Medium Egret or Gray Heron, but instead within seconds we heard the call of the Mariana Crow. We followed the calls and quickly came across a family of three birds, welcoming us to the island. Biggest Year-bird 882. That was easy! Moving right along.

We spent the rest of the first day checking the shoreline and other hotspots until driving up into the foothills in search of Rota White-eye. The place we wanted to go had a checklist from four days earlier with Rota White-eye and Pacific Swift, an Asian vagrant. We felt lucky. Every time we got out

279

of the car, we knew we could find something unusual since this island does not get eBird reports often. We thought we could increase our chances of finding birds by walking the rugged roads rather than driving (and we didn't want to risk damaging the rental vehicle). As we walked, I scanned the cliff face above us hoping something interesting would be circling the high ridge. I spotted something large flying overhead.

Mariana Myzomela
23 Dec 2023, Rota, Commonwealth of the Northern Mariana Islands

"Here's something!" I called out to get my dad's attention. As I tried to get my binoculars to focus, I thought could this be some weird seabird, or a raptor? Dad got on it first. "It's a bat." A bat?! I then learned that the island of Rota was home to the Mariana Fruit Bat, with a wingspan like a Black Vulture. These things flew all over the island at all hours of the day and were pretty cute despite their monstrous size. After hiking for six miles, we had not seen a single Rota White-eye. These birds might end up being more difficult than we anticipated.

The next morning, we tried our luck at Guam Rail, once considered to exist only in captivity. A local ornithologist gave us coordinates for a reliable spot that is near where these birds have been reintroduced to the wild. On the brink of extinction, they are a highly sensitive species, and recent projects to improve the population brought them to Rota. We got to the location before sunrise and slowly drove the single lane dirt roads hoping to spot one running around. Strike one.

We didn't have much time to search for the rail because we had arranged to meet with local ornithologists to search for an Abbott's Booby. This odd-looking species is long-winged and gangly in appearance and is often mistaken for an albatross or frigatebird. An individual wandered far from its nesting grounds on Christmas Island to Rota about a year before but had not been seen since February 2023. We knew our chances were slim, but we had to try. At 7:30 AM we met up with Keith, Rachel and Julia at the trailhead. They were team members that elected to come to the island for a remediation project for Mariana Crow, one of the rarest species on Earth, with fewer than 200 remaining in the wild. They led us through the forest on an under-developed trail that Dad and I would have missed without their help. The forest was dense, and the hike was slow, buggy and hot. After about 35 minutes, we emerged to a scene I will never forget. The trail opened onto a narrow ledge that overlooked the Philippine Sea and a forest hundreds of feet below, with hundreds of boobies nesting in the treetops.

My interest in finding the lone Abbott's Booby in a trove of Red-footed Booby and Brown Booby diminished as I was overwhelmed by the beauty of it all. Dad on the other hand started announcing a group strategy to search the colony. I took photos, videos and selfies with my cell phone, and tried to record the different seabirds that came floating up the cliff face to check us out while keeping an eye out for the vagrant Abbott's Booby.

Ninety minutes passed quickly, and we accepted the fact that most likely the misplaced Abbott's Booby was out patrolling the sea, possibly hundreds of miles away, perhaps flying back to Christmas Island to celebrate Christmas!!

We said goodbye to the prehistoric view and trudged through the jungle back to the car. Strike two.

Tired and slightly disappointed in our lousy luck so far, we decided to check out some vagrant traps before making another run for the white-eye. We headed to the airport to scan the fields for possible shorebirds or waders. It was a slow process, and most of the heads popping up from the grass were Pacific Golden-Plover. Finally, we caught a break. I spotted a snipe. Snipes in this part of the world are tricky, but there was a high probability we could turn it into an Asian vagrant that was new for my dad's list. We studied the bird as best we could, and after some deliberation, we agreed that this was a Swinhoe's Snipe (883). A clutch double in the gap!

Now it was time for another crack at Rota White-eye. This time we used improved intel to determine our search location. We drove higher in elevation to some better habitat. Again, we walked for miles in search of our target. We stumbled across a massive coconut crab, rats and the largest monitor lizard I've ever seen, easily six feet long, but no white-eye. The consolation prize was an incredible sunset view overlooking the Wedding Cake Peninsula of Rota. It was a valiant second effort for Rota White-eye, but nonetheless a swing and a miss.

That evening we celebrated Christmas Eve together with our new ornithologist friends, by sharing a delicious pizza dinner, Dad's treat. Christmas did not seem like a major holiday on Rota. Or maybe we were just focused on our mission.

Our third and final day on Rota started with another unsuccessful attempt at finding Guam Rail. Strike two (if you count the at-bat last evening). With only a few hours to spare before our flight back to Saipan, we had to go for the white-eye again. This time we picked a spot that had the most eBird reports of this species ever. It was almost a guarantee. We followed navigation to the pin but were stopped short. The road had degraded, and the ground was too wet to even attempt driving over. If we got stuck out here, we'd risk missing our flight, or worse. We luckily managed to get the car out of the muddy tracks and to a safe parking spot. Then we took off on foot. The clock was ticking.

Now on foot, we again hit more roadblocks. The path had turned into a creek bed and water was rushing down the mountain. I first tried to keep my feet dry by tiptoeing through the mud but eventually gave up and fully submerged my running shoes & socks in the murky water.

"This white-eye is kicking our ass," I said.

We stopped and spished at every good patch of jungle, habitat that the bird preferred, but all we heard was silence. Time had run out. We walked back shaking our heads. Who knew we didn't have the bat speed to catch up to the Rota White-eye's proverbial pitch. Strike three, we're out. Back to Saipan and Guam.

22 Dec 2023, Rota, Commonwealth
of the Northern Mariana Islands

CHAPTER 50
Return to Guam

W e returned to Guam on December 26, 2023, after spending our final night in Saipan in style at the Coral Ocean Resort. We had booked the short flight on a United Airlines jet for about $300 each. Before returning our rental car, we drove around to the Saipan Airport pond for one last attempt to see the Common Greenshank that had been reported there in recent days. We got excited when a shorebird arrived, but it turned out to be Wood Sandpiper, the most common sandpiper wintering on the island.

United Airlines' procedures were slow and cumbersome compared to S.T.A.R. Marianas Air. And because CNMI and Guam are different territories, we needed to go through additional customs inspections. The short flight took up much of the morning.

My friend Tom Hall, who had accompanied me for the Gambell (Alaska) gamble in June, had worked in Guam years ago. He informed his former colleagues there of my Biggest Year project. They recommended that I contact Martin Kastner. I had emailed him. He responded with some general guidance about birding in the region and offered to help find our target species and join us for birding December 26, 2023. He was waiting for us at the airport when we arrived at 10:30 AM.

Martin was a great birding guide. We headed south from the airport following the coast. In the harbor area, we found a Black-naped Tern. From the harbor, we crossed the island to the east shore, where we visited Jeff's Pirate Cove restaurant for lunch. Birding the grounds didn't turn up much: Black-bellied Plover, Pacific Reef-Heron, Yellow Bittern. Next, we visited the Layon Landfill where we found Pacific Golden-Plover, Wood Sandpiper, Green-winged Teal and Northern Pintail. We searched some grasslands for Blue-breasted Quail but found none of these tiny introduced birds. We heard

284

the call of another exotic species introduced to Guam for hunting, the Black Francolin. We ended the day by hiring a boat for $200 to take us to tiny Cocos Island, just a little over a mile off Guam's southwest shore. Here we found Micronesian Starling and Guam Rail (884), both critically endangered and vulnerable to the Brown Tree Snake infestation on Guam.

White Tern
19 Dec 2023, Guam

In 2023 Martin was a doctoral candidate with Virginia Tech University, working on recovery of critically endangered bird species. He developed a nest box for the Micronesian Starling that has positively impacted the recovery of that native population on Guam. He also coordinated a volunteer effort to control Brown Tree Snake on Cocos Island which greatly benefited the population of Guam Rail there.

After birding all day with Martin, we met his lovely wife and young daughter (Mel and Nora) and some of his friends (all of whom were involved with endangered species studies) at a popular pub. The building next to the

285

outdoor seating area hosted a huge mural of the Guam Rail, which for two decades was extinct in the wild, i.e., only surviving in captivity, until it was reintroduced to Cocos Island in 2010. Perhaps the Guam Kingfisher could be brought back from extinction next. I understand some of the beautiful cinnamon and cobalt kingfishers were recently transferred from captivity to a wild setting at Palmyra Atoll.

At sunrise the next morning, I boarded the first of three United Airlines jets that would take me half-way around the globe to Boston where I would have one more chance to find Dovekie before the end of the year. Nick headed the opposite direction to Japan where he celebrated his 30th birthday by seeing more birds.

Special thanks to Martin Kastner for spending the day with us and providing much other useful information throughout our trip to Guam and the Northern Mariana Islands. Guam and the CNMI had produced 25 species for my Biggest Year effort. I was hoping for a bigger yield but apparently, I arrived about 20 years too late! The full trip list of 62 species is in the eBird trip report here: https://eBird.org/tripreport/298614.

Pacific Reef-Heron
19 Dec 2023, Guam

CHAPTER 51
Race to the Finish Line

$\mathcal{A}$s I prepared to return to the US mainland, I checked the eBird standings for ABA Area, ABA Continental and Lower 48. I used the *Explore* tab in eBird.org and then clicked on *Top 100* and selected among the list for *Major Regions*. I hoped to see USA and Territories included in the list of major regions but I would have to be patient.

While I was vacationing in the South Pacific, a new competitor was rapidly rising in the standings. Gino Ellison from Lynnfield, Massachusetts, was diligently working on adding new species to his Big Year and had moved into third place (by six species) in all three of the standard competition categories. I was now in fourth place in all of those categories. David and Tammy McQuade had also increased their ABA Area totals and were firmly out of reach, occupying first and second place.

I would have to work hard and efficiently to catch Gino, and hope that he had hung up his binoculars for the final week of competition. The number of possible adds for my ABA Area list was limited. These included five species in Texas, three in California, a couple of vagrant waterfowl plus Dovekie in the Northeast, and two or three pelagic species offshore in the Atlantic Ocean. Also, there was one rosy-finch in my home state of Colorado that had eluded me. I also considered species I had already seen in Alaska but I could add to my Lower 48 list. Species in this category included Rusty Blackbird, Rock Sandpiper and Yellow-billed Loon.

My departure ticket from Guam only got me to Honolulu, so I extended it to Boston, with arrival scheduled for 2:30 PM on Wednesday, December 27, 2023. My plan was to try to find Dovekie, a tiny seabird, from shore. I consulted with my long-time friend Alf Wilson, who told me that a week earlier, during a Christmas Bird Count, Rick Heil had counted more than 1,200 Dovekie from Andrew's Point, a rocky promontory in Rockport on Cape Ann north of Boston.

Flock of Assorted Rosy-Finches
27 Dec 2023, Estes Park, Colorado

Dovekie had also been seen from other vantage points along the Cape Cod shoreline during the same period. Winds were strong from the east that day. Subsequently there were no reports anywhere along the Massachusetts coast. Fortunately, the forecast included stormy weather Wednesday night so I was hopeful for finding in-shore Dovekie on Thursday. Dovekie were known to occasionally seek shelter from the wind in harbors where they were much easier to find.

Dovekie is a fish-eating, black and white, diving bird in the family Alcidae, which also includes murres and murrelets, auks and auklets, puffins, guillemots and Razorbill. All these birds use their wings as flippers to propel themselves through the water. Underwater cameras have captured alcids in deep water while foraging for fish. They appear to fly under water. If I missed the Dovekie in Massachusetts on December 28, my backup plan was a pelagic boat trip scheduled for December 29 from Ocean City, Maryland.

The United Airlines flight departed Guam at 7:35 AM on December 27, 2023, and landed in Honolulu, more than 3,700 miles to the east across the International Date Line, shortly before 7 PM on December 26. I was encouraged when I realized that I had gained an extra day for birding. Unfortunately, much of that day was spent on an airplane.

The Boston flight departed Honolulu at 9:15 PM on December 26 and landed in Denver at 6:30 AM. As the plane descended it occurred to me that I might need an extra day in Texas on the final day of the year, and thus would miss out on another opportunity to chase Black Rosy-Finch in the Colorado mountains. Conditions in Colorado were overcast with a thin layer of fresh snow on the ground, reasonably good for feeder-happy finches. What if I didn't get on the connecting flight to Boston and instead searched for finches? I could probably get on a later flight to Boston. The 2:30 PM arrival in Boston was too late anyway to find Dovekie the same day as the short winter days lost adequate light for birding by 4 PM. I presumed I could pick up my checked bag at the baggage office in Boston. This would have to be a quick chase. The next flight to Boston was a couple hours later. I called my speedy friend *Danica Patrick* from the airplane at 4 AM Mountain Time and explained the proposition. She was all for it.

"I will pick you up at the airport at 7 AM," Kathy Kay said. Was she expecting my call? It seemed that way.

I hurried off the plane and speed-walked to the passenger pick up area of Denver International Airport where Kathy was already waiting for me. She revved the engine as I climbed into the copilot's seat, no time for pleasantries.

"Where to, Cap'n?"

"Golden," I said. "I have two hours before the next flight leaves for Boston."

We arrived in Golden at 7:45 AM, but the flock of rosy-finches was absent from the feeding station. We called the homeowner who confirmed that the flock of 65 rosy-finches had visited briefly at 7:15 AM and included several Black Rosy-Finch. My friend Thomas Heinrich arrived a few minutes later, having cycled from Boulder to Golden (more than 20 miles). He is a dedicated *green birder* who had grown up near me in Eastern Massachusetts before settling in Colorado. Thomas watched the feeders as we searched the neighborhood by automobile for the missing finch flock. He also told us of his intentions to search for a staked-out Rusty Blackbird about ten miles away at Wheatridge Greenbelt. I called my friend Scott Rashid in Estes Park.

"A flock of Gray-crowned Rosy-Finch was here all day yesterday with an immature Black. They are still here this morning," reported Scott.

I asked Thomas to call if the flock showed up in Golden. We sped off toward Estes Park. Thomas called 20 minutes later, but it was too late. We were well on our way to Estes.

Scott welcomed us as we arrived. Scott and I had spent a fun week of birding together in Arizona in March. He was thrilled to help me add another species this late in the game. He pointed out the pale gray finch in the flock perched in the tree overlooking his feeders. This was the immature Black Rosy-Finch (Biggest Year-bird 885). I snapped a photo.

We did not stay long. I had missed the Boston flight but presumed there would be another during this busy travel season.

"Where to?" Danica asked.

"Wheatridge Greenbelt." We sped off again.

At Wheatridge we quickly found and photographed three gorgeous Rusty Blackbird, which I needed for my Lower 48 list. I showed them to Thomas who had just arrived.

"Do you have Barn Owl yet?" Kathy asked. "There are a couple of roosts near the airport."

Yes, but I still needed a photo. We found one of the owls inside an airport hangar, but it did not pose for photos. Kathy had spent the entire day with me. I thanked her profusely for supporting me in my Big Year efforts.

"Glad to help, Komar. If you want to go on the pelagic off Maryland let me know and I will pick you up wherever you are, even Boston." I didn't take her offer seriously at the time, but I think she might have done so, if I'd asked.

Daylight was waning by the time I got back to the United Airlines check-in counter. For some reason (Christmas spirit?), United Airlines honored my boarding pass from the morning flight and issued me a new ticket. I arrived in Boston at midnight. My bag was waiting for me at the United baggage office. What a relief! When I did not board my original flight in Denver, I received a message from United Airlines informing me they had cancelled my flight. I was worried they might have returned my bags to my starting point in Hawaii or even worse, Guam.

I invited my mother Karen to join me for the Dovekie hunt on Thursday, December 28, 2023. The weather was rainy with brisk winds from the north. Alf Wilson joined us at Andrew's Point on Cape Ann. Few birds were flying. In the surf we spied Common Eider, Harlequin Duck and several species of scoter, a type of sea duck. But no alcids. We split up to cover more territory. Alf went toward Annisquam. Karen and I went toward Gloucester Harbor. Other than one Razorbill in the harbor, there was no sign of any alcids.

The pelagic trip off Ocean City (Maryland) on December 29 was full and travel logistics were complex so I didn't count on a cancellation and instead headed a day early to South Texas where E. J. Raynor, a friend from Fort Collins, Colorado, had offered to drive for me. He was chasing some of the same birds I was. I was able to find a last-minute flight on Southwest Airlines from Boston to San Antonio, with a change of planes in Nashville. I arrived shortly after midnight in the wee hours of December 29, 2023. I found out later from Kathy Kay, who was on the Maryland pelagic, that hundreds of Dovekie, as well as Cory's Shearwater and Black-capped Petrel, were seen from that boat. I regretted missing that opportunity.

Rusty Blackbird
27 Dec 2023, Wheatridge, Colorado

CHAPTER 52
Last Stand in Texas

W ith three days to go in the ABA Area Big Year competition, I was still in fourth place, six species behind Gino Ellison who was picking up birds in Arizona and California. Nonetheless I would try to maximize my species number, and get my camera on those that I had not yet photographed.

There were four ABA Code 3+ vagrants on winter territories in the lower Rio Grande Valley I needed: Gray-collared Becard in Brownsville, Crimson-collared Grosbeak in Weslaco and, at Santa Margarita Ranch near Roma, Bare-throated Tiger-Heron and Mottled Owl.

My friend E. J. Raynor was already in Brownsville when I arrived in San Antonio close to 1 AM on Friday, December 29, 2023. I figured I would rent a car at the airport, find a cheap hotel, then drive four hours to Weslaco for the grosbeak and then meet E. J. in Brownsville at the end of the day. For the following evening, we had reserved a guided hike at Santa Margarita Ranch in hopes of hearing nocturnal species, including the recently-reported Mottled Owl and the Bare-throated Tiger-Heron.

This plan had some kinks. First, the car rental center was closed until 6 AM. I tried reserving a car online but payments did not go through. I slept a bit on the hard floor of the rental center. Second by 6:15 AM, I figured out there were no cars available (after all, it was the busiest travel week of the year). Third, just one Greyhound bus was heading south this morning from San Antonio departing at 6:30 AM. Fourth, the taxi I found arrived at the bus station at 6:33 AM. Too late. The bus had already departed.

There I was, stranded at the downtown bus depot in San Antonio. I was also losing valuable time. Maybe I could hook up with a local birder or birding group that also was headed to the Valley. I reached out to a few birding friends in the San Antonio area. Laura Keene was the first to respond.

Miraculously, she offered to lend me a car. Wow. She saved the day. By 9 AM I was on the road heading south. Laura had an epic Big Year in 2016 and empathized with me. She reported 815 species in the ABA Area that year.

I arrived at Frontera Audubon Sanctuary in Weslaco at 2 PM. The grove here was dense and full of birds, many of which were visiting a network of feeding stations and watering holes. E. J. had found the Gray-collared Becard in Brownsville after four hours of searching earlier in the day. He met me at Frontera to help me find the Crimson-collared Grosbeak. But the grosbeak wasn't interested in being found. After an hour of searching, E. J. returned to Resaca de La Palma State Park in Brownsville to search for another over-wintering vagrant there, Roadside Hawk. I stayed on at Frontera until it closed at 4 PM. I was rewarded with a cooperative Golden-crowned Warbler (ABA Code 3) which was almost too close for photography. Most of my photos were out of focus but one came out pretty well, certainly an improvement over the blur of yellow and gray I obtained November 3, in Harlingen, Texas.

I headed to Brownsville hoping to meet E. J. at Resaca de La Palma State Park. Light was fading fast by the time I reached the state park; dusk had settled in. The place was still crawling with birders. With the fading daylight, the bird activity had died down. A couple of Great Horned Owl were hooting. E. J. had gotten great looks at the Roadside Hawk and had moved on to view parrots roosting at Oliveira Park in Brownsville. I met him there after the parrot activity subsided. He was with Fort Collins birders Paul Gordy and Dilka Murtazina. We had dinner nearby. I promised to meet Paul and Dilka the next morning at Resaca de La Palma to look once again for the Gray-collared Becard.

On Saturday morning, December 30, I joined the throng of birders looking for Texas's first state record Gray-collared Becard. This bird, from Southeast Mexico, was originally found by my friend Brandon Nooner while he was looking for other reported rarities (Roadside Hawk, Blue Bunting, Tropical Parula), on November 5, 2023, a fine example of the *Patagonia picnic table effect* in action. This refers to the phenomenon that a rare bird attracts many birders who in turn find more rare birds.

I had only been there 20 minutes when I saw birders begin to run toward a small crowd in the visitor center parking lot. Sure enough, they were on the Gray-collared Becard (ABA Code 5, Biggest Year-bird 886). I snapped a photo. I began to search for other rarities with Paul and Dilka, but E. J. kept me on track.

Gray-collared Becard
15 Dec 2023, Brownsville, Texas
Photo by Richard Taylor

"We should go to Frontera now. You may need extra time to find the Crimson-collared Grosbeak."

E. J. arrived first and quickly spotted the grosbeak in a shrub with red berries where it frequently forages in the mornings. But it flew off into the thicket before anyone else could see it. I joined the search party.

After about 30 minutes walking the maze of trails without luck, I crossed to the other side of the thicket and sat down at one of the feeding stations. I struck up a relaxed conversation with an older man who was also taking a break on the bench. While conversing, I noticed a dark tanager-sized bird perched in a shrub about 30 feet from us.

"That's the grosbeak!" I exclaimed.

It was dark olive-green with a black head, bill and throat, a female Crimson-collared Grosbeak (ABA Code 4, Biggest Year-bird 887), a resident of tropical forest in Northeast Mexico. I snapped a photo.

Next, E. J. and I visited the National Butterfly Center in Mission, Texas. A friendly birder pointed out an Eastern Screech-Owl in a nest hole. We also saw the resident Audubon's Oriole (rare) and its hybrid offspring (with Altamira Oriole).

After checking into our hotel at Rio Grande City, we visited Roma Bluffs World Birding Center, which offers a bird's eye view of the Rio Grande River between the US town of Roma and the Mexican town of Ciudad Miguel Alemán. The sun was setting and I was watching for Red-billed Pigeon flying to roost. One flew by heading toward Mexico. I tried to photo document it but my Nikon P950 was not up to the task.

Now for the big event. We were signed up for a guided nocturnal field trip to Santa Margarita Ranch later that evening. At 7:30 PM, 25 customers (paying $75 each) assembled along the US-Mexico border wall. From there, we carpooled to another spot where there was a huge open gate in the wall. Our guides (Zach Johnson and Ryan Rodriguez) escorted us along a two-track ranch road that paralleled the river. We heard spontaneously calling Eastern Screech-Owl and Great Horned Owl. Bare-throated Tiger-Heron (888, ABA Code 5), a Mexican vagrant that had taken up residence at the ranch, responded to an imitation vocalized by Ryan who was talented beyond his 16 years. At 11 PM, the Mottled Owl, another vagrant from Northeastern Mexico, had not yet been detected. Zach stopped the group one last time to listen. He played a recording for Long-eared Owl and Tawny-collared Nightjar, *on spec*. He did not play the recording for Mottled Owl because this evening's tour was stipulated as *no recordings* for the Mottled Owl. I nodded off to sleep during the quiet moment of listening and did not hear what Zach later described as distant song of the Mottled Owl. Several customers however were more alert than I was and did hear it, including E. J. and

Kathy Kay, who had flown to Texas after the Maryland boat trip to join this tour. Kudos to them. The Mottled Owl was Kathy's 20th owl species observed in the Lower 48 states in 2023.

There was a moment of excitement a few minutes later. Ryan, who was at the rear of the group, saw a mid-sized owl fly into a small tree along the two-track. It flushed a noisy Plain Chachalaca that was roosting in the tree. At that moment, about six different Eastern Screech-Owls called loudly, in excitement. Alas, the offending owl never did reveal itself. Later I listened to my audio recordings for Eastern Screech-Owl and Bare-throated Tiger-Heron. The screech-owls are a unique subspecies from South Texas known as McCall's Owl. It may one day get split off as a full species. Indeed, its calls sound slightly different from the owl in my back yard in Colorado. I was surprised to hear a couple of different owl sounds in the background of my recordings. One was a single bark that sounded like the first note of the song given by Mottled Owl. I sent it off to Zach Johnson, my brother Oliver in Honduras, and Andrew Spencer, a sound technician for the Macaulay Library of Bird Sounds. All agreed with my assessment. It's risky to hang your hat on one distant bark but out of desperation I decided to count Mottled Owl for my Biggest Year (889). Fortunately, I noticed that the sonogram I recorded was a strong match to the final note in a typical series of barks that comprise the typical song of Mottled Owl.

Another owl call in the background of my tiger-heron recording was a brief mourning hoot. To me it sounded like a single hoot of Long-eared Owl or possibly even Stygian Owl, another potential stray from Northeast Mexico. Again, my team of sound experts agreed with me, but which owl was it? That one I decided to leave in the checklist as owl species.

One of my goals of this final visit to Texas was to photograph species that I had not yet documented, such as Blue Bunting, Morelet's Seedeater and Red-billed Pigeon. On the morning of Sunday, December 31, while I was still packing up, E. J. called me. He had gotten an early start at Salineño Wildlife Preserve and had a perched Red-billed Pigeon. And he had seen a Morelet's Seedeater. Of course, these birds had moved on by the time I arrived, but it was as good a place as any to look for photo opportunities. I ended up spending the entire morning there. Highlights were Green Kingfisher, Ringed Kingfisher, Zone-tailed Hawk and Morelet's Seedeater (no photo, unfortunately).

While I was exploring along the river, I misplaced my cell phone. Retracing my steps, I could not find it. I recounted my dilemma to Bob Bowman and Lois Hughes, two snowbird volunteers from Maine and Iowa, respectively, who maintain the feeders at the wildlife preserve. They offered to help me find the cell phone and with their assistance, calling my phone from various points along my route, I found it! After that fiasco, I sat with them by the feeding station for a while. I was tired. It had been a long day, a long year.

"Are you really going to try to drive to San Antonio today?" Bob said to me. The prospect of driving four hours was daunting.

"I reckon not," one of us said.

By now it was 2:30 PM. Laura Keene, the owner of the car I had borrowed three days earlier, sent me a Facebook post of a possible Lesser Yellow-headed Vulture in La Feria, a couple hours away. If confirmed, it would represent a first record for the USA. This species lived in the tropics of Middle America and South America. It is almost identical to Turkey Vulture and would be easily overlooked in South Texas. One of these birds straying to Texas was long overdue. I remembered a lovely birding spot I visited earlier in the year called La Feria Nature Center. I called E. J. who had headed to South Padre Island hours earlier. He agreed to meet me there. We both arrived at dusk, too late to find any vultures. It was time to end my quest and go home.

EPILOGUE
A Year to Remember

As I drove north from the Valley on January 1, 2024, I pondered my achievement. I felt very fortunate to be able to see this adventure through. I considered it my personal *walkabout* or sabbatical. I wondered what new adventures lay in store for me in the years ahead.

My final tally was 889 species for the USA and Territories, 11 short of my goal of 900. A complete chronological list of the birds I found during my Biggest Year appears at https://www.bohannonhallpress.com/. I wondered what I could have done differently to make up the shortfall. There was some pretty low hanging fruit that I failed to take advantage of during the course of the year. First, I should not have missed any ABA Code 1 species but I did miss one, Cory's Shearwater. I missed a chunk of ABA Code 2 species as well, including Spectacled Eider, Himalayan Snowcock, Red-legged Kittiwake, Dovekie, Black-capped and Mottled Petrels, Yellow Rail, Gyrfalcon, Akohekohe, Maui Parrotbill, Aniauniau, Akekee, Palila, Arctic Warbler and Connecticut Warbler. Some ABA Code 3+ vagrants had been staked out for weeks or even months but I never made the attempt to find them. This category included Common Shelduck in Pennsylvania, Steller's Sea-Eagle in Maine, Northern Lapwing and Pink-footed Goose in Massachusetts and, in Florida, Yellow-headed Caracara and Fork-tailed Flycatcher.

Then there were nemesis species I tried hard for that gave me the slip, including Yellow-green Vireo, Yellow Rail, Connecticut Warbler and Dovekie. Which one deserves the dubious honor for worst nemesis? You pick. My vote goes to the Dovekie, which has evaded my detection for more than five decades! Yellow Rail was a close second in this competition.

And finally, there were the big misses, species that got away from me before I could definitively identify them. In this category I include Cook's Petrel in California, Black-capped Petrel in Florida, Cory's Shearwater in Puerto Rico, Little Curlew in American Samoa, Short-tailed Nighthawk in

Puerto Rico, Stygian Owl in Texas, Crimson-fronted Macaw in Florida, and Palila in Hawaii. Of course, I may not have seen any of those, but I have strong suspicions for all.

Based on those considerations, I believe that observing 900 species within a year in the USA and Territories is certainly possible. I allowed some distractions to interfere with my mission. For example, I participated in two baseball tournaments which took up eight days. I could have been birding instead. I also left the region for a week in February (guiding in Honduras) and a week in November (family vacation in El Salvador). Had I redirected those periods to my mission, I may have achieved my goal. Furthermore, I would have scored higher in the ABA Area and Lower 48 competitions. I believe I could have won those competitions, especially if they had been my primary goal. Of course, I spent 30 days birding in the territories, outside the ABA Area. What could I have achieved if those seven weeks of distractions were available for birding in the ABA Area?

I did not keep track of miles driven or flown. But I can tell you I submitted 1,210 eBird checklists within the USA and Territories in 2023 and at least one eBird checklist each day of the year. I spent parts of 17 days at sea. Within the Lower 48 states, I visited Texas the most (eight times) followed by Florida (six times), California and Massachusetts (five times each) and Arizona (four times). My goal for ABA Code 3+ species was 40 and I surpassed it, eventually tallying 66 ABA Code 3+ species.

There will be some people who doubt that I saw or heard all the birds I reported. To address their doubts, I included photos and sonograms in my eBird checklists, and provided links to my trip reports in eBird, where those checklists are accessible to all.

In the end, I photographed 808 species of birds. These photos are on public display at https://pbase.com/quetzal/bigyearphotos. Of the species I did not photograph, I audio-recorded 50, and noted witnesses for an additional 26. I saw only five species without witnesses or physical documentation. These were Audubon's Shearwater (Florida), Blue Bunting (Texas), Newell's Shearwater (Hawaii), Black-headed Gull (Massachusetts), and Indian Silverbill (Puerto Rico).

Looking back, I have lots of wonderful memories from my Biggest Year. First there are the birds. My favorite was Ross's Gull at Gambell, Alaska. Then there were the places. Nome, Alaska, qualifies as my favorite birding destination. A close second was the Kaulana Manu Nature Trail on Hawaii. It's the closest thing to an enchanted forest I can imagine. And last, but not least, the people I met along the journey were so dear to me. I have many to thank (see *Acknowledgments*).

There are a few strategy changes I might recommend to the next Big Year birder. Spend more time in Alaska and more time on the open ocean. I think most of the species that separated the McQuades from me came from those two places. But ultimately, I have no real complaints. Leading the group tours during the first half of the year was a great way to share this adventure with friends and helped soften the financial burden of my Biggest Year.

Long-tailed Jaeger
29 Aug 2023, Larimer County, Colorado

Birding every day all year long was living a dream. Perhaps the one regret I had was that I didn't have time to bird for the sake of birding. I had to constantly move on to chase the next staked-out target. Although I enjoy the chase, I enjoy even more finding birds myself and sharing my discoveries with others. One of my most memorable experiences of 2023 was in late

August when I identified a juvenile Long-tailed Jaeger from Paul Gordy's fishing boat at Boyd Lake in Loveland, Colorado. I shared the rare sighting with the local Northern Colorado birders, many of whom were able to see it. It wasn't even a year-bird for me.

In the ABA Area competition, I finished with 796 species, achieving fourth place. I was 18 species behind the leaders (David and Tammy McQuade) and eight species behind the third-place finisher Gino Ellison. I finished the ABA Continental competition in a similar position with 741 species. In the Lower 48 competition, I finished with 707 species in third place, just seven species behind the McQuades. These competition results are based on eBird data. Over the years, the results may change slightly as taxonomic updates become reflected in changes within the eBird database. For the official ABA-vetted totals, I subtracted a dozen species considered "provisional" from my ABA Area list total (see table). These are mostly exotic species or new country records not yet judged.

TABLE

List of 12 species observed that were not yet considered countable by the American Birding Association.

Provisional Bird Species	Location
Helmeted Guineafowl	Hawaii, Texas, Puerto Rico
Budgerigar	Arizona
White-eyed Parakeet	Florida
Blue-crowned Parakeet	Florida
Burrowing Parakeet	California
White-fronted Parrot	Texas
Red-lored Parrot	California
Orange-winged Parrot	Florida
Tanambar Corella	Hawaii
Cattle Tyrant	Texas
Swinhoe's White-eye	California
Lavender Waxbill	Hawaii

Acknowledgments

I have many people to thank for my success during 2023. Foremost is my supportive family, particularly my wife Elena Maribel.

I thank the customers who signed up and paid to attend my tours: Joe Burns, Phil Cafaro, Michael Costello, Patricia Cullen, Irene Fortune, Greg Goodrich, Tom Hall, Cliff Hendrick, Dana Hiatt, Kathy Kay, James Nealon, Kelly Ormesher, Greg Osland, Lori Pivonka, Sue Riffe, Pamela St. Clair, Anna Troth, Alfred Wilson, Sandy Winkler, Charles Wood, Bud Younts and Howard Youth. Some of them attended more than one.

I thank several professional and volunteer tour leaders who served as guides for me and my tour groups or drove during these guided tours. They are Adrian Burke, Eric DeFonso, Eli Gross, Steve Heinl, Steve N. G. Howell, Eric Hynes, Jack Jeffrey, Zach Johnson, Logan Kahle, Joe Kipper, Aaron Lang, Forrest Luke, Larry Manfredi, Jim Millensifer, Peter Pyle, Scott Rashid, Sue Riffe, Ryan Rodriguez, Julio Salgado, Mandy Talpas, Raymond VanBuskirk, John Vanderpoel and David Wade.

For valuable information on finding birds, I thank Peter Alden, Linus Blomqvist, Peter Crosson, Louie Dombrowski, Richard Fray, Brian Gibbons, Frank Haas, Jesse Huth, Nathan Johnson, Martin Kastner, Alex Lamoreaux, John Malenich, David McQuade, Sherman Wing and Craig Ziolkowski.

The following individuals I thank for accompaniment while birding: Noah Arthur, Skyler Bol, Jay Breidt, Josh Bruening, Phil Cafaro, Kyle Carlsen, Jim and Brenda Carpenter, Yaron Charka, Paul Gordy, Cliff Hendrick, Mark and Joanie Hubinger, Marshall Iliff, Bill Kaempfer, Kathy Kay, Russel Kokx, Elena M. Komar, Karen Komar, Nick A. Komar, Oliver Komar, Adrian Lakin, Stephan Lorenz, David and Tammy McQuade, Dilka Murtazina, Brandon Nooner, Greg Osland, Lori Pivonka, Scott Rashid, Graham Ray, E. J. Raynor, Valentina Roumi, John Shenot, Archer Silverman, Alex Smilor, Richard Taylor, Kenna Sue Trickey, John Vanderpoel, David Wade, Cole Wild and Alfred Wilson.

Special thanks to the following individuals who went above and beyond expectations in their support of me during my Biggest Year effort: Manuel Amador, Andy Bankert, Brad Benter, Bob Bledsoe, Thomas Ford-Hutchinson, Kathy Kay, Martin Kastner, Laura Keene, Elena M. Komar, Beto Matheus, Thane Pratt, Ellen Schwenne, Richard Taylor and Sally Waterhouse.

I'm sure I inadvertently left out some names from these lists for which I apologize.

Thanks to my editors Oliver Komar and Richard (Rick) Taylor for dedicated work making my book better. In Richard Taylor, I was very lucky to find a professional editor and author who happens to be an accomplished birder and who has visited most of the spots I mention in the book. His experience was invaluable when it mattered.

I also want to thank Rip Coleman at Bohannon Hall Press who personally typeset and formatted *The Biggest Year in American Birding* and made many useful suggestions along the way. Sarah Robin Coleman, a skilled professional artist, painted the beautiful bird illustrations that help give this book its distinctive character.

Finally, thanks to you, my loyal readers. Knowing that folks were following my story through my weekly blog was inspiration for me to keep going.

Kirtland's Warbler
21 Jun 2023, Adam's County, Wisconsin
Photo by Sue Riffe

Index of Birds

Razorbill, 47, 48, 49, 50, 53, 144, 145, 146, 238, 249, 289, 291
Red Avadavat, 217
Red Crossbill, 53, 72, 76, 160, 163, 164, 174, 181
Red Junglefowl, 97, 210, 220
Red Knot, 21, 90, 122, 127, 129
Red Phalarope, 18, 127, 236
Red-bellied Woodpecker, 40
Red-billed Leiothrix, 213
Red-billed Pigeon, 170, 225, 296, 297
Red-billed Tropicbird, 193, 238
Red-breasted Merganser, 19, 130
Red-breasted Sapsucker, 20, 21, 56
Red-cockaded Woodpecker, 88
Red-crested Cardinal, 213, 255
Red-crowned Parrot, 19, 25, 27
Reddish Egret, 19, 60
Red-eyed Vireo, 88, 115, 147, 170
Red-faced Cormorant, 122
Red-faced Warbler, 139, 172, 175
Red-flanked Bluetail, 56
Red-footed Booby, 195, 196, 212, 217, 219, 261, 269, 281
Redhead Duck, 15
Red-headed Woodpecker, 88, 110, 141
Red-legged Honeycreeper, 97
Red-legged Kittiwake, 139, 299
Red-legged Thrush, 34
Red-lored Parrot, 302
Red-masked Parakeet, 59, 98
Red-naped Sapsucker, 68
Red-necked Grebe, 48, 126, 164
Red-necked Phalarope, 84, 127, 179
Red-necked Stint, 127, 129, 238
Red-shouldered Hawk, 19, 149
Red-tailed Tropicbird, 217, 220, 276
Red-throated Loon, 51
Red-vented Bulbul, 92, 260
Red-whiskered Bulbul, 59, 97, 213
Rhinoceros Auklet, 58, 80, 84, 236
Ring-billed Gull, 13, 51, 52, 54, 62, 150, 181, 187, 230, 253
Ringed Kingfisher, 28, 298
Ring-necked Duck, 15
Ring-necked Pheasant, 40
Rivoli's Hummingbird, 68, 70, 172
Roadside Hawk, 25, 228, 229, 294
Rock Ptarmigan, 121, 131
Rock Sandpiper, 56, 121, 238, 287
Rock Wren, 45
Roseate Spoonbill, 27
Roseate Tern, 36, 96, 144, 146
Rose-breasted Grosbeak, 46, 115, 147
Rose-ringed Parakeet, 58, 213

Rose-throated Becard, 25, 28, 228
Ross's Goose, 20
Ross's Gull, 20, 135, 136, 142, 238, 253, 301
Rosy-faced Lovebird, 67, 175
Rota White-eye, 279, 280, 282, 283
Rough-legged Hawk, 40, 131
Royal Tern, 150, 185, 193
Ruby-throated Hummingbird, 30, 145
Ruddy Quail-Dove, 37, 202, 203, 238, 250
Ruddy Turnstone, 90, 255, 261, 263
Ruff, 36, 56, 58, 59, 120, 121, 187, 188
Ruffed Grouse, 41, 42, 47
Rufous Hummingbird, 87, 171
Rufous-backed Robin, 18, 67, 73, 175, 209
Rufous-capped Warbler, 70, 71, 73, 173, 174, 176
Rufous-crowned Sparrow, 60, 106
Rufous-winged Sparrow, 70
Rustic Bunting, 134
Rusty Blackbird, 126, 238, 287, 290, 291
Saffron Finch, 198, 210
Sage Thrasher, 21
Saipan Reed-Warbler, 276
Saltmarsh Sparrow, 139, 144, 145
Samoan Myzomela, 261
Samoan Starling, 261
Sanderling, 90, 102, 143, 255, 261, 263
Sandhill Crane, 44, 64, 141, 145
Sandwich Tern, 34, 185
Savannah Sparrow, 70, 142, 143
Say's Phoebe, 21
Scaled Quail, 72, 78, 175
Scaly-breasted Munia, 18, 19, 21, 35, 60, 92, 97, 210
Scaly-naped Pigeon, 34
Scarlet Ibis, 36, 37, 198, 203, 238
Scarlet Tanager, 96, 149
Scissor-tailed Flycatcher, 88
Scott's Oriole, 106
Scripp's Murrelet, 19, 80, 83
Seaside Sparrow, 90, 248
Sedge Wren, 141, 142, 248
Semipalmated Plover, 90, 127, 134
Semipalmated Sandpiper, 35
Sharp-shinned Hawk, 15, 35
Sharp-tailed Grouse, 76, 158
Sharp-tailed Sandpiper, 103, 104, 187, 212, 238, 271, 277
Shiny Cowbird, 34, 98
Short-billed Gull, 14, 54, 56, 63, 126, 127
Short-eared Owl, 40, 44, 123, 158, 213, 214, 227
Short-tailed Albatross, 124
Short-tailed Hawk, 72, 73, 94, 154
Short-tailed Nighthawk, 200, 201, 203, 299

Photo References

All photos by Nicholas Komar except:

Common Crane, Lewellen, Nebraska by Cole Wild	page 65
Crescent-chested Warbler, Big Bend National Park, Texas by Brandon Nooner	page 107
Nick Komar and Tom Hall, Gambell, Alaska by Oliver Komar	page 131
Ross's Gull, Gambell, Alaska by Oliver Komar	page 135
American Flamingo, St. Mark's NWR, Florida by Nicholas Alexander Komar	page 169
Nick Birding near Tutuila, American Samoa by Oliver Komar	page 262
Gray-collared Becard, Brownsville, Texas by Richard Wilks Taylor	page 295
Kirtland's Warbler, Adam's County, Wisconsin by Sue Riffe	page 304

About the Artist

Sarah Robin Coleman was first inspired to become an artist by her talented grandmother, Alice Clynese Winston, who began giving her lessons in color theory, perspective and composition when she was only a child. Sarah went on to earn a degree in history and fine arts. Her oil, watercolor and acrylic paintings hang in private collections across the country. Her distinctive illustrations and cover designs enhance many of the Bohannon Hall Press publications.

Sarah is also currently working in watercolor to produce a delightful collection of en plein air images depicting scenes from her life that range from an antique car parked at a favorite hamburger hangout in College Park to a gathering of soldiers honoring WWII heroes at Camp Toccoa, Georgia.

Birds have always been a favorite subject and appear in many of her creations. Her images convey unique artistic perspectives and deeply emotional responses to the amazingly diverse collection of winged wonders gracing our planet.